Bordering

Bordering

Nira Yuval-Davis
Georgie Wemyss
Kathryn Cassidy

polity

First published in 2019 by Polity Press

Polity Press
65 Bridge Street
Cambridge CB2 1UR, UK

Polity Press
101 Station Landing
Suite 300
Medford, MA 02155, USA

ISBN-13: 978-1-5095-0494-7
ISBN-13: 978-1-5095-0495-4 (pb)

A catalogue record for this book is available from the British Library.

Library of Congress Cataloging-in-Publication Data
Names: Yuval-Davis, Nira, author. | Wemyss, Georgie, author. | Cassidy, Kathryn, author.
Title: Bordering / Nira Yuval-Davis, Georgie Wemyss, Kathryn Cassidy.
Description: Cambridge, UK ; Medford, MA : Polity, 2019. | Includes bibliographical references and index.
Identifiers: LCCN 2018050593 (print) | LCCN 2018061750 (ebook) | ISBN 9781509504985 (Epub) | ISBN 9781509504947 (hardback) | ISBN 9781509504954 (paperback)
Subjects: LCSH: Emigration and immigration--Social aspects. | Border security--Social aspects. | Internal security--Social aspects. | Freedom of movement--Social aspects. | BISAC: SOCIAL SCIENCE / Sociology / General.
Classification: LCC JV6225 (ebook) | LCC JV6225 .Y88 2019 (print) | DDC 363.28/5--dc23
LC record available at https://lccn.loc.gov/2018050593

Typeset in 10.5 on 12 Sabon
by Fakenham Prepress Solutions, Fakenham, Norfolk NR21 8NL
Printed and bound in Great Britain by CPI Group (UK) Ltd, Croydon

For further information on Polity, visit our website: politybooks.com

We dedicate this book to all those who are stuck in grey-zone bordering scapes anywhere across the globe.

Contents

Acknowledgements

We developed our theoretical and methodological framework on bordering and carried out the bulk of our fieldwork while taking part in the EUBORDERSCAPES project (http://www.euborderscapes. eu) funded by the European Community's Seventh Framework Programme 2012–2016.

We would like to thank all our partners from twenty-two universities in nineteen different countries in and around Europe for participating the many stimulating conferences and discussions that took place during these years. Special thanks to James Scott and Jussi Lane from the University of Eastern Finland who capably and tirelessly administered this very large and complicated project.

Special thanks also to the nine international teams who constituted with us Work Package 9, Borders, Intersectionality, and the Everyday, led by Nira Yuval-Davis. We cooperated closely and produced two special issues of the journals *Ethnic and Racial Studies* (*Racialized Bordering Discourses on European Roma*, 2017) and *Political Geography* (*Intersectional Borders*, 2018) in which we were able to pursue some comparative studies of our subject. Earlier versions of sections of chapters 1 and 3 were published in the special issue of *Ethnic and Racial Studies*, parts of chapter 4 were published in *Sociology*, and parts of chapters 3 and 5 were published in the special issue of *Political Geography*. The material has since been updated and restructured around our developing argument; hence this book has been worked on and written exclusively by us, working in Britain.

We would like to thank the School of Social Sciences at the University of East London, and especially the Centre for Research on Migration, Refugees and Belonging (CMRB), which provided us with a home during the project. We would also like to thank the central research administration team at the university and especially Jamie Hakim, for being such a supportive research administrator and media researcher for our team. And we want to thank all the national and international scholars who took part in the research seminars series on Bordering, which we ran at CMRB during the project.

Nira Yuval-Davis would also like to thank the Centre for Gender Studies at the University of Umea in Sweden. The Centre enabled her, as a part-time visiting professor, to apply for and be a formal partner in the research project.

Our work would not have been possible without the close relationships we have developed with various grassroots organisations working on different aspects of bordering. With three of them – Migrants Rights Network (MRN), Southall Black Sisters (SBS), and the Refugee and Migrant Forum of Essex and London (RAMFEL) – we cooperated formally in producing the film *Everyday Borders* (2015), directed by Orson Nava and produced by Georgie Wemyss (see https://vimeo.com/126315982).

Our work would also not have been possible without the very many other individuals and organisations who helped us to get insights into different aspects of bordering, who put us in touch with the people we interviewed, and who facilitated the bordering encounters we observed. Among them are Doctors of the World, Sue Lukes, Migrant Voice, the Everyday Borders Consortium, Hackney Migrants' Centre, Roy Millard, Emad Chowdhury, L'Auberge de Migrants, and Secours Catholique.

We owe a special debt to the many regular and irregular border crossers and workers who gave us the angle of their situated gazes on what bordering meant to them in and between Calais, Dover, Folkestone, and East and South London.

At Polity, we are grateful to John Thompson, who encouraged us to propose the project, and to the editorial team, which showed patience when the result of the EU referendum and the election of Trump in 2016 forced us to delay completion, as we sought to incorporate these events and embed the significance of bordering to governance and belonging in the context of contemporary political earthquakes.

Importantly, we want to thank our families and our close friends for their continuing practical and emotional support. As we are migrant families, bordering has been a subject close to all our hearts.

1

Introduction
Framing Bordering

Introduction

The argument of this book is that borders and borderings have moved from the margins into the centre of political and social life. We aim to show how bordering has redefined contemporary notions of citizenship, identity, and belonging for all, affecting hegemonic majorities as well as racialised minorities in their everyday lives while creating growing exclusionary 'grey zones' locally and globally.

> The borders ... are dispersed a little everywhere. (Balibar, 2004: 1)

When Étienne Balibar made his famous comments on the change of bordering technologies in Europe at the beginning of the noughties, he was referring to the spread of border checking points from the territorial borders at the edge of states into a multiplicity of locations, especially in the metropolis – in train stations, sweatshops, restaurants – wherever border agencies feel that there is a chance to catch 'irregular' or 'undocumented' migrants. Similarly, borders have been moved away from the territory of their state into the territories of other countries: not only are US border checks taking place in Canadian airports and British ones in Eurostar terminals in continental Europe, but consulates in most countries have effectively turned into passport and visa checkpoints. In this way, the deterritorialisation and reterritorialisation of borders have been taking place globally.

As analysed in this book, these debordering and rebordering practices have marked a fundamental change. This change has been

1

caused not just by the technologies that have been employed in bordering processes, but also by the political projects of governance and belonging that underlie them. As will be discussed here, these political projects themselves emerged as a result of, and in response to, neoliberal globalisation and its associated double crisis of governability and governmentality (Yuval-Davis, 2012). The growing centrality of borders and bordering in the contemporary political and social order has in its turn had a profound effect on global social inequalities, which are multiscalar (Mezzadra and Neilson, 2013).

Controlling national borders has acquired in the second decade of the twenty-first century a political and emotional poignancy that it has not had since the end of the Cold War, or even earlier. After decades in which the importance – or even existence – of borders was seen as waning in a world increasingly dominated by the rise of globalisation – economic, cultural, political (Hudson, 1998; Wonders, 2006) – rebordering the states has become a symbol of resistance to the pressures that emanate from neoliberal globalisation. Thus Donald Trump, whose promise to build a wall along the border between the United States and Mexico played an important role in his election victory in 2016, argued in his 2018 lecture to the UN General Assembly: 'We reject the ideology of globalism and accept the doctrine of patriotism' (*Guardian*, 25 September 2018).

Discourses regarding the control of national borders have been central to political projects in the West as well as in many other parts of the world (Geschiere, 2009). Such discourses relate to the control of immigration at a time when the 'migration and refugee crisis' is being described as the most serious one since the end of the Second World War (Geddes and Scholten, 2016). They also relate to trade agreements, tariff controls, and protection from competing cheap imports and from the 'chipping away' of state authorities by global institutions such as the International Monetary Fund (IMF) and the World Trade Organization (WTO) (Sassen, 2015a). Some of the more 'creative' solutions suggested by the British government as to how to resurrect the United Kingdom's borders, especially regarding the passage of goods to and from the Irish Republic to Northern Ireland, show how complex, contested, and torn between the demands of the polity and those of the market these bordering processes have become. They also show how bordering has become dependent to a considerable degree on digital and virtual technologies. This is also a central facet of the other, related political bordering discourse, namely the securitisation discourse: the demand that the government should 'keep our nation safe' (Andreas, 2003) from 'global terrorism'. Therefore borderings, regarded as spatial and virtual processes – dynamic and shifting, multiscalar and multilevel – that construct, reproduce, and contest borders, make a considerable contribution to a variety of local, regional, and global political projects of governance and belonging. They determine individual and collective entitlements and duties as well as social cohesion and solidarity. As such, bordering can be considered a pivotal 'structure of feeling' (Williams, 1977) as well as of hegemonic social imaginaries (Taylor, 2004).

Thus we argue that, in order to understand contemporary local and global political and social relations, the management of social solidarity and social difference, and the regulation of labour and of the economy at large, we need to analyse the bordering processes and technologies that are used as discourses and practices in different, multiscalar locations. The present book shows how, in this historical conjuncture, bordering processes weave together arenas of social, political, and economic configurations in complex and contested ways, which cannot be understood while remaining within the boundaries of more traditional subdisciplines such as social policy, international relations, migration studies, social identities, or race and ethnic studies. In recent years there has been a lot of discussion on the limitations of national methodologies (e.g. Beck and Sznaider, 2010; Büscher and Urry, 2009). We argue that bordering studies, which originally emerged in the very different fields of geography (Newman, 2006; Paasi, 2012) and cultural studies (Anzaldúa, 1987), play a crucial role in the understanding of contemporary global–local society – or 'glocal', to use Brenner's (1998) term – and need to be studied in a holistic (if complex) interdisciplinary way. At the same time we argue that, to fully understand the role of bordering in contemporary society, we need to encompass in our analysis of macrosocial structures and processes the gazes of differentially situated individual and collective social actors.

In this introductory chapter we present and explain the theoretical and methodological framing of our approach to bordering as well as the overall context in which we see borderings as operating today.

We start by locating bordering in-between the political and the sociocultural or, more specifically, at the intersection of political projects of governance and belonging.

The section that comes after this examines the paradoxical roles that borders and borderings play in contemporary neoliberal globalisation, as they are both a constitutive part of this process and a response to its effects. It demonstrates how these roles affect contemporary hierarchies of inclusion and exclusion, and thus glocal inequalities.

The following sections expand on our methodological and epistemological approach to the study of bordering. We first discuss the processual turn in border studies and then argue for the addition of an everyday, situated intersectionality approach that should contribute to a comprehensive and valid understanding of bordering.

Bordering: In-between the political and the sociocultural

Doreen Massey (1994: 149) used the term 'power geometry' to address new images of space, highlighting that such analysis includes 'how different social groups and different individuals are placed in very distinct ways in relation to ... flows and interconnections'. Henri Lefebvre (1991) has argued that space is the ultimate locus and medium of struggle, and therefore a critical political issue. Border work (Vaughan-Williams, 2008; Rumford, 2008, 2013) is thus about producing, controlling, and regulating (as well as resisting and contesting) such spatial power geometries, producing discourses and practices related to borders that continuously divide – and connect (Donnan and Wilson, 1999) – territorial, social, and economic spaces.

In consequence, borders need to be seen as constitutive parts of the world rather than as segmenting a pre-given 'natural' whole. Importantly, bordering is not only about who moves and who does not, but also about who controls whose movements. In other words, some of the crucial analytical as well as political questions related to bordering concern the understanding of the 'who', 'how', and 'why' of the construction and control of specific borders in specific times and spaces.

Bordering, then, is continuously happening. Different kinds and levels of bordering connect apparently unrelated social, political, economic, and ecological phenomena – from the governance of international trade, climate change, and criminalisation of particular people to social and economic inequalities within and between states. Most importantly, as Nash and Reid (2010) claim, state bordering processes acquire a double meaning, as processes related on the one hand to state territorial boundaries and on the other to symbolic social and cultural lines of inclusion and difference, material and imagined, physical and cultural. As Popescu (2012) argues, borders can be regarded as dynamic and creative discontinuities that play a

4

crucial role in encouraging the multiple, complex interplay between political and territorial and between cultural and identitarian processes. They are based both on collective historical narratives and on individual identity constructions of self in which difference is related to space but not reducible to it. Given these characteristics, borders and bordering need to be seen as material and virtual processes that existed even before digital technologies came to play such crucial roles in contemporary borderings. And, to understand them fully, we need to incorporate into our analysis both everyday vernacular (Jones and Johnson, 2014) and situated and intersectional (Yuval-Davis, 2015a) perspectives. On these we will expand towards the end of this chapter.

Barth (1998) and others following him have argued that what is crucial in processes of ethnicisation and racialisation is the existence of ethnic (and racial) boundaries rather than that of any specific 'essence' around which these boundaries are constructed. Any physical or social signifier can be used to construct the boundaries that differentiate between 'us' and 'them'. State borders are but one of the technologies used to construct and maintain these boundaries. Henk van Houtum and his colleagues (van Houtum and van Naerssen, 2002; van Houtum et al., 2005) have argued that all bordering processes are a combination of ordering and othering. Indeed, as will be shown throughout the book, bordering has a double character, as a political project of governance and as a political project of belonging.

In the empirical chapters of the book, we show that political projects of governance and belonging tend to be entangled and to support and shape each other in concrete social and political situations. However, in this introductory chapter we consider it useful to separate these strands.

Bordering constitutes a principal organising mechanism in constructing, maintaining, and controlling social and political order. This mechanism includes determining not only who is and who is not entitled to enter the country, but also whether those who do would be allowed to stay, work, and acquire civil, political, and social rights. Different political projects of governance determine in different ways the differential criteria for these different entitlements and the individual and collective duties of those governed, be they formal citizens or not. While these bordering constructions might seem to affect only those who were not born in the country, they actually affect the society as a whole, both materially and normatively. They determine what everyone should expect as a citizenship

5

entitlement or as a duty, especially when one compares oneself to people of different origins and formal citizenship status whom one encounters in everyday life. In this way bordering affects all members of society, although in different ways, according to their situated positionings as well as according to the racialised imaginary and the normative social order.

Bordering processes, which are related to different functions of governance, are multilayered. This is true not just in relation to different levels of state, or in relation to regional and global institutions of supra-state borderings, but also within the state borders. In different states there are different spatial and governance hierarchies of territorial borders – of neighbourhoods, cities, country regions, and federal states. For example, in the United States individual states are known to interpret differently the US constitution regarding the rights of undocumented migrants (Park, 2015) and in Britain there is much talk of 'postcode lottery' – a term that refers to the ways in which the spatial location of citizens' places of residence determines at least a part of their rights and duties (Press Association, 2016).

Thus there are many situations in which the spatial governance of internal borders acquires an importance of its own. Of course, these spatial borderscapes intersect with ethnic and other social categorisations that hold among a country's population, to establish a shifting and contested hierarchy of citizenship statuses and entitlements to different state resources.

Nevertheless, national borders have important roles in establishing territorial, national identities; they also constitute the bedrock of international social order. As Häkli (2015) has pointed out, 'the border is in my pocket': more and more frequently and in more and more places, people are asked to prove the legitimacy of their stay within particular state borders by showing their passports and visas.

The decisions, however, regarding the criteria for selecting such people are not intrinsic to the bordering technologies in operation but rather reflect the political, economic, social, cultural, and security interests linked in various ways to the states' and supra-states' governance. In other words, when we study contemporary borderings, we need to pay close attention not just to their mode of operation and their discursive imaginaries but also to the particular roles they play in particular political projects.

As mentioned above, van Houtum and van Naerssen (2002) correlated the terms 'bordering', 'ordering', and 'othering' – which Popescu (2012) calls 'borderology' – to refer to the interplay between contemporary social and political ordering and border-making. Physical borders are there not only by virtue of tradition, wars, agreements, and high politics; they are also made and maintained through other cultural, economic, political, and social activities, which are aimed at determining who belongs and who does not.

It is for this reason that particular constructions of bordering constitute not only particular political projects of governance but also particular forms of political projects of belonging. Processes of bordering always differentiate between 'us' and 'them', those who are in and those who are out, those who are allowed to cross the borders and those who are not.

Different political projects of belonging would construct the borders as more or less permeable, would view those who want to cross the border as more or less of a security or cultural threat, and would construct the borders around different criteria for participation and entitlement for those who do cross them. Thus bordering constructions are intimately linked to specific political projects of belonging, which are at the heart of contemporary political agendas and whose contestations are closely related to different constructions of identity, belonging, and citizenship.

It is important to differentiate between belonging and the politics of belonging (Yuval-Davis, 2011). Belonging relates to emotional (or even ontological) attachment, about feeling 'at home', comfortable, and (although feminists who have worked on domestic violence would dispute this) 'safe' (Ignatieff, 2001). It is a material and affective space that is shaped by everyday practices and social relations as well as by emotions, memories, and imaginaries (Blunt, 2005: 506). This construction of belonging as being at home is also linked to views on who has a right to share the home and who does not belong there, that is, views on bordering. As we shall see later on, technologies of everyday bordering and securitisation that are supposedly aimed at making people feel safe by keeping out those who do not belong can end up undermining these feelings of safety and raising instead a sense of precarity.

Belonging, especially in terms of self-identification, tends to be naturalised (Fenster, 2004). It becomes articulated, formally structured, and politicised only when it is perceived to be under threat in some way. The politics of belonging comprises specific political projects aimed at constructing a sense of belonging to particular collectivities, which are themselves being assembled through these projects and placed within specified boundaries. For example, in specific nationalist political projects of belonging, people of colour or foreign-born persons can or cannot be part of the nation. Other kinds of projects decide whether people who support, say, the right to abortion can be part of a particular religious community, and so on.

As Antonsich (2010) points out, however, these boundaries are often spatial and relate to a specific locality or territoriality and not just to constructions of social collectivities, which brings us back to issues of bordering. In addition, as Back and Sinha (2018) emphasise (and see also Andersson, 2014), when considering issues of belonging we need to allow for the importance of the temporal dimension. These authors argue that we cannot understand migration without an appreciation of the experience of time in an unfolding life. The debate about belonging is often coded so as to refer to those seen to 'really belong' because they and their kin have put 'time into' society. Migrants, by contrast, are viewed as itinerant, passing through.

Facing the challenge of global reflexivity (Beck, 2007) expressed by quickly shifting markets, social relations, and political conditions, many non-mobile residents find it rational to claim that they really belong – to a social community, to a network of friends (including social media; see Metykova 2010), or to a particular place. However, there is a considerable gap between such claims and actual projects of 'making belonging come true'.

This is particularly true when we relate to the most common political project of belonging, which is that of state citizenship. As Sahlins (1989: 271) claims, borders are 'privileged sites for the articulations of national distinctions' and, hence, of national belonging. While regional, ethnic, racial, and religious differences might be crucial signifiers of belonging, when people travel to other countries they are usually identified, both formally and informally, through their nationality or state citizenship. Or at least this tended to be the situation until the global war on terrorism and the recent refugee crisis, when many, especially among those of Muslim background, started to be identified everywhere through their presumed religious affiliation, although at the moment of writing this identification is a subject of political campaigning but in most countries is not (yet?) embedded in law.

However, an 'undesirable' racial or religious belonging is not as important in everyday borderings as the construction of people as non-belonging.

Following Arendt (1943), Agamben (1998) has pointed out that refugees (or, more accurately, those who are seeking refuge but do not have the legal status of refugee) are constructed around a major paradox: 'that precisely the figure that should have incarnated the

8

rights of *man par excellence*, the refugee[,] constitutes instead the radical crisis of the concept' (Agamben, 1995: 116). Agamben claims that, 'in the nation-state system, the so-called sacred and inalienable rights of man prove to be completely unprotected at the very moment it is no longer possible to characterise them as rights of citizens of a state' (1998: 2). He sees refugees as a modern embodiment of 'bare life' that in the ancien régime belonged to God and in the classical world was clearly distinct (as *zoē*) from political life (*bios*), which in the modern world relates to a person's nationality. 'By breaking up the identity between man and citizen, between nativity and nationality, the refugee throws into crisis the original fiction of sovereignty' (Agamben, 1995: 177).

Given the recent refugee crisis and the fact that thousands of refuge seekers have been allowed to drown in the Mediterranean, let alone die in many other locations on the globe (such as in the Mexican desert) on their way to a secure haven, Agamben's prophetic words are a powerful vindication of the ways in which political projects of governance affect political projects of belonging. However, as Bousfield (2005), Zembylas (2010), and Yuval-Davis (2011) point out in somewhat different ways, one should not equate being deprived of legal status and civil rights to lacking subjectivity as well as agency to resist. Nor should we assume that being an outsider with no rights of citizenship means that those who seek refuge do not have other attachments and forms of belonging, or other political projects of (self-)governance. American Latino/a researchers discuss empowering identities and cultural performances by (postcolonial) migrants as 'border performantics' (Aldama et al., 2012; see also Gonzales and Sigona, 2017). The bordering scape of the 'Jungle' near Calais discussed in chapter 5 will illustrate this claim.

Having discussed the relationship, in bordering processes, between the political and the sociocultural, between governance and belonging in general terms, we now contextualise contemporary borderings within the hegemonic social order of neoliberal globalisation.

Bordering and neoliberal globalisation

It seems perhaps paradoxical that we are writing a book on bordering at a time when, for many, it was expected that borders would have become an irrelevance; after all, many of us are living more transnational lives than ever before, and the volume of transnational flows is so great. Borderings – their supposed disappearance as well as their proliferation – are central to the global and local operations of neoliberal globalisation in several different ways.

Scholte (2005) claims that most of the characteristics that are usually considered to typify globalisation – internationalisation, liberalisation, universalisation, westernisation – have existed previously under the rule of different empires and the spread of international capital and trade. Only the 're-spatialization with the spread of trans-planetary social connections' (Scholte, 2005: 3) is distinctive and a key to contemporary historical development.

Globalisation can therefore be understood as a widening and deepening of webs of interconnectedness and implies 'a heightened entanglement of the global and local' (Inda and Rosaldo, 2008: 11). This time–space compression (Harvey, 1999), the specific respatiali-sation of the present globalisation, has been possible as a result of the microchip revolution, which has brought about major changes in the speed and cost of global transport (Dicken, 2003; Rodrigue, 2006) and, even more, in global communication, especially the Internet (Block, 2004), creating what Castells calls 'information societies' (Castells, 2000 [1998]: 21) that build transnational political and cultural ties (Tsing, 2002: 457; Ong, 2006; Inda and Rosaldo 2008). Indeed, the intensity and immediacy of this connectivity and the potential for rapid change it releases not only enable greater mobility but can be linked to some of the imagery frequently encountered in popular and political discourses on contemporary migration to (and within) Europe and other western countries, such as 'flood', 'swarm', and the like – metaphors that in turn exacerbate fears among 'autochthonous' Europeans and the sense of threat that migrant mobilities present.

Contemporary globalisation has taken place under the hegemony of the neoliberal political and economic order. The economic processes inherent in neoliberalism's globalisation have been part of an imperi-alist project that serves to reconcentrate wealth according to particular class interests, creating inequalities and uneven development (Harvey, 2007a, 2007b; Petras and Veltmeyer, 2001; Saad-Filho and Johnston, 2005). In this new world order, integration is achieved through struc-tural and policy reforms that have gained global dominance since the 1970s and are driven by a range of neoliberal policies, including market deregulation and expansion through privatisation (Petras and Veltmeyer, 2001: 12–13). These neoliberal restructurings serve to distinguish the contemporary period of capitalist expansion from other periods in history when globalising tendencies were also in evidence.

According to Bob Jessop (2013a), neoliberalism took over from ordoliberalism, which was the hegemonic political economic system in the West after the Second World War; others, such as Esping-Andersen (1990), called it welfare capitalism. In ordoliberalism, the capitalist economic system was controlled by a strong state, which could limit and regulate the forces of the market.

According to Wendy Brown (2015), neoliberalism is essentially a form of governing that sees democracy at best as an obstacle and at worst as an illegitimate intervention into the rule of the market. In neoliberalism, the rule of the market is understood as a form of governance that should be applied everywhere, not just to marketised goods but to education, prisons, the organisation of the state, and so on. So neoliberalism treats popular sovereignty, or decisions based on human agreement and deliberation, as inappropriate interference with the efficient market and the price mechanism. 'Business' is viewed as a means to displace the messiness of politics and democracy. Globalisation, which was facilitated by the microchip revolution, is not, then, identical to neoliberalism but has become one of its main tools, facilitating mass movements of goods, finances, and people and destabilising local, regional, and global political and social relations.

In this context of neoliberal globalisation, particular places, territories, and scales have an advantage over others for capitalist accumulation, and certain cities and city regions have a privileged position in this spatially differentiated global order; positioning is therefore relational (Massey 1994; Sheppard 2002). The rise of what is called the economy of flows (Lash and Urry, 1994) has been highly uneven in terms of benefits. While global elites have been rapidly incorporated into a world community, others have found themselves included under much less favourable, even exploitative conditions; some places and people have been excluded from these developments or completely marginalised. As we explore further in the book, economic changes resulting from neoliberal reforms cannot be simply summarised as 'decline' or 'advantage'; the situation is far more complicated. While some places are devolving into economically marginal areas or 'grey zones' (Yiftachel, 2009; 2011), possibilities for the development of new connective social and economic activity may still exist. We assume – as does Gough (2002) with respect to the contemporary city – that neoliberal globalisation creates not only fragmentation but also opportunities for new forms of socialisation.

Increasing evidence indicates that globalisation processes are not homogeneous in their effects, but diverse and context specific, as well as often ambiguous, contradictory, unstable, and limited in their impact (Kingfisher and Maskovsky, 2008; Ward and England, 2007). As a result, scholars have shown a growing concern to explore 'actually existing neoliberalism' (Brenner and Theodore, 2002). Places and regions are constantly vying for ways to engage in economic activities and to connect with, even manipulate or subvert, centres of power. In almost all cases, inhabitants are not just passive receivers, as the seemingly marginalised both act on and transform this global complex (Nagar et al., 2002: 265; Lindner, 2007; Woods, 2007).

These developments – and the different degrees of access gained around them by different populations and segments of populations – have been crucial in shaping and structuring some of the central characteristics of contemporary neoliberal globalisation. Bordering processes have been affected by these developments in several ways, all major and all different, and have themselves caused, in turn, some significant social, economic, and political effects.

First, the time–space compression associated with globalisation has made physical and virtual mobility and connectivity much easier (Urry, 2007). This has resulted in a dramatic rise in the volume of global border crossers. Overall, the rise in cross-border mobilities of not just people but goods, services, and capital is often framed as unprecedented (O'Byrne, 2001). At the same time, these developments have also facilitated the installation of sophisticated systems of surveillance both at physical border zones and everywhere else, in and outside state territories, via satellites and other virtual and digital means (Broeders, 2007).

Secondly, neoliberal globalisation, like previous imperial globalisations but probably even more so because of the mobility and communication technological developments, has made the global economy much more interdependent and at the same time diversified. The expansion of global capitalism can be characterised by the flexibility of labour (e.g. part-time or contracted work, which is much less protected in terms of labour conditions and workers' rights) and of labour markets, as well as by the creation of new markets, and new ways of organising production and of arranging and coordinating the international financial system (Harvey, 1989: 147–72). In this neoliberal restructuring of capitalism, the role of the state is no longer that of a basic unit for the accumulation of capital, trade, and investment—which now take place transnationally.

As Mezzadra and Neilson (2012) point out, this required a proliferation of bordering to operate as labour regulators. As these and other scholars argue (see e.g. Brambilla et al., 2015), global neoliberalism relies on complex and shifting flows of heterogeneous labour force and differential rates of pay for different kinds of labour in different parts of the world, where various bordering processes are vital as regulatory mechanisms. Moreover, while neoliberal companies depend on global mobility, there is a huge disparity, although also degrees of mutual dependency, between different kinds of labour that are filled in by people of usually different genders, education, and origin and who are subject to differential regimes of bordering permeability.

This creates a system of transnational stratifications constructed through people's accessibility to different kinds of passports and visas (to be discussed in chapter 2); and these different kinds dictate cross-border mobility, transforming borders into a virtual computer firewall (Rumford, 2006). Mezzadra and Neilson use the examples of mutual dependence among careworkers and global finance workers to illustrate this point; but, as will be seen in the bordering scapes presented in chapters 3–5, a variety of participants depend on different bordering encounters, and this dependence often cuts across not only the national–transnational, the skilled–unskilled, or the public–private, but also the legal and the nefarious.

Thirdly (and this point is closely associated with the second), global economic interdependence under neoliberalism has increased and polarised social and economic inequalities both globally, between the North and the South, and within each society. The capabilities required for globalisation have developed within the context of (western) nation-states and reached tipping points in which they were transformed by and became part of the new assemblage of the global economic and political order (Sassen, 2006). Globalisation reshaped and expanded capitalism, which is centred on surplus accumulation. The growth of transworld spaces has encouraged major extensions of capitalist production, including in areas of information, communications, and finance biotechnology. Notable shifts occurred in the ways in which processes of surplus accumulation operate – for example offshore arrangements and transworld corporate alliances – towards what Sassen calls 'hypercapitalism'. Hypercapitalism – or neoliberalism – is, however, driven by the same impulses that drove nineteenth-century imperial capitalism and found new fields for the 'primitive accumulation of capital' through the appropriation of capital and goods from the public sector – spectacularly so in the postcommunist countries, but also in the 'developing' (or industrialising) world and in the West, thanks to the spreading control

13

of neoliberal market norms in more and more sectors of the state (Massey, 1995).

This state of affairs has created at least three different social processes with profound effects on contemporary bordering scapes. It created a global economic elite, executives and directors of multinational companies in which, significantly, there is also a growing minority of women and of people from the Global South, especially from what is known as the 'tiger economies' (Poon, 1996). This economic elite is constantly on the move, establishing its operations in different countries according to the suitability of the different locations in terms of infrastructure, labour force, and tax regimes.

Neoliberal globalisation has also created larger and larger territories – mostly, but not exclusively in the South – where the local economies were destroyed and no alternative systems have been created. As a result, there is a growing number of people, especially young men, who are desperate to migrate to areas of economic growth and are prepared to face any hardships for it, but on arrival have no skills to offer, except casual labour under the living wage (Triandafyllidou, 2016). These are the people whom Kofi Annan, former UN secretary general, has branded 'people on the move'. Although the UN has recently established an interagency committee on migration, there is no international legislation that compels nation-states to allow them entrance to their territories, as in the case of refugees and asylum seekers fleeing from zones of armed conflict and from governments' oppression; and the more pressure is created by these people as they try to migrate in growing waves, the more punitive the bordering regimes developed by different states become (Fekete, 2009). To a large extent, the growing number of people in 'limbo-scapes' and 'grey zones' (which will be discussed in chapter 5) is an outcome of this process. The humanitarian discourse that is often used when camps are formally established by the UN, international aid organisations, and NGOs, is often contradicted by draconian measures taken by different states and regions to block migrants from entry. Such measures range from razor wire through detention camps in deserts and islands to mass expulsions to a third country.

Another way in which neoliberal globalisation has affected bordering is via its effects on states' governability. As discussed in chapter 2, neoliberal globalisation emerged during a period of global optimism, after the fall of the Soviet Union and the supposed victory of democracy and freedom (the 'end of history' to quote Fukuyama, 1992), in a cosmopolitan world in which social, national, and state borders were on the wane and the state as 'container of power' (Giddens, 1985; Taylor, 2004) was going to be over. States were seen as withering away, becoming weaker and less able to impose their will on other social, economic, and political carriers of power.

With the growing hegemony of neoliberal ideologies and policies and the strengthening of neoliberal global market forces, more and more agencies and the state apparatus in increasing numbers of countries have been privatised or restructured, either fully or in part (Jessop 2013a, 2002; McBride, 2005). In this way labour protections were loosened at a time when contemporary societies were becoming increasingly diverse, layered, and interconnected (Gonzales and Sigona, 2017). This does not mean that states stopped being important to neoliberal globalisation – all over the globe, the entire infrastructure in which corporations operate is after all, at least nominally, under the control of individual states. For the purpose of taxation all corporations are registered in particular states (which is often not where their main operations take place). The United States has had a special role in the development and running of neoliberal globalisation (Panitch and Gindin, 2012).

Saskia Sassen (2006) has concluded that, rather than weakening states overall, neoliberal globalisation has exerted on them a kind of pressure that caused some important internal changes. One such change is that the executive powers of governance have been strengthened at the expense of the legislative powers. With the privatisation of the state, a lot of the regulative tasks of the legislative branch have been lost; at the same time the executive branch negotiates virtually on its own with other national and supranational governance executives (the EU, the UN, the World Bank, the WTO) as well as with private, national, and especially transnational corporations. The struggle of the British parliament to be included significantly in the Brexit negotiations is a clear illustration of such a shift. Some would say that the inclusion of so many corporate executives in Donald Trump's postelection cabinet represents an even further stage in this transformation, in which corporations give up on the 'middlemen' and enter state politics directly.

Yuval-Davis (2012), however, argues that Sassen's position is somewhat overoptimistic and that liberal democratic states have not only shifted the internal balance of powers, but also suffered overall from a certain depletion of their powers. As the banking crisis has shown, with the growing entanglement and dependency of local and global markets and of local private and public institutions, various states have been forced to bail out banks and large corporations for fear of total economic collapse, while at the same time the governability of state agencies, their ability to reinforce regulations on that same private sector, is severely limited.

This is ultimately the result of a basic legal relationship between corporations and states in which companies have the status of fictional citizens. This status, carried by the famous 'Ltd' affix, enables the people who run these companies to escape responsibility for the results of the actions of their corporations. Moreover, while states were forced to bail out banks in order to avoid major economic collapses, states themselves – such as Ireland, Greece, and others – were forced to cut their budgets severely, against the interests of their citizens, because (among other reasons) they have become dependent on their credit assessment, which is carried out by the global financial market. These practices started, however, not in the Global North but in the Global South, through the enforcement of 'structural adjustments' programmes by the IMF and the World Bank. They began more than a decade earlier and had similar results (Bello et al., 1994).

A global crisis of governmentality has followed this crisis of governability (Yuval-Davis, 2012); this is because, when people feel that their interests are not pursued by their governments – even by the most radical ones, such as the Syriza party, which came to power in Greece – they are disempowered and deprived. After a while they also stop buying the neoliberal ideology, which tells them that it is their responsibility if they fail to be healthy and wealthy, to provide for their families, and to become incredibly rich and famous. This disenchantment has triggered forms of resistance that have employed everyday bordering both as a rhetoric and as a practice to 'regain control' – to use a popular Brexit slogan – and have articulated autochthonous claims of belonging (Geschiere, 2009; Yuval-Davis, 2011) as social and political triggers to 'reborder' the state and to keep its resources exclusively for those who 'really belong'.

The combined crisis of governability and governmentality at a time of growing global mobility and of deeper heterogenisation of the local population as a result of migration brought with it also the major crisis of multiculturalism as the technology of control over diversity and discourses of diversity, which became hegemonic in the North after World War II and during the period when the welfare state flourished. Carl Ulrik Schierup et al. (2006) claimed that multiculturalism was an ideological base for transatlantic alignment whose project was the transformation of the welfare state, in late modernity or postmodernity, into a pluralist state in which cultural diversity rights would be incorporated into the more traditional

16

welfare social rights (see also Rex, 1995). However, as Brown (2009) stated, multiculturalism can also be described as a technology of controlling and regulating aversion via tolerance. With the double crisis of governability and governmentality in the new millennium, this technology is gradually giving way to policies that encourage a 'hostile environment' (to use the British government discourse in the run-up to the 2014 and 2016 Immigration Acts). We call such policies 'everyday bordering'.

Thus everyday bordering has come to replace multiculturalism as the hegemonic governance technology for controlling diversity and discourses of diversity, using often both securitisation and racialised discourses of belonging. In everyday life, bordering has developed as a technology of control of diversity by governments, which allegedly have been seeking to reassert control over the composition and security of the population. Instead of being found at the edge, separating and connecting one state to another, borders have now spread so as to be everywhere. Airports, train stations, even places of work, worship, and living can be borders. Borders can be situated in embassies as well as at the heart of metropolitan cities. Any place has become a borderland; and borderlands can no longer be determined exclusively in relation to specific territories and states.

In different and new contexts, citizens are required to become untrained and unpaid border guards, and more of us are falling under suspicion as illegitimate border crossers. Therefore the relationship between bordering as a top-down political project and everyday processes of 'othering' or constructing 'us' and 'them' – which is in any case linked to political boundary-making – is also intensifying. This tendency, which has been developing since before 9/11, is now institutionalised and legalised in many states. This happened in recent years, especially after the refugee crisis of 2015. More material and legal walls have been erected between and within states to prevent 'undesirable' migrants from entering or staying in this or that country. Promises to this effect, which have been central to the electoral success of Trump in the United States, Orbán in Hungary, and others elsewhere, signal the transition, in political discourse, from what Nancy Fraser (2017) calls 'progressive neoliberalism' – which has used the discourse of human rights, at least rhetorically – to outright exclusionary nationalist discourse.

In the United Kingdom, through the 2014 and 2016 Immigration Acts (as we detail in chapter 4), landlords, employers, teachers, and doctors are responsible for verifying that their tenants, employees, students, and patients are legally in the country and, if they fail,

17

they may be fined or even go to prison, unlike those who are trained and paid to do this job. In this way, far from supporting a multicultural society of convivial diversity, this technology of control breeds suspicion, fear, and boundaries sensitisation both among those who belong and among those who do not. Brexit only enhances this sense of differentiation and hierarchisation among people and has become a model for right-wing autochthonic movements throughout Europe. Similar trends are evident in the Global North (e.g. the United States) and in the Global South (e.g. India).

Thus neoliberal globalisation, which seemed to many to facilitate a cosmopolitan 'borderless' world, has used bordering in its global regulatory work, by cooperating with and exploiting, in differential and hierarchical ways, different population groupings, states, and spaces across the globe. However, as Alpa Parmar (2018) has observed, contemporary borderings should not be seen as introducing new divisive imaginaries. Rather she views borders across western liberal democracies as mirrors that reflect, deflect, and obscure the image of western democracies, their attitudes to race, and their emotions about racial others. One needs at the same time to analyse the transformative function of borders in conjunction with their aim to preserve, all across the world, those local and global hierarchies, both racial and colonial, that govern mobility for some but not for others.

In the next chapter we present an overview of the main historical developments that have brought bordering to the centre of contemporary global political discourse as it is today. However, before turning to this task (and to the more detailed ethnographic borderscaping cases of the following chapters, which will illustrate the main features of contemporary bordering), we need to say a word about the methodological and epistemological framework of our analysis.

From borders to bordering: The processual turn

The outsourcing of borders (Yuval-Davis et al., 2016) has been part of the dynamics of contemporary mobile borders, which involve processes of debordering and rebordering (Newman and Paasi, 1998; Popescu, 2012; Szary and Giraut, 2015), in other words the deterritorialisation of borders from fixed border zones and their relocation in a multiplicity of spaces spread throughout civil society – especially in urban settings, which have become official and unofficial border checkpoints (Balibar, 2004; Vaughan-Williams, 2008). Bordering takes place inside and outside, as well as along the official borders of the state. In school textbooks as well as on official maps and globes, state borders are marked as fixed linear contours that are usually recognised by international law and in international relations as marking the official edges of the territory or space over which one single state has control – a naturalised 'homeland'. This hegemonic imaginary (Bürkner, 2018; Jessop, 2013b), however, covers political, social, cultural, and economic realities that are much more complex and less stable than official discourses would want us to believe and reflect global as well as regional and national power relations.

The literature of border studies – what has recently been called 'borderities' (Szary and Giraut, 2015) – tends to contrast the imaginary construction of 'borders' as fixed lines with that of 'bordering' as a process, as an attribute of different temporalities, and discusses 'borderings' as multiple and mobile processes specific only to the post-Cold War and neoliberal globalisation period. The term 'borderscapes' has tended to be used as a very specific descriptor of contemporary bordering processes under global neoliberalism (e.g. Perera, 2007; Mezzadra and Neilson, 2012). Brambilla (2014: 19) argues that the notion of borderscapes seeks 'to express the spatial and conceptual complexity of the border as a space that is not static but fluid and shifting; established and at the same time continuously traversed by a number of bodies, discourses, practices and [internal and external to the state] relationships'.

However, we argue that all bordering processes, in all times and places, need to be analysed in such a way, although, of course, there are technological and other specificities to what is currently happening. For this reason, we use in this book the term 'bordering scape' to refer to any spatial zone in which specific bordering processes are taking place. Such a zone can be found along a particular state border or at the heart of a metropolitan city; in a particular mountain area or in a whole state, region, or the globe. In other words, bordering scapes appear at a multiplicity of spatial scales – the scales at which specific bordering processes take place.

We argue that, although it is true that bordering processes have changed significantly during the period we cover here (and chapter 2 discusses this aspect in detail) and that both political and academic discourses have tended to describe them in this way, we do not see borders as having always fitted in with this hegemonic imaginary perfectly and without contestation and, to the extent that they have, such a fit reflected more of a moment of strong hegemonic control than an inherent characteristic.

19

Not surprisingly, the borders that have been constructed as completely straight lines, with the least regard for local geographical and social contexts, belonged to countries under colonial rule, where borders were decided by regional or global superpowers rather than through any bottom-up political processes. This situation is reflected in the history of border delineations of states as different from one another as Zambia, Thailand, or Finland.

Moreover, the continuous linear construction of borders along the edges of states' territories – a construction that invites the image of states as containers (Taylor, 1994) whose territories exclude one another – is, as Ben Anderson (1991) has pointed out, of relatively short historical duration. In premodern times, state borders consisted of points of contact rather than continuous lines; and, as has become clear in the Afghanistan War, for instance, in certain parts of the Global South, especially in mountainous areas, such continuous lines do not exist on the ground in our days either. Even when they do exist, they can be contested as a result of national political conflicts in which two or more states (or stateless national collectivities) claim ownership on territories that are included in the borders of another state, such as in Kashmir or Crimea. In extreme cases, such as in the states of Israel or Northern Cyprus, most or all borders lack official international recognition.

As Mustasaari (2016) points out (and see also Yuval-Davis and Stoezler, 2002), the construction of meanings and the imaginaries about borders can range from representing them as desired barriers against the demonised 'other' and as means of exclusion to a conception of the border as an institution that maybe is in need of reform but is essential to economic survival. Border narratives should be read through their historicity and relationality. Bordering practices and social divisions affect each other, are constantly changing, and can both include and exclude certain collectivities. The 'border' and the divisions stemming from it are fluid, contextual, and spatially manifest in the community and its relations with the state (Aure, 2011).

Two terms that have been commonly used to describe bordering spatial zones are 'frontiers' and 'borderlands'. Mezzadra and Neilson (2012) and Weizman (2012), link the notion of frontiers directly to the bordering processes that dominate colonial expansion. In consequence, frontiers are elastic and can be controlled through mobile techniques. Frontiers can be observed in India during the days of the East India Company, in the Wild West of North America, and in other settler societies and occupied countries, for example during the Napoleonic Wars, under Nazi occupation, or in the Palestinian territories occupied by Israel. The frontier bordering scape is important when we analyse the notion of bordering as an illustration of the fact that the elasticity and mobility of bordering processes and the different technologies of control that constitute them are not unique to colonial contexts; they are rather central to the territorialised, deterritorialised, and reterritorialised ways in which states construct their hegemonic powers. Indeed, Donnan and Wilson (1999) see all borders as formative frontiers of identities, nations, and states.

Borderlands is the term used in the literature (e.g. Baud and van Schendel, 1997; Doevenspeck, 2011) to designate spaces in which the lives of the local population are formed as well as controlled by the dual and competing political, cultural, and economic bordering realities on the ground. Borderlands are specific territorial zones in which the geographic state borders themselves become embedded in the everyday lives, identities, and livelihood of the people who live in them, so that the border largely defines the spatial understanding of the local context and the social and cultural meanings attached to them.

Unlike the traditional notion of borders, the spatial imaginary of 'borderlands', like that of frontiers, has been not linear but territorial and spatial, related to areas of land and to population groups that live near and often across state borders. It draws attention to the ways in which people who live in border zones often differ, politically and culturally, from most other population groups in the country. This difference can be due to the ethnic and national origins of border people – a social and political factor that was disregarded in the historical processes of constructing official state borders; one could look for example not only at the Saami people but also at other minorities who live on either side of the state borders dividing Sweden and Finland. The difference can also spring from the fact that a specific border economy often develops in these areas, so that people who live near state borders make their livelihood by trading across the border, legally or not (Cassidy, 2013).

Cultural studies scholars who studied borderlands – especially the one between the United States and Mexico (e.g. Anzaldúa, 1987; Rosaldo, 1997) – pointed out an important cultural characteristic of the people who inhabit such spaces. This is cultural hybridisation, a feature that many have seen as reflecting more general cultural developments in postmodern times (Bhabha, 2015 [1994]; Lavie and Swedenburg, 1996).

21

These processes of hybridisation, as well as all cultural, political, and economic cross-border activities, take place in a global and regional context in which power relations between two neighbouring states and among the borderland people on the two sides of the border are not symmetrical and generate a variety of personal, political, and economic conflicts and resistance. In discussing the emergence of hybrid communities such as the 'new Mestiza', for example, Anzaldúa (1987: 19) rightly emphasises that such border-lands are abundant with the 'hatred, anger and exploitation [that] are the prominent features of this landscape'.

The spread of a hybrid border culture in the population as a whole is a phenomenon triggered by, but not confined to, cross-border migrations and echoes the more general need to theorise bordering processes in a relational way. Sassen calls it an 'analytic borderland': 'A heuristic device that allows one to take what is commonly repre-sented as a line separating two differences, typically seen as mutually exclusive, into a conceptual field – a third entity – that requires its own empirical specification and theorization' (Sassen, 2006: 379).

As will be discussed in more detail in chapter 5, it is important to observe, as part of this overall change, what happens to border zones that become 'post-borderlands' – communities that continue to depend on borders for their symbolic and territorial identities yet have lost their political and economic *raison d'être* as gatekeepers in particular bordering zones. Given their character, post-borderlands are specific bordering scapes that emerge as just one of the 'grey zones' typical of neoliberal globalisation.

There is a complex – or even paradoxical – relationship between the notion of borders and the notion of migration. On the one hand, migrants and immigrants are embodiments of the permeability of borders, of the multicultural, cosmopolitan nature of contemporary society, especially in metropolitan societies. On the other hand, as discussed above, more and more border work is aimed at blocking migrants – or rather certain kinds of migrants, who are deemed to be dangerous, 'undesirable', or just redundant to the country's economic needs – from crossing a border and becoming members of the society on the other side. This is the bordering 'firewall' in action; we will take a closer look at it in chapter 3. At the same time, whereas business and professional elites are able to move across the globe with growing ease and frequency thanks to technological and political developments – the 'frequent flyers' club, to use Calhoun's (2003a) expression – millions of other people, most of them from the Global South, who want to cross borders are blocked from doing so. As will be discussed in chapter 5, it is for this reason that more and more migrants join the ranks of those suspended in in-between 'limbo spaces' – another type of grey zone produced by neoliberal globalisation – either before or after they cross the borders. Thus more and more would-be migrants, instead of being border crossers, become an embodiment of the border itself (Dona, 2015). In the grey zones they inhabit it is hardly possible to plan and build any life project, even a medium-range one (Edkins, 2000; Manjikian, 2010; Hyndman and Giles, 2011, 2016).

As Yiftachel (2009) and others have pointed out, these grey zones exist not just around borders but also in big cities and other spaces in which the power of the state is being fragmented from below and new relations of power, of governance, and of belonging prevail. These grey spaces should be seen as important contemporary bordering scapes that highlight not just the complexity but also the failure of state governance, in more and more spaces. While the disenchantment of dislocated traditional working-class citizens in post-borderlands of the North (Cassidy et al. 2018a) is largely focused on their hope that control of borders and immigration will solve their systemic crises, migrants are increasingly 'stuck' in the in-between in their everyday lives, and grey zones multiply, reaching into more and more spaces in the Global South and North. When we discuss migrants in limbo spaces, and the grey zones within and outside state territories, the need arises to examine again the notion of citizenship and its relation to both human and civil rights.

Borders and boundaries, then, should not be viewed just as an application of top-down macro social and state policies; they are present in everyday discourses and in the practices of different social agents, from state functionaries to the media and all other members of society (Wemyss et al., 2018; Wemyss and Cassidy, 2017; Yuval-Davis et al., 2018; Yuval-Davis, Varjú et al., 2017). Importantly, we need to understand that these everyday bordering processes are not just national but are global processes, as they 'enable the channelling of (global) flows and provide coordinates within which flows can be joined or segmented, connected or disconnected' (Mezzadra and Neilson 2012: 59). In consequence, as we mentioned early in the chapter, borders need to be seen as constitutive of the world rather than as dividing an already made one, as differential border controls regulate labour no less than the production and distribution of goods and services in different parts of the world. Moreover, borderings affect people profoundly, not just in their countries of origin or destination but frequently in the many countries in which they stop or are detained on the way. Border guarding is organised on a country basis; what is more, it uses organisations like Frontex and private companies that guard regions rather than just individual states. Security datasets are shared between states as a matter of routine.

Although when discussing the specific effects of bordering we focus on particular locations and times, we need to contextualise them with the help of a multiscalar gaze on policies, discourses, imaginaries, and the situated views of those people who, while participating in a particular bordering encounter at a certain time, also carry with them bordering experiences from other places. It is from this perspective that we need to evaluate everyday borderings.

Everyday intersectional bordering

We regard the analysis presented in this book as part of a wider turn in contemporary social theory that requires 'a shared understanding of practices as embodied, materially mediated arrays of human activity' (Schatzki, 2001: 1). Narratives and practices of everyday lives – this is the place where the nature and transformation of the subject matter of these practices needs to be studied. Ben Anderson (1998) called this methodological approach 'the inverted telescope'. The idea is to use microscale everyday bordering practices in order to both conceptualise and visualise what borders are at a more general level.

Borderings are therefore practices that are situated and constituted in the specificity of political negotiations as well as in the everyday life performances of these negotiations, being shifting and contested across individuals and groupings as well as in the constructions of individual subjectivities. As Paasi and Prokkola (2008) argue, borders can be found everywhere in society, in various forms of 'banal flagging' of the national in everyday life (Billig, 1995). Emotional bordering is loaded in national flag days and in other national iconographies and practices – and this is the 'location' of the borders. Active border work may deconstruct established and existing forms and codes of national socialisation in some locations. On the other hand, borders are also crucial to what can be called the discursive landscape of social power constructions, which manifest themselves in material landscapes, ideologies, and national performances all over the territory. We argue that all these can be found in the everyday.

While Sarah Pink (2012: 143) argues that the everyday is 'at the centre of human existence, the essence of who we are and our location in the world', we would argue that the definitions of who we are and what our location in the world is are, both, constructed by discourses and imaginaries of particular bordering political projects of governance and belonging that are affected by the situated positionings, identifications, and normative value systems of the specific social agents that take part in this 'everyday' social dynamics. This is especially true of the ways in which discourses and practices of bordering are interwoven into the everyday lives of contemporary people, particularly in metropolitan cities (Jones and Johnson, 2014; Yuval-Davis et al., 2018).

Back (2015: 820) argues that the study of everyday lives necessitates developing an eye for detail and attentiveness to the 'seemingly unimportant'. This links to the assumed equivalence between 'the ordinary' (seemingly unimportant) and 'the everyday' (Hall, 2015: 865) in much of the literature on the everyday. Featherstone (1992) dichotomises between 'everyday life' and 'heroic life'. We argue, however, that 'everyday life' encompasses and has the capacity to routinise also extraordinary (or 'heroic') lives, as the lives of many of the border crossers we have encountered have been, especially the 'irregular' ones among them (see chapter 5). We would also question the construction of the dichotomy stated by Neal and Murji (2015: 817) and implicit in 'co-constituting' the everyday 'as a site of resistance' and as 'a site of normativity', since the notions of normativity and resistance depend on the different discourses of belonging of the participants in these everyday situations.

Rather than describing everyday lives as random 'babble of multiple tongues' (Featherstone, 1992) or as 'what is left over' after all the distinct, superior, specialised, structured activities have been singled out by analysis (Lefebvre 1991: 97), we must define them as a totality. Therefore we argue that 'everyday life' cannot be understood unless we employ a situated intersectional analysis that encompasses the different ways in which people understand and experience their lives (Yuval-Davis, 2015a).

It is not possible to carry out 'an objective' analysis of any social situations of 'the everyday'. Rather any epistemological attempt 'to approach the truth' (Collins, 1990) necessitates a dialogical process that should encompass the differently situated gazes, the knowledge, and the imagination of the social actors involved. Such an approach differs both from positivist approaches, which assume one 'objective' truth (usually determined by the researcher), and from relativist approaches, which assume a different and autonomous truth for each different social positioning. To achieve this dialogical process, we have used a specific methodology of intersectionality, which Yuval-Davis (2015a) calls 'situated intersectionality' in order to differentiate it from other intersectionality approaches.

As a theoretical approach to the study of social inequality, intersectionality can be described as a development of feminist standpoint theory, which claims, in somewhat different ways, that it is vital to account for the social positioning of the social agent – the researcher or the researched – and to challenge 'the god-trick of seeing everything from nowhere' (Haraway 1991: 189) as a cover and a legitimisation of a hegemonic masculinist 'positivistic' positioning. Situated gaze, situated knowledge, and situated imagination (Stoetzler and Yuval-Davis, 2002) construct differently the ways in which we see the world. At the same time, it is important to remember that people with the same social positionings would develop different identifications and emotional attachments, as well as different normative values, and all this would affect the situated gazes of particular social actors at any particular moment.

Lesley McCall (2005: 1771) and others argue that intersectionality is 'the most important theoretical contribution that women's studies, in conjunction with related fields, has made so far'. While the term was originally used by Kimberlé Crenshaw (1989: 139), scholars in different academic fields and activists from different parts of the globe developed intersectionality in somewhat different ways (see Lutz et al., 2011; Hancock, 2016; Collins and Bilge 2016; and the two special issues dedicated to intersectionality, *European Journal of Women's Studies*, vol. 13, issue 3 of 2006 and *Signs*, vol. 38, issue 4 of 2013).

While much of this development is linked to black feminist politics (Brah and Phoenix, 2004), we argue that our analytical and political approach to situated intersectionality should be applied to all people of all times and spaces. Only in this way can we avoid the risk of exceptionalism, which would reinforce the view of marginalised and racialised women as 'a problem' and, with that, also the practice of their surveillance.

Intersectionality analysis relates to the distribution of power and other resources in society and does not reduce the complexity of power constructions to a single social division – as has been prevalent, for instance, in sociological stratification theories, which privilege only class divisions. Situated intersectionality views different social divisions as discourses and practices that are ontologically different and irreducible to one another but that, in any concrete situation, are mutually constituted and shaped. They form the particular, nuanced, and contested meanings of particular social locations in particular historical moments and within particular social, economic, and political contexts, in which some social divisions have more saliency and effect than others.

The ethnographic methodology on which the empirical illustrative bordering scapes we are using in this book are based has encompassed observations, individual and collective interviews, and contextual analysis of policy documents and the press. It is aimed to capture the multilevel complexities of different bordering processes by focusing on a range of everyday situated intersectional encounters at the 'internal border'. Through careful contextualisation of these everyday bordering encounters we were able to link the level of macropolitics that legitimises the internal borders with related media coverage of immigration and thereby to identify the issues and the lived bordering experiences of differently situated people in multi-scalar ways.

By analysing various individual perspectives on these internal bordering processes, we are able to see how the people involved construct and reconstruct the border, as well as their own identities and claims of belonging, through the creation of sociocultural, political, and geographical distinctions. The capture of such multilevel complexity necessitates a methodological approach that is sensitive to broader contextual processes and recognises the shifting nature of connections between research subjects and multiple sites, times, and spaces. This is particularly important in metropolitan areas, where the volume of connections to other places and the intersections among them lead to a plurality of encounters with bordering processes, seen from differently situated perspectives. As Manson (2001: 59) points out, complexity theories insist that it is impossible to understand changes in complex global systems without reference to the relatively simple local interaction between system components over time.

Our research, therefore, has not been concerned only with 'agonistic' encounters such as those between the UK Border Force – which is required by law to take on border-guarding roles – and its targets, but relates also to convivial encounters that are threatened by the encroachment of the border further into everyday life in pluralist society. Our fieldwork was carried out in the United Kingdom at the Dover–Calais border zone and in London, from May 2013 to June 2016, during the period in which the British Immigration Act 2014 was being drafted and debated inside and outside parliament. The Act was passed in October 2014 and our fieldwork continued as the Act's legislative requirements were introduced over the following twelve months.

The richness of the material we collected during this four-year research project cannot be contained even in a book-length monograph. Moreover, given our methodological approach, we need to evaluate vernacular meanings of bordering, which are based on specific intersectional dialogical encounters in wider spatial, temporal, and scalar contexts. For this reason, after the next chapter, in which we present, in a wide brush, what we believe to be the most significant developments in bordering in recent times, we focus on nine constructions of contemporary everyday bordering scapes that we believe are crucial to understanding contemporary local and global bordering.

Outline of the book

After this introductory chapter, the next one explores borderings as global historical processes. It examines the impact of various developments of Westphalian 'nation-states' on bordering, as well as on political empires and settler colonial societies; and it also considers how these have been transformed under the new world (dis)order of neoliberal globalisation. The chapter locates the growing political importance of contemporary bordering discourses within the context of the double crisis of governability and governmentality in neoliberal globalisation. It examines the history of border-crossing documentation forms such as passports and visas and provides an overview of the main developments and shifts in bordering matters during the last century.

Chapters 3 to 5 focus on some of the main facets of contemporary bordering processes that are described in the introductory chapters. Each chapter begins with a discussion of globally significant contemporary borderings that situates the empirical material in its international context. They then present selected empirical bordering scapes in specific times and places, mainly in the United Kingdom (but elsewhere too). Each chapter will introduce three illustrations of bordering scapes, using the methodological and epistemological lens of everyday situated intersectionality to study them.

Chapter 3 elaborates on the notion of borders as computer firewalls that pre-select who would be allowed to cross the border, who would be blocked from doing so, and under what conditions. The first two illustrative bordering scapes that the chapter focuses on are international border-crossing control points and registrations of marriages as internal border-crossing control points. Thirdly, the chapter discusses internal and international border crossing by two racialised minority groups in the United Kingdom where the intersection of political projects of governance and belonging is particularly visible: Nepali families associated with the British Army; and European Roma communities.

Chapter 4 views contemporary borderings that can be found everywhere and everyday as a constitutive part of people's citizenship and belonging. It illustrates both the centrality of contemporary borderings in constructing people's identities and access to public and private resources and the effects that these borderings have on cohesion and solidarity in society as a whole. Bordering scapes 4, 5, and 6 in this chapter focus on different aspects of the 'hostile environment' that the British state has constructed for migrants, especially in the 2014 and 2016 Immigration Acts, examining in particular the fields of employment, housing, and education.

Chapter 5 examines the growing impact of borderings on constructing indeterminate in-betweenness and grey zones for a larger and larger number of people who live in continuous limbo states, inside as well as outside state borders. Bordering scape 7 focuses on the limbo space of the 'jungle' in Calais, made up of people who attempted to cross the border into the United Kingdom but got stuck there owing to United Kingdom's offshoring (i.e. relocating) its border with France to Calais and surrounding areas. Bordering scape 8 focuses on the continuous bordering experience of those who live in the United Kingdom but have not yet managed to get a permanent residency status, being caught in the gaps and conflicts between international law, which protects the rights of forced migrants, and the British policy of creating a hostile environment for those who 'do not belong'. The last bordering scape studies lives that are spent in the grey zones of the 'stayers' and examines Dover as a 'post-borderland' bordering scape, left behind by the privileging of global cities and the complex debordering processes related to multiscalar political and economic changes in the Global North.

Chapter 6, the conclusion of the book, sums up our main arguments: the constitutive role of borderings; their reflection of intersecting political projects of governance and belonging; their major role in controlling and widening multiscalar social inequalities; and the need to encompass differentially situated gazes in order to understand the meanings of bordering fully. The chapter concludes with reflections on transversal political alliances and on some of the possible directions that situated resistance to the injustices caused by contemporary borderings should take.

2

Bordering, Governance, and Belonging

An Historical Overview

Introduction

In the previous chapter we looked at our conceptual and methodo-logical approach to the study of bordering. Here we contextualise, historically and spatially, the contemporary bordering scapes that will be presented in the main body of the book (chapters 3–5). We have organised this chapter chronologically. The first half looks at premodern and modern bordering up to the end of the Cold War. The second half focuses on the rise of neoliberal globalisation and contemporary borderings.

Our aim here is to produce a more nuanced and complex analysis of historical borderings that will challenge the assumption that their contemporary proliferation is somehow inevitable. Just as in the 1980s, when the Conservative slogan 'there is no alternative' (TINA) became the rallying cry and basis for Margaret Thatcher's sweeping reforms, which were grounded in neoliberal ideologies, we find ourselves living in a time when governments across the Global North are claiming that 'there is no alternative' to dominant paradigms of border securitisation and internalisation; and these paradigms have in turn led to the multiplication of border(ing)s and of their disruptive and intrusive extension into all areas of our lives, as more and more of our resources were devoted to such efforts. In this chapter we explore and elucidate the proposition that, far from there being no alternative to the current situation, throughout history there have been many alternative forms of delimiting territorial control and many examples of political projects that do not involve such demarcations. We seek to challenge the idea of the 'inevitability' of contemporary bordering that underlies current approaches. In doing so, we trace the history of bordering itself and, more specifically, its entanglement with the governance of belonging. We give borders their own 'biography' (Megoran, 2012), recognising that territorial borders should be afforded a narrative and a history. We show that the very idea of bordering or attempting to delimit control over a particular territory can be differentiated across space and time; and we seek to avoid a Eurocentric analysis of bordering. At the heart of our discourse here lies a critique that attempts to disentangle bordering from imperialism and neoliberalism, which have shaped so much of contemporary global society, and in particular to emphasise the ways in which migration, the very threat that everyday bordering legislation in the Global North is trying to eliminate, is a direct result of the deliberate approaches to governance employed by these states in their expansionism – alongside the relentless drive of the market that their policies have so clearly enabled. Indeed, as de Genova (2017) has argued, borders produce migration; without them there is only mobility.

Premodern borderings

Historically, there were attempts to delimit territory and create forms of borders such as lines via linear fortifications. Yet the vast majority of scholars seem to argue that these early kinds of border fortification were often permeable to trade and other cross-border interactions (cf. Whittaker, 1994). Early fortifications never delimited an entire territory; they were selective. While the very existence of the Great Wall of China, for example, might appear to confirm the ancient roots of boundary-making on territory, it is perhaps more useful to think of it as the exception rather than the rule. We can conceive of it more as a spectacle of power than as a real attempt to control movement across a territory.

Popescu (2012) suggests that early borders were defensive and commercial. They had one of two roles, and sometimes both: to control trade and to deter barbarian invaders. As such, they did not seek to mark the sovereignty of the state, which was much more closely linked to peoples and individual subjects. Therefore these imperial borders can be viewed as a temporary form of demarcation,

31

as borders generally have been throughout history. Yet in ancient imperial China and other ancient civilisations, unlike today, one fully expected borders to be challenged, since rulers saw it as their divine right to extend their influence over more subjects. As Benedict Anderson (1991) points out, usually these borders were not continuous and the boundary stones set at strategic crossing points were often some distance away from those of the neighbouring state, in a borderland zone.

It has been argued that the introduction of the concept of lines into border-making can be traced to the shift from tribal to territorial law – that is, from *ius sanguinis* to territorial sovereignty. 'Sovereignty is territorial; hence it must have a certain known extent' (Kristof, 1959: 271). However, this does not mean that each frontier was produced and understood in the same way; indeed, it is difficult to find any form of universality that could be applied to premodern frontiers. As Kristof (1959: 275) suggested, '[a] boundary does not exist in nature or by itself. It always owes its existence to man' – and in consequence he posits that similarities in the way of life often shaped the emergence of frontiers. Such a view clearly overlaps with the idea of a convergence between sociocultural boundary-making and political border(ing)s, discussed in chapter 1.

Some interpret these early, loose boundary formations as one stepping stone on the way to more fixed or permanent entities (Kristof, 1959). However, Barfield (2001) argues that attempts to establish frontiers were not so much civilisational – or even about finite control – as they were defensive; at least in Central Asia they arose from clashes between pastoral nomads and more settled agrarian societies. The pastoral nomads offered an alternative system to the one developed through Chinese territorial expansion and sedentarism. In Mongolia and elsewhere to the north, animal husbandry economies led to the development of very different forms of governance and control, focused on a confederacy that sought to distribute rather than capture wealth for its leaders. Nonetheless, the nomads were dependent upon access to and exploitation of Chinese goods (Barfield, 2001), which meant that any ruler had a responsibility to secure his subjects' access to these goods. The Mongols' mobility and use of horse cavalry made them unexpectedly difficult opponents for the much larger Chinese Empire. This led to the development of a symbiotic relationship between the nomads and the Chinese, or what Barfield calls 'shadow empires'.

In the premodern era there were, in fact, no delimited boundaries between Europe and Asia. According to Perdue (1998), the limitations of early boundary-making can be attributed, at least in part, to the undeveloped state of map-making. Indeed, map-making and cartography have long been a focus area for historians interested in understanding bordering. Like maps, walls have long been associated with the very notion of borders, and this link was apparent in the premodern era; thus in Chinese the same word means both 'wall' and 'city', as if to testify to the fact that one was unthinkable without the other. Walls were defensive, being intended to protect the ruler, but they also marked the limits of a settlement. However, it was not only ancient China that saw this conflation of wall and city; medieval Europe saw it too – witness for instance the fact that the Germanic noun *borg*, which designated a fortified place (bourg, borough), also came to be understood as referring to a town or a city (Nightingale, 2017). Yet Nightingale (2012, 2017) has argued that continued or exclusive focus on what surrounds a city – the wall – as its key borderscape obstructs from view the many borders and divides that existed *within cities* throughout history. Of course, the materiality of urban spaces involves numerous forms of borders – walls, barriers, fences; however, more important and significant for those living in cities, argues Nightingale (2012), are the many invisible borders that separate or even segregate populations within urban areas, most frequently on the basis of colour and race.

An examination of other premodern empires enriches our under-standing of the emergence of differing administrations of mobility within and beyond territories. In the Roman Empire as in other premodern empires, there was generally a continuity in adminis-trative functions across the captured territories: existing structures were retained, at least where the locals cooperated. However, the specific contribution of the Roman Empire is the legal notion of 'Roman citizen': no other premodern empire (such as the Persian) had anything equivalent. This notion of citizen of an empire involves a multilayered construction of citizenship, which differentiated between the levels of the Roman political project of belonging as much as it unified them (Mathisen, 2006).

Popescu (2012) argues that borders in the medieval era were characterised by ambiguity, owing to the complex overlapping of multiple territorial units. Medieval Europeans were also subject to different forms of authority (Brenner and Theodore, 2002), the most universal of which at that time was undoubtedly the Christian Church. Indeed religion was central to boundary-making in Europe throughout the Middle Ages; in particular, as Islam gained ground elsewhere, Christian religion gave focus to the process of othering that created European positionalities during the period. Conklin Akbari (2009) has argued that representations of Islam in Europe during the later Middle Ages focused not only on the different religious identity of the 'Saracens', but also on the ways in which this identity was linked to the body and to bodily diversity. So, while the crusades may have sought to capture territories in the Middle East and to reverse the challenge presented by Turkish gains in Byzantium, the wars could not and would not have been fought without an understanding of Islam as other. Therefore these representations of Islam and the Orient that bordered Muslim peoples and their bodies were critical to the shift of political borders in the Middle Ages.

Modernity and bordering: The long eighteenth century

While Europe may to some extent have been united against the threat posed by Islam and its rulers during the crusades, Christianity faced its own internal battles after the Protestant Reformation (1517), which led to over a century of internal conflicts; the Peace of Westphalia (1648) was only the first step in resolving these. Yet, as well as recognising three separate Christian traditions, Westphalia has become a key moment in narratives of the history of borders. The right of self-governance over a particular territory is often seen to lie in the European treaties of Westphalia (Popescu, 2012; Brunet-Jailly, 2012). This *logic* is central to border-making, as it is the legitimising principle of the nation-state, but the extent to which the treaties themselves can actually be seen to support the notion of sovereignty has been a source of debate among historians. Braun (1996) has demonstrated the ways in which the treaties actually recognised both the territorial authority of individual rulers and the overall sovereignty of the Holy Roman Empire. This double recognition is evident in the fact that the Holy Roman Empire itself continued to exist after 1648, while the estates granted territorial authority still continued to raise taxes and to contribute to the functioning of the empire itself. Thus the absolute power over defined territories with which borders are generally synonymous in the contemporary period (particularly as it has appeared in recent debates in the United Kingdom ahead of, and since, the referendum to leave the European Union) is not granted in these treaties.

The emphasis on territory in the Peace of Westphalia may bear evidence to a changing conception of the state, from rule over people to rule over territory, but is hardly a definitive indication of sovereign statehood, as the territory functioned as a basis for negotiations, not as an explicit or implicit endorsement of the idea of sovereignty in the terms of the treaties (Croxton, 1999). When it comes to legislation, there was also a shift over time in the wording of treaties; while the initial focus had been on trying to create comprehensive lists of all that would be subject to the authority of a particular ruler, by the time of these treatises there had been a move towards wording that sought to convey general rights and prevent contravention. However, such universal or generalised control was often not absolute, but in fact still punctuated by small spaces and territories of alterity, for example bishoprics and independent cities.

Walby (2003) has argued that the nation-state cannot be viewed as dominant materially during this period. Nations were more in the nature of projects that were becoming, but never fully realised in terms of territory. Such projects were based upon the development of myths of common heritage (Smith, 1986), but few achieved territorial stability. Walby's analysis focuses on three key ideas: there were more nations than states; some so-called nation-states were in fact empires for much of this period – the 'long' eighteenth century; and, finally, polities continued to defy nation-state boundaries, just as those of the Holy Roman Empire did after the treaties of Westphalia.

After a period of absolute monarchy in which the unity of French territorial governance was established, the French state that emerged after 1789 sought to create consistency between its territorial expression and the identity of those dwelling within its borders. After the revolution, however, the classical connection between ruler and subject had been lost and the new state supposedly belonged to all those who lived within it – or, as it came to be imagined, the nation. France at this time was very far from being constituted of one nation. Indeed, from 1792 to 1815, and particularly under Napoleon from 1804 on, the French Revolution became linked to a drive to unsettle existing borders and boundaries in Europe through expansionism, which led to the collapse of the last remnants of the Holy Roman Empire.

After the defeat of Napoleon in 1814 and 1815, his opponents had to seek legitimation for their opposition to the ideals of the revolution, which for the first time in modern Europe had introduced the concept of citizenship rights. The victors – Britain, Austria, and Russia – were concerned with maintaining the status of their rulers, and therefore the Peace of Paris (1814) and the Treaty of Vienna (1815) very much sidelined the claims of the nation (for example in Poland) in favour of the state (Barkin and Cronin, 1994). The bartering of territories between the victorious sovereigns reflected an approach to border-making by the European states that stretched across the world in the nineteenth century.

The empires forged through European colonial expansion contributed to the strengthening, centralisation, and homogenisation of the developing European states (Tilly, 1992). While the conquest of territories beyond Europe and the imposition of borders all over the globe by European powers had been occurring since the Portuguese and Spanish Empires of the fifteenth and sixteenth centuries, the colonial expansion of Britain and France dominated the early nineteenth century; and other European nations competed with them to accumulate territory as the century progressed. Any attempt to imagine the 'nation-state' as an autonomous 'container' (Taylor, 1994) needs to be placed in this historical context.

The multilayered global histories of conquest, European settlement, enslavement of Africans, plantation and mining industries, destruction of the Indian cotton industry and creation of new markets for European goods (to give a few examples) contributed heavily to the Industrial Revolution across Europe (Wolf, 1982). They also constitute histories of borders imposed and maintained to regulate trade, to facilitate the collection of customs and land revenues, to order the global mobility of labourers, and to filter citizens and subjects according to racialised hierarchies. One example of the colonial imposition of borders occurred at the Berlin Conference of 1884: there European leaders partitioned the African territory, which led in turn to the creation of linear borders between colonies claimed by competing European states. During the same period, populations living under colonial rule were grouped into categories defined by constructions of class, religion, and ethnicity, some groups having the land they were associated with divided by colonial borders, while others were incorporated into colonial administrative systems and travelled and studied in the metropoles (Young and Brown, 1995). The inequality inherent in colonialism – where conquest, settlement, and rule were justified by ideologies of European superiority and colonised territories were sites of contest over European nationalist projects – is thus part of the biography of borders (Megoran, 2012).

In North America, the period is synonymous with the expansion of settler colonialism, the advancement of the American frontier. The two main frontiers (Spanish and English) marked not only the brutal dispossession of Native American lands by European settlers and the forced removal of their inhabitants to so-called 'reservations', but also the development of racialised hierarchies and systems

36

that denied non-Europeans full citizenship and ensured that they were not included in the politics of belonging that shaped the new nations (Janiewski, 1995). One emergent political project included the development of an 'American' identity, which was based upon heritage and race (European, white) but was distinct from European national identities (Turner, 1996). However, the frontier was not only racialised; it also represented in some areas a move away from European urbanisation and economic development and towards a reified agrarian life – a 'retarded frontier' (Dunaway, 1996) that marked a step backwards according to the discourses of industrialisation and capitalism. This shift also brought with it cultural change, which was gendered as well as racialised, the settlers ushering in European patriarchal households that replaced systems of female and indigenous control (Janiewski, 1995).

To return to our earlier example of China and the nomadic peoples to its north, the effective end of the nomadic empires was a key global event in the seventeenth and eighteenth centuries (Perdue, 1998). It also put an end to an age of fluidity that explained how this region had resisted the Chinese dynasties' threat for centuries. Michel Foucher (1998) has argued that this development did not exist in Europe after Westphalia, but that the modern bordered state emerged on the edges of the giant Eurasian empires, namely through the treaties negotiated between the Eurasian empires. For example, the Treaty of Zuhab between the Ottoman and Safavid Empires in 1639 was the first in a series of eighteen treaties between the empires that carved up much of the Caucasus and concluded only in the nineteenth century. This clearly reflects that treaties were an increasingly used form of bordering practice; but it also demonstrates that the permeability and dynamism of early modern frontiers remained.

Russia, too, began to attempt to stabilise its borders in Asia with the Ottomans, Tatars, Kalmyks, and others from the mid-seventeenth century on. However, this does not mean that there were not challenges to these processes from within the territories claimed. One of the key issues for subjects of the Tsardom of Russia and, later, Russian Empire was the imposition of serfdom. While serfdom can be traced back to the Kyivan Rus, it came to dominate from the late 1500s, numerous laws being passed in the seventeenth century to prevent flight and to end free labour among the peasantry. Consequently, some populations sought to defy serfdom through flight to Russia's more remote and depopulated areas, including the Ukrainian steppe and Siberia. Perhaps the most well-known among these groups was that of the Cossacks, who came under Russian rule after the 1654 Treaty of Pereyaslav (Toje, 2006). In the Russian Empire we can see a shifting politics of belonging in relation to the Cossacks, whose refusal to accept serfdom initially placed them at odds with the tsar's regime. Their later inclusion enabled them to retain a distinct identity, thanks to their military service to the empire.

One of the key shifts that enabled the intensification of both internal and external bordering processes during this period was the development of surveying and mapping techniques – particularly under the rule of Louis XIV of France in the seventeenth century. These technological advances not only led to new data being captured and stored, but also framed emerging political projects of belonging through the inclusion of social and cultural data in ethnographic atlases. As we shall see below, maps and atlases fed into growing administrative structures that sought to regulate belonging and border territory.

In addition to map-making, the development of administrative systems also laid the groundwork for the extension of fledgling passport systems. Throughout history, populations have proved to be convertible into wealth and military strength, and rulers have consequently been interested in identifying and controlling the movements of their subjects. In thirteenth-century England, the Magna Carta forbade all but peers, notable merchants, and soldiers to leave the kingdom without a licence. So the focus was on losing subjects as property rather than on preventing people from coming in. In the late medieval period, France developed a state-defined idea of a 'foreigner' for the first time; however, it was the early modern state that started to be preoccupied with the idea of entry into a territory.

In France, after 1789, the revolutionary government embarked on a programme of geographical administrative reform that led to the creation of departments. This process pushed the reach of the state out to 'national' borders. France's declaration of freedom of movement was undermined by fears and gatherings of émigrés and opponents of the regime at its borders, and several departments (particularly on the borders) began to reintroduce passport controls and checks. A heated debate developed in which it was clear that citizens were being asked to accept some controls on their liberty in order to stop brigandry and protect the wider liberties won by the revolution. From the beginning, these controls classified people into categories such as being 'suspicious', being 'ill-intentioned', and 'lacking means' – that is, being without a job or a sponsor. Here we can trace an early form of filtering: the supposedly honest or right-minded would remain unencumbered or 'unbordered'. Not all revolutionaries agreed with the reintroduction of these controls. However, it is also clear that, rather than being based upon a uniform or shared ideology, this reintroduction was context-specific, fluctuated, and was not always driven from the centre.

By the mid-nineteenth century, a number of European countries, including France, had begun to issue travel documents for all citizens whenever they had need of them. However, this phenomenon was not universal. Britain and the United States did not follow suit (Davis and Guma, 1992), and many elite British travellers became frustrated with the increasing checks made by other European states (O'Byrne, 2001). This was particularly true of Italy, which by that time had also introduced (alongside Turkey) requirements for entry in the form of a visa. In the United Kingdom the 1905 Aliens Act introduced systematic immigration controls upon entry into the country (Wray, 2016). For some historians (see Juss, 1993 and 1997), the influence of the Act was symbolic rather than material, in that it put a stop to any freedom of movement. The First World War provided the main impetus for the world's major powers to introduce stricter regimes of passport control (Davis and Guma, 1992: 61). The 1914 Aliens Restriction Act, rushed into being after the outbreak of the war, led to greater restrictions, abolishing exemptions for religious persecutees and placing controls on all aliens. As well as controls on entry, powers of employment and deportation were extended (Holmes, 1991); and this led to almost 50,000 repatriations, primarily of Germans, during and immediately after the war (Bloch and Schuster, 2005). Gendered norms were written into the 1914 British Nationality and Status of Aliens Act, as women's citizenship was tied to that of their spouse; thus British women would become aliens upon marrying an alien (Baldwin, 2001). The 1915 Defence of the Realm Act made passports a prerequisite for all British citizens who left or entered their own territory. In most states the use of passports had been standardised after the Great War, although in the United States such a duty was not legislated until 1941. The passport requirements were retained after the end of the war and became part of a wider political project of belonging, focused on 'redefining and building a sense of nation' (O'Byrne 2001: 402). In consequence, passports have become a potent symbol of the nation-state and are central both to imagining it and to its materialisation through nation-building processes (Benedict Anderson, 1991); passports are key elements in the bordering practices that delimit the boundaries of the state and the conditions of belonging to it. While almost all nation-states have come to use the passport as a legal document, its symbolic use in nation-building varies across the world.

Bordering in the aftermath of the First World War

The end of the First World War saw a period of turmoil and civil wars that brought about some major transformations in governance and belonging all around the world. It signified the collapse of four major empires – the Austro-Hungarian, the German, the Russian, and the Ottoman – as well as the extreme weakening of a fifth one, the Chinese. This has had a major effect on borderings globally. The colonies of the Ottoman and German Empires, especially in Africa and the Middle East, were redistributed among the Allies (although Japan, also an ally, did not benefit similarly, which eventually led it to invade China and fight against the allies in the Second World War). The Baltic countries and Poland gained independence, while the Soviet Union re-annexed parts of Ukraine as well as Armenia, Azerbaijan, and Georgia at the end of the Russian Civil War that followed the October Revolution of 1917.

The end of the First World War also signified the consolidation of the United States as a leading world superpower. Woodrow Wilson, the American president at the end of the war, was determined to use the Allies' victory to establish, in the Treaty of Versailles, a new world order, in which such a world war could not happen again. He oversaw the creation of the League of Nations.

The League of Nations (Northedge, 1986) established the right of national self-determination as a cornerstone of international law and world governance. The principle of national self-determination assumes a world in which different nations will reside side by side, separated by national borders. As Barkin and Cronin (1994: 120) claim, '[f]or Wilson, a legitimate nation-state was one that represented a defined national population and whose government was accountable to its people'. In other words, nation-states were liberal democratic political projects of governance and belonging.

However, while such nationalist imaginaries naturalise the trinity people–government–homeland, they do not account for the fact that different nationalist movements often claim ownership to territories, especially in the borderlands, which other nationalist movements claimed as well. As a result, international borders kept being challenged and changed several times (Rothschild, 2017).

Nationalism and the old and new nations that were established as independent states in the aftermath of the First World War were only a part of the political and ideological picture and map at the time, which, as mentioned above, also saw the communist movement rising to power in the former Russian Empire; but they were active, like other socialist political movements, all over the world (McDermott and Agnew, 1996).

The dismantling of empires, the universal legitimation of the right for national self-determination, and the growing popularity of socialism and communism have also had a major impact on the growing wave of anticolonial movements all over the world. It was a time in which the nationalist imaginaries of 'authentic' independent nations developed – a process that, as Chatterjee (1993) has argued, is a necessary condition for any anticolonial struggle for national independence to be successful. Many of these movements in the Global South were led by colonial elites educated in Europe who drew on ideas of modern nationalism that incorporated the existing, already imposed borders in their battles for independence. Contests over which ethnic or religious collectivities would define or control the newly independent states or the rights granted to groups defined as indigenous or as descendants of colonial mobile labourers are characteristic of many struggles, both before and after independence (Wimmer, 1997).

While the relative power of socialist and communist political movements grew all over the world, fear of a communist victory, especially in Europe, has been one of the major reasons that many industrialists and financiers, in their need for protection and legitimation, have given for the rise of fascist movements in different countries in Europe in the 1930s. One of the main roots of the success of the Nazi Party was what many perceived as a national humiliation after the First World War. Especially important was the economic burden of the Versailles agreement, which forced Germany to pay heavy reparations for the damages incurred in the First World War, for which it was held responsible. The situation became especially acute after the Great Depression of 1929, in the aftermath of the stock market crash that put an end to the postwar economic boom of the 'roaring twenties'.

While the United States overcame the crisis via the New Deal policy imposed by President Roosevelt (Hawley, 2015), most countries did not fully recover until after the Second World War. However, the Weimar Republic – that is, the unofficial name of the German state between the two world wars – was hit particularly strongly by the financial crisis; it had astronomical rates of inflation, and even the financial support provided by the United States at the time had only a very limited effect. The Nazi Party was seen as the only party that could save Germany's economic and political problems as well as prevent the communists from gaining power (Shirer, 1991).

Fascism (Eatwell, 2011; Mann, 2004) came to power between the two world wars in several states in Europe (and even outside, e.g. in Brazil). It was seen as the miracle solution to all the woes caused by the devastation of the First World War, fast industrialisation, and urbanisation, as well as to the harsh economic conditions imposed during the Depression and to the rising popular unrest. What is more, it fuelled strong feelings of national pride and opened the prospect of a utopian future.

Although there have been differences among fascist movements and states, there are also some common characteristics. Fascism is a strong nationalist collectivist ideology, which claimed to be able to modernise society, supply work for everyone, and at the same time preserve the strong moral values of family and community. The centralised state was organised in a militaristic fashion, around sectorial branches of the economy, with no space for any autonomous class politics. In Nazism more than in any other fascist ideology, the emphasis on a wholesome, healthy society contained a strong purging element of cleansing society from all those who seemed to threaten or corrupt it in any way, especially racially and sexually.

Fascist movements have had strong expansionist bordering policies and dreams of building empires. The League of Nations proved ineffective in preventing this. Germany, which resigned from the League in 1933, after Hitler came to power (Japan resigned a few months later), argued that it needed to expand its territories for what was claimed to be the need for its 'living space', Lebensraum. This eventually led to the outbreak of the Second World War.

Bordering in the aftermath of the Second World War

The political and social world order was transformed after the Second World War, and this has had profound effects on local and global bordering processes, including major displacements of populations that crossed borders and settled in different states. In Europe, the end of the war saw the largest population movements in European history. Millions of Germans fled or were expelled from Eastern Europe – mainly to West Germany, where they received automatic citizenship rights, but also to other countries, especially in Latin America. Hundreds of thousands of Jews, survivors of the Holocaust, sought secure homes beyond their countries of origin all over the globe, including in the Zionist Yishuv in Palestine, which was established as the State of Israel in 1948. Also, many people from Eastern European countries sought escape from the newly installed communist regimes (Kirk and Huyck, 1954). The United States was initially reluctant to accept refugees and opened its doors only after 1948, increasing the number of refugees from the original 200,000 only under the effects of the Cold War.

Outside Europe, in addition to the influx of refugees from Europe, other major refugee crises sprang out as a result of anticolonial struggles. In particular, the partition of Southern Asia in 1948 into the two separate independent states of India and Pakistan (the latter divided into Pakistan and Bangladesh after the war in 1971) caused an 'exchange' population movement estimated as involving 14 million people (Zamindar, 2007). In Palestine, the establishment of the Israeli state involved the displacement of 600,000 Palestinians, who became refugees in territories ruled by other Arab states (Pappe, 2007).

Several major developments can be seen as contextualising bordering processes in the era after the Second World War. These developments have closely affected and influenced one another. The first one to mention here is the establishment in 1945 of the United Nations (UN) and its associated agencies, which have played major roles in overseeing issues related to militarised conflicts, refugees, and displaced populations. The UN was founded as a more effective replacement to the League of Nations. It has a Security Council with five permanent representatives from the world's superpowers (Taiwan represented China until the reconciliation between China and the United States in the early 1970s) and ten rotating members from the other member states, who all take part in the General Assembly. Members of the Security Council have the right of veto so as to discourage defection from the UN when global tension grows (as happened with the League of Nations).

A Universal Declaration of Human Rights established the normative framework for common international and national legislation, as a part of which it guaranteed refugees the 'right to seek and to enjoy in other countries asylum from persecution' and forbade any 'arbitrary deprivation of nationality'. International courts for human rights and war crimes that followed the Nuremberg Trials after the Second World War sought to exercise international authority in this domain.

In spite of its many imperfections and chronic (and worsening) financial pressures, and although often blocked in its various humanitarian missions by political conflicts, the UN has been active in many social and political fields. It has played crucial roles in looking after refugees and displaced populations via its agencies, namely the United Nations High Commissioner for Refugees (UNHCR) and, for the Palestinian refugees, the United Nations Relief and Works Agency for Palestine Refugees in the Near East (UNRWA).

Secondly, until 1989, world politics (and this includes political activity related to the UN) has been constructed around the Cold War – which on occasion became a proxy for 'hot wars' in countries like Korea (1950–3) and Vietnam (1955–75), dominated by the United States and the Soviet Union as the two major superpowers. The spheres of influence that emerged after the Yalta Conference in 1945 shaped the world order for almost half a century, until the collapse of the Soviet Union in 1991. As far as bordering goes, one of the most important developments during the Cold War era was the Iron Curtain, whose territorial manifestation was the Berlin Wall. Except for specific government-controlled cases, free movement outside the Soviet bloc was forbidden to Soviet citizens. The 1951 Geneva Convention on Refugees, which defined the notion of 'refugee' and accorded this category of people specific rights, was initially aimed at catering for refugees who escaped from the Soviet bloc (Carruthers, 2005).

Another major development during these years has been *decolonisation* and the establishment of independent states in most territories of the former empires. The 'special relationships' of these states with their 'mother countries', however, continued to be influential, especially in the British case, through the Commonwealth. During the Cold War, both sides of the bipolar world offered economic and social aid as part of the global competition to consolidate global spheres of political influence. The rise of the third world after the Bandung Conference in 1955 was an attempt by the postcolonial states to use that competition for forging a more autonomous political space for themselves. However, given the colonial nature of most postcolonial borders, in addition to international pressures, nation-building processes in these countries have often been heavily contested along ethnic, religious, and tribal grounds, and this fact has often caused militarised conflicts and large numbers of displaced and refugee populations within and across borders. It has also affected the local economies, which have often developed dependencies on aid (Moss et al., 2006).

Another development, this time economic, during this period has been the Bretton Woods Agreement of 1944, which dominated world economy until its unravelling during the 1980s. In order to prevent another financial crisis like the pre-Second World War Great Depression, representatives of forty-four allied nations gathered in Bretton Woods in New Hampshire in July 1944 and set up a system of rules, institutions, and procedures designed to regulate the international monetary system. They established the International Monetary Fund (IMF) and the International Bank for Reconstruction and Development, which is today part of the World Bank. The United States, which controlled two thirds of the world's gold, became the international guarantor for keeping the cost of gold at $35 per ounce. The Soviets declined ratifying the agreement, but throughout the 1950s and 1960s, the financial regulations of Bretton Woods supported international economic growth, the development of welfare states, and the trend of lowering social and economic inequalities.

However, the 1960s saw growing breaches of the agreement, as banks in the City of London and other banks on the international scene devised increasingly 'creative' ways to use alternative sources of gold rather than that of the United States to accumulate new wealth. In 1971 the United States unilaterally terminated the fixed convertibility of the US dollar to gold, and from then on the dollar became the reserve currency used by many states (this kind of currency is often known as 'Eurodollar' or 'petrodollar') (Bullough, 2018). In this way national borders became gradually more permeable to the mobility of money, goods, and people.

Welfare states can be seen as a product of all the developments described above. They evolved in different ways and to various extents in states across the globe, but especially in Europe and the Anglo-Saxon world (Esping-Andersen, 2013). Citizenship rights' entitlements have been inspired by international human rights discourse, but also affected by socialist movements that fought to give workers social and economic rights, in an alternative model to the state socialism of the Soviet bloc. The expanding economies of the welfare states required growing labour power; hence these states invited migrant workers from the postcolonial countries, offering rights of settlement especially to members of their former empires. As Rex (1996) and Schierup et al. (2006) have argued, multiculturalism was a hegemonic ideology and policy of dealing especially with non-European migrants, and it aimed to strengthen the welfare state. Things changed when the postwar economic boom started to decline and national and global inequalities consequently increased again.

In the 1980s further deregulations, initiated by Reagan and Thatcher, triggered the hegemony of neoliberal globalisation, which, together with the collapse of the Soviet Union and the end of the Cold War in 1989, once again brought about a reconfiguration of global politics, economy, and bordering, privatised more and more sections of the welfare state, and increased social and economic inequalities. These shifts took place concomitantly with the growth of one of the world's largest trading blocs, which later became one of the key de- and rebordering projects of the late twentieth and early twenty-first century: the European Union.

The Common Market or the European Economic Community (EEC) had started to form in 1950, when it had six original members: Belgium, France, Germany, Italy, Luxemburg, and the Netherlands. The United Kingdom, Ireland, and Denmark joined in 1973. Around that time, after the oil energy crisis, there was also a beginning of subsidising poorer regions in Europe and developing progressive environmental and labour legislation. During the 1980s the poorer southern European countries joined the EEC and in 1986 the European Single Market was established, facilitating free movements of goods and finance as well as people and services among the members.

The collapse of state socialism and EU enlargement

The collapse of socialist governments in Europe in 1989, followed by the fall of the Soviet Union in 1991, led to a series of de- and rebordering processes that reshaped the continent. These processes included the opening up of the formerly state-dominated economies to global capitalism and the often violent emergence of new nation-states, some of whose territories remain disputed. The most significant rebordering took place within the former Soviet Union, where the republics declared independence and began to develop national administrative systems that led to struggles over who did and did not belong. The movement of populations during the Soviet period had left behind many minority groups within the newly independent states; consequently there were struggles over minority rights, particularly in relation to ethnic Russians and Russian speakers. In Estonia and Latvia, claims of ethnic and linguistic discrimination threatened potential membership of NATO and of the European Union (Ozolins, 2003). Both countries sought to exclude Soviet-era 'settlers' by awarding citizenship only to those who had been citizens

46

in 1940 and to their descendants. For residents without automatic rights, the acquisition of citizenship involved passing a national language test.

In addition to rebordering through citizenship policies, there were violent conflicts related to the rights of national and ethnic groups, which became territorial in their focus and caused secessionist movements. Examples include the breakup of the former Yugoslavia, as well as ongoing frozen conflicts in Moldova and Georgia. While the reasons for the emergence of secessionism are specific to populations and regions, the vacuum of power left by the collapse of socialist institutions and external involvement, often from the Russian Federation, formed a common backdrop. Many territories with frozen conflicts in the region operate as de facto states, occupying an in-between position and having a corresponding status in the world order (Blakkisrud and Kolstø, 2011). As for the states themselves in which these frozen conflicts are located, these de facto states have influenced wider bordering processes that take place in the region by preventing the wider state from joining NATO and by inhibiting accession to the European Union.

The de- and rebordering processes that emerged after 1989–91 during the period of transition from socialism to market democracy (Stenning, 2005; Sokol, 2001) were socially and spatially differentiated (Bradshaw and Stenning, 2004). Debordering was very uneven, particularly in its relations with the market democracies of Western Europe and North America. Barriers to trade and investment were removed much more rapidly than those that controlled the movement of people. And when debordering began, it was often one-sided, most Central and Eastern European countries (CEE) offering ninety-day visa-free travel to people from EU member states, the United States, and Canada, while flows the other way were strictly controlled and generally restricted to tourism and highly skilled or seasonal worker schemes. The deep and long transitional recession (Kornai, 1994) that emerged led to 'hub-and-spoke' (Gowan, 1995) relations between East and West, whereby the West extracted economic benefits from the debordering of CEE and rebordering emerged from new discursive performances of 'the East', as well as from growing disparities between East and West and within CEE countries. As a result, the optimism about a 're-unified' Europe that followed the collapse of state socialism quickly became embroiled in the complexities of shifting relations and in the bureaucracy of EU accession.

From the founding, through the Treaty of Paris in 1952, of the first iteration of what was to become the European Union after the

Maastricht Treaty in 1993, there were a number of enlargements to it; and the end of the Cold War contributed to European debordering even before the accession of CEE states. For example, the reunification of Germany in 1990 extended membership of what was then called the European Community to the former German Democratic Republic (DDR). In addition, Austria, Finland, and Sweden, which had remained neutral during the Cold War, were able to join the Community. The wider enlargement of the European Union into CEE was governed by the Maastricht Treaty, which was replaced in 2009 by the provisions set out in 2007 in the Lisbon Treaty. 'Enlargement' has become synonymous, in popular discourse, with the inclusion of the CEE countries in the Union in 2004 and 2007, when several states joined the expanded Schengen area. However, the debordering of some CEE states through EU membership has been accompanied by the rebordering of those that have not joined the Union – and also by the emergence of new inequalities, to which Pisano (2009) refers globally as the 'golden curtain'.

Neoliberalism and its crises

Francis Fukuyama greeted the end of the Cold War with his now infamous treatise that hailed the 'end of history' (Fukuyama, 1992). Fukuyama's claim was based upon Marx's historical analysis, which argued that communism would follow and lead to the end of capitalism. While Fukuyama's analysis was heavily critiqued, the question he raised was important in terms of what may come next to challenge not just capitalism, but neoliberalisation after the fall of socialism in the countries of Central and Eastern Europe and in the former Soviet Union. While communist countries remained in Asia and Latin America, there was an overall sense that not only would they struggle to survive without the support of the Soviet bloc, but also those that did continue to maintain a socialist ideology would need to open up and adapt to the principles of market economics. In a nutshell, there would be a global geopolitical and geoeconomic reconfiguration that had to involve a range of de- and rebordering processes.

The economic reforms carried out by Pinochet in Chile in the 1970s were hailed as supplying a global role model. Neoliberal globalisation freed finance to be mobilised and used in new ways; and, as discussed in chapter 1, these created a reconfiguration of the state and the domination of the private sector over the public, while continuing to depend on different states' provision of the necessary

48

legal authorisation, infrastructure, and other services. The IMF and other international organisations were used to pressurise postcolonial and post-Soviet states so as to integrate them into the highly uneven global market; the goal was to carry out 'structural adjustments' as a result of which the prioritisation of the public sector and of social provisions for citizens would give way to opening the borders to the operation of multinational corporations, which was to create small local neoliberal elites (Bello et al., 1994). The devouring of public goods in southern states was later directed also at northern ones, producing – after the bailout of the 2007–8 banking crisis and the follow-up of austerity regimes – the double crisis of governability and governmentality discussed in chapter 1.

States and their borderings need to be viewed as effective regulators in the global economy. As Sassen (1995: 31) argues, there is also a need for strategic sites within national territories that bring together vast resources and infrastructure and point to the limits of mobility within globalisation. The (im)mobilities, at varying scales, of these sites are discussed throughout the remaining chapters. Top global financial cities have not lost their importance; they remain key nodes. A lack of local knowledge can inhibit global capital from maximising the possibilities that exist in host countries; and, if global capital is to overcome this limitation and become embedded, local human resources are needed. So what we see emerging is neither a borderless world nor one in which national dominance is inevitable. Nation-states have both driven neoliberal globalisation and adapted to it, but at the same time we have witnessed the increasing importance of transnational and hybrid forms of governance. This is especially important when we examine two new sectors of the global economy, the securitisation economy and the green economy, which have become new sources of profitability by way of making profit from what is seen as necessary costs.

Indeed the rise of neoliberalisation, which Giddens (1998) argues marked the end of the 'welfare consensus', alongside the collapse of state socialism, also invited questions about the future of social democracy or about the continental European model, which has been seen as a key alternative to Thatcher's and Reagan's neoliberal policies of the 1980s and has shaped much of the United Kingdom's relationship with the European Union. While Giddens was advocating for a 'third way' based on social democracy, many of the countries that emerged from the collapsed socialist regimes of Central and Eastern Europe had already followed advice (Sachs, 1990; Aslund, 1992) that promoted a swift 'opening up' to global markets as part of a programme of debordering from 'the West' (Pickles and Smith, 1998).

Of course, the reconfiguration of the bipolar world extended well beyond Europe. The structural adjustment policies, which conditioned international aid for countries in the Global South on the adoption of deregulation policy reforms, have attracted many international investments since the late 1980s. While overall these reforms increased social inequalities, local elites have largely benefited from them in states known as 'emerging economies'.

The states known earlier as 'the BRICs' (Brazil, Russia, India, China) are considered to be major economic powers in the future of global neoliberalism. There are predictions that, by 2050, China and India will become the world's dominant suppliers of manufactured goods and services respectively, while Brazil and Russia will become similarly dominant as suppliers of raw materials. Due to lower labour and production costs in these countries (which now include a fifth nation, South Africa), many companies have also cited BRICS as a source of foreign expansion opportunity, in other words as promising economies in which to invest. In 1990 the BRICS accounted for 11 per cent of the global GDP; in 2014, this figure had risen to nearly 30 per cent.

The economic growth of the BRICS has been framed as presenting a challenge not to the global capitalist economy, but to liberal principles (Stephen, 2014). While the Cold War period has been predominantly characterised by separation and isolation, bordering and rebordering, the rise of the BRICS led to increasing debordering and economic interdependence, as states and businesses in the West sought to profit from this growth. However, the BRICS model of growth has also, in different ways, reintroduced the state, or state-led developmentalism, disrupting to some extent the dominance of the Washington Consensus in the global economy. The growing political conflicts with Putin's Russia and the 'trade wars' with China indicate growing divisions in global political power relations – divisions unprecedented since the end of the Cold War.

As in the Cold War, there is an ongoing 'shadow war' that is taking place in the Middle East, especially in Syria, and in which Russia supports the Assad regime and the United States some of its opposition. However, significant as it may be to contemporary global politics, this war is not a militarised confrontation dominated by two global political powers. The conflict between Iran and Saudi Arabia as regional powers is no less important to understanding the war in Syria than the renewed regional ambitions of Erdoğan, Turkey's president, the national liberation struggle of the Kurds, and, of course, the rise of ISIS, the Islamist jihadist movement (Yassin-Kassab and Al-Shami, 2018). It is also important to remember that the war in Syria has started among the protests of the Arab Spring, the wave of resistance movements across the Middle East that brought initial hope and then devastating despair to people all over that area.

While there were obvious problems with the neoliberal-led 'transition' in CEE, and while the adaptation of the Washington Consensus to the BRICS countries presented challenges related to neoliberalisation, clearly the most extensive crisis of neoliberalism has sprung from the 2007–8 global financial crisis. This crisis very much highlighted a number of points that antiglobalists had been making regarding economic interconnectivity. The global reach of the crisis was made possible through increasing interdependence in the international system, as well as through the attendant dependence on internal systems within banks rather than on strict regulatory frameworks designed to manage risk in relation to the expansion of credit (Claessens and Kodres, 2014; Wellink, 2009). These processes are directly linked to the crisis of governability to which we refer in the first chapter. Cross-border banking not only rapidly extended the global reach of the financial crisis, but also increased the complexity of any form of coordinated response. The crisis was facilitated through the wider trend of financialisation, which has been linked to the expansion of financial capitalism in the period since the 1980s. Financialisation, although contested, refers broadly to the growth in financial instruments that facilitate capital accumulation at a time when the profit derived from production capitalism in reducing. The process is heavily embedded in neoliberalism, and particularly in the development of financial services – both in larger states, for instance the United States and the United Kingdom, and in smaller nations such as Iceland and Ireland. Crotty (2009) argued that the 2008 crisis was part of a cyclical boom and bust process that neoliberal policies have created. In his view, deregulation in particular has facilitated the growth of financial markets through high-risk financial innovation. When these innovative products fail and governments bail out financial institutions, further innovation and expansion begins and the regulation intended to manage the risk associated with this process fails to keep up with the speed of change.

Since 2008, very little has changed in terms of the 'new financial architecture' that Crotty (2009) has argued led to the crash. The key reason for this is that neoliberal policies continue to dominate and low regulation remains. The incentivisation that led to excessive risk has not been addressed by regulatory change. In terms of the financial products being sold, complexity obscured transparency to such an extent that even experts within the banking sector could not determine a 'fair price' for some securities (Tett, 2009).

Within Europe, the crisis also sowed the seeds of contestation, which in turn fuelled elements related to the rise of populism. This was caused in part by seeming frustration with and among national governments, which failed to respond in a meaningful way, so as to protect the interests of their people. However, the situation highlighted not only the difficulties of neoliberalism but also those of ordoliberalism in the context of Greece and the Eurozone crisis. The Eurozone crisis demonstrated that a solution that may be of benefit to the overall Eurozone could and did have extremely negative consequences for particular member states. Bulmer (2014) has argued that Germany's ordoliberal principles took precedence over its commitment to European integration when it supported the imposition of austerity politics on Greece. The Eurozone crisis highlighted the need for stronger oversight and greater control over domestic economies and the banking sector; and, in this sense, it further deepened the divide between Britain's neoliberal-driven response and that of the member states in the Eurozone. Indeed, London's exceptionalism as a global financial centre and the impending regulation from Brussels were key drivers of debates in the lead-up to the United Kingdom's EU referendum. So, while the United Kingdom has sought recovery through further debordering and the rolling back of the British state, Brussels, and Berlin in particular, have moved towards increased regulation and controls.

The rise of absolutist movements

The rise of extreme right autochthonic and fundamentalist religious movements has been a response to the governmentality crisis of neoliberal globalisation; but it has deeper roots, too. These movements feed off localised problems and grievances, but are also linked to the crisis of modernity – of social orders based on a belief in principles of enlightenment, rationalism, and progress. Both capitalism and communism – and in the Global South postcolonial national independence, too – have proved unable to fulfil people's material, emotional, and spiritual needs and have prompted people to seek solace in reified notions of history, religion, and morality as defensive anchors of personal identity (Sahgal and Yuval-Davis,

1992; Cowden and Sahgal, 2017; Fitzi et al., 2018). Autochthonic politics of belonging can take very different forms in different countries and can be reconfigured constantly even in the same place. Nevertheless, its discourses, like those of all varieties of racialisation and boundary construction, always appear to express self-evident, even 'natural' emotions: protection of an ancestral heritage, fear of being diluted or contaminated by foreign influences, and so on – and yet they often hide very different notions of ancestry and contamination, entangling religious and secular discourses (Yuval-Davis, 2011). Geschiere (2009) called this paradox 'the turn of the global to the local'. As Marine Le Pen, leader of the French Front National, has stated, 'the right–left divide makes no sense anymore. Now the real division is between nationalism and globalization' (*Guardian*, 22 March 2011). And President Trump, in his annual lecture to the UN General Assembly, argued: 'We reject the ideology of globalism and accept the doctrine of patriotism' (*Guardian*, 25 September 2018).

Although neither Le Pen nor Trump are religious individuals, they have found solid political support among the Catholic right in France and the evangelists in the United States. Jouet (2016) has argued that Trump's authoritarian black-and-white message is deeply appealing to evangelical fundamentalists in a country where 42 per cent of the population considers itself 'creationist'. These same evangelical Christian movements are now travelling south, as fundamentalists make substantial inroads within and outside the Catholic Church across Latin America and Africa.

In Europe we have seen the rise to power of autochthonic authoritarian political movements; in countries such as Austria, Hungary, Italy, and Poland they are part of the government, whereas in others such as Denmark, Finland, France, Germany, and Sweden they have come to play the role of major opposition parties. Either way, they have deeply affected the national discourse on migration, the European Union, and liberal democracy.

In India, Prime Minister Narendra Modi, while opening the country to an extreme form of neoliberalism, has also been majorly involved in its Hinduisation and, as a governor of the Indian state of Gujarat, in the massacres of Muslims carried out there in 2002 (IIFJIG, 2003).

The construction of 'the Muslims' as the main 'other' is one of the common denominators of many of these autochthonic movements – in India, in Europe, in Israel, in the United States, and also in some postcolonial African countries where religious affiliation and ethnic or tribal belonging overlap. Traditionally, since the times of the Arab Empire, then of the Ottoman Empire, Muslims were constructed in Europe as the enemy outside (while Jews and Roma were the main enemies within), and there is a growing dominant discourse of the fear of the 'Islamisation of Europe' (Kaufman, 2017). This cultural attitude has been affected by the discourse of 'global war on terrorism' and affected it in its turn (Bhatt, 2007).

Contemporary Islam is far from being homogenous and there is an ongoing fight among its different schools, such as the Sunni majority and the large Shia minority, which controlled the first successful Islamist revolution in Iran in 1978. Many of the Islamist fundamentalist religious activities have been part of national autochthonic movements (e.g. in Egypt, Palestine, and Sudan), and much energy has been put into campaigns for states with Muslim majorities to adopt sharia as the state law and to establish sharia courts where they did not exist. Many of these campaigns have, however, a transnational missionary character; its most articulated expression is the ideology of ISIS (the Islamic State in Iraq and Syria, also known as IS or Daesh), whose aim is to establish a caliphate, a Muslim state that ideally would embrace Muslims from all over the world as members of the Muslim *ummah* (community). Hence the ISIS has campaigned and encouraged the recruitment of fighters from everywhere, using sophisticated social media and other forms of IT.

ISIS was originally a splinter group of Al Qaeda ('The Base'), an international group of fundamentalist Sunni Muslims and Salafi jihadists (Maher, 2016), most of them from Saudi Arabia, who fought with the Taliban against the Soviets and then against the Americans in Afghanistan. The organisational structure of Al Qaeda, which had a loose network, has helped to spread its mode of activities all over the world. Al Qaeda's primary enemy has been the West (Boko Haram, the name of one of its splinters in Nigeria, means 'No western education'). Besides, Al Qaeda claimed responsibility for the 9/11 attack and regards the killing of non-Muslim non-combatants as part of its religious duty. Nevertheless, it is important to state that much of the fight of these groups is aimed at members of rival versions of Islam, such as the Shia, as well as at 'blasphemous' members of their own.

These political and military struggles (the 'new wars' discussed below) in the North as well as in the South have had a major impact on contemporary bordering. The ban that President Trump has imposed on travellers from several Muslim states is just one example.

Bordering in the context of the violent conflicts, neoliberal developments, and ecological crises of the Global South

The spread of neoliberal globalisation has created new types of continuously changing organised violence and ecological crises that have forced people from across the Global South to move within and across state borders and continents.

The rise of twenty-first-century 'new wars' is linked to the weakening of authoritarian states as they open up to neoliberal processes and to the wider world. The characteristics of these new wars, as argued by Mary Kaldor (2013), continue to affect borderings, both locally and globally. In new wars, specific ethnic, religious, or tribal groups seek to gain state power and resources by directing violence, including sexual violence, at civilians and by forcing the displacement of populations with opinions or identities that differ from theirs. They achieve this through violent methods, which partner, for example, state armed forces with warlords or private security contractors funded by transnational smuggling, private finance, and the 'taxation' of foreign aid, and equip them with communication technologies that facilitate the spread of fear and panic, encouraging targeted populations to leave their homes. Thus, while new wars rarely extend the existing territorial state borders, bordering through the denial of citizenship and belonging to minorities and through the forcible displacement of populations across borders is central to their methodology. This can lead to demands for new territorial borders, as minorities seek to secede.

Population displacement is therefore, on different continents, a common characteristic of wars that grew out of the long reach of neoliberalism into recently independent nation-states and economies created through different colonial histories of conflict, occupation, border-making, labour migrations, and independence struggles. For example, in Central Africa, the new wars in Rwanda, Burundi, Uganda, and most recently in the mineral-rich Democratic Republic of Congo have produced the displacement of millions of people (Castles et al., 2013: 175), as specific groups used identity politics and other strategies to gain control of the state, its power and its resources. In East Africa, the wars in Eritrea, Somalia, and Sudan that resulted in the rebordering of territories created through colonialism have also caused the mass displacement of populations with identities and politics that challenged the dominant groups. In Sudan, in 2003, the state government and the military allied themselves with the Janjaweed militia to destroy the non-Arab population in the

55

region of Darfur. Two million people were displaced and put into camps in Sudan and neighbouring countries.

In Asia, the continuing conflicts in Afghanistan, Sri Lanka, and Myanmar have led to huge displacements of populations and, in some cases, to forced statelessness. Six million people left Afghanistan after the Soviet invasion in 1979, most of them finding refuge in neighbouring Pakistan and Iran. Since the takeover of the Taliban in 1989, the events of and after 9/11, and the intensification of old and new war hostilities, millions more left, planning to work in the Gulf states and to seek asylum in the Global North. In Sri Lanka the mainly Hindu Tamil minority sought to create an independent Tamil state within the Buddhist Sinhalese-dominated island state. Following the Tamil surrender in 2009 after twenty-six years of war, it was estimated that 274,000 people were internally displaced and that 141,000 left the country as refugees, joining the already existing global Tamil diaspora (UNHCR, 2011, 2017). The largest growing forced migration across state borders is that of the Rohingya Muslim minority from Buddhist-majority Myanmar, where the government claims that the Rohingya are illegal migrants from Bangladesh and denies them citizenship. Their political marginalisation and the violence perpetrated against them by state and non-state actors have increased since independence in 1948. Since 2012, over 100,000 Rohingyas were forced to move to internal camps (Ibrahim, 2016) and over 1 million fled by boat to South-East Asian states and – most significantly – across the border to Bangladesh in 2017 (UNHCR, 2016b). In Bangladesh, Rohingyas remain stateless, confined to camps, and dependent on aid.

In the Americas, rebordering has been enabled via the inter-connections of violent conflict and the inequalities created by neoliberal globalisation, on the one hand, and, on the other, the US-controlled businesses and political interests that managed the economies and political discourses within the territorial borders of the United States as well as of other states (Harvey, 2007a). The US-backed military regimes of Central and South American states during the 1970s and 1980s and the associated wars in countries as different as El Salvador and Chile led to the displacement of thousands of people. Dictatorships facilitated the introduction of neoliberal regimes through IMF structural adjustment policies and through the repatriation of profits, which contributed to increased inequality in rural–urban and South–North migration (Castles et al., 2013). The violent conflict and demand for migrant workers in US-controlled factories in the north of Mexico as well as in the

United States prompted Central Americans and Mexicans to move to the north.

Ecological crises that force the mobility of indigenous peoples and slum dwellers, for example, have also affected bordering, past and present alike. Migration may be forced by the intersections of climate change and processes of globalisation, including the construction of dams, power plants, and middle-class housing projects. In 2011, drought in East Africa led to over 100,000 nomadic pastoralists joining other refugees from the war in Somalia in the UNHCR-run Dadaab complex in Kenya that had been set up in 1992 (Al-Jazeera, 2011). Marginalised groups of people from lower socioeconomic backgrounds who migrate across borders become targets of exclusionary bordering discourses and practices that build on identity politics and on fear creation (i.e. on fostering fears of new wars). For example, residents of Dadaab are not protected by the Kenyan government, are not entitled to Kenyan identity cards, and can be victims of fears about Al-Shabaab terrorism. In India people suspected of being Bangladeshis who crossed the border to find work after losing land to floods and changing river courses, or as a result of neoliberal developments in their multiple manifestations, have become the subject of bureaucratic bordering campaigns whose aim is to register and deport 'foreigners'.

Journeys towards the 'global migration crisis'

The continuing new wars, forced displacements, and unemployment across the Global South are the recent background to the migration crisis that hit the European headlines in the summer of 2015, and to the Mexico border and deportation debates that dominated Trump's campaign in 2016. A key element of bordering 'EU'rope and the United States has consisted of discourses of the United States, the European Union, and national governments of members states, alongside the mass media – discourses that desensitise many EU and US citizens to how the Mediterranean and the deserts of the Mexico border are turned into racialised mass graves (de Genova, 2017; Heller and Pezzani, 2017). In both cases – that is, the migration crisis and the Mexican border – the spectacle of masses seeking to cross sea and land borders obfuscates histories of centuries of colonial occupation and bordering, together with the wars and structural adjustments that characterise neoliberal globalisation. The media and political discourses hide not only the heterogenous identities of the migrants, but also complex and dangerous journeys that could have taken many years and included numerous stages.

Those who arrive in the Global North are a minority of people forced to move, and many of those who travel transnationally will have spent time in limbo, in camps, or trying to work in third countries. The most forcibly displaced people in Africa remained on that continent, without citizenship, often in camps in adjacent states (of which Dadaab is just one). While women and children may remain in overcrowded camps run by UNHCR, many young men have avoided or left them in order to find work on the continent or move to Europe (Jaspers and Buchanan-Smith, 2018). One million people displaced from El Salvador, Nicaragua, and Guatemala during the wars of 1974 to 1996 were forced to live either elsewhere in their own countries or in camps in neighbouring countries, registered as refugees or as undocumented migrants. Since then poverty, overcrowding, and sexual violence in the camps and permanent state and gang violence continue to push Central Americans on to Mexico, the United States, and Canada, where they face inconsistent and shifting bordering policies that respond to the political contests within each state (García, 2006; Holmes, 2018). Since 2014 the United States has outsourced US border control to the Mexican government, so that in practice the Mexican–American border has shifted 3,000 kilometres south, to the narrowest part of Mexico, where the movement of people can be more easily controlled (Romero, 2016).

In 2011 uprisings against autocratic regimes in North Africa and the Middle East became known as the Arab Spring (Howard et al., 2011). As the initial protests pushed for more democracy, social media and the Internet provided the means for organising demonstrations and facilitated a transformation of politics, allowing for networks to be developed and for ideas to flow across borders (Howard and Hussein, 2013). The instability that followed the Arab Spring included the beginning of the war in Syria, which has displaced more than 11 million Syrians, half of whom have been forced to leave the country to find refuge in the neighbouring states of Turkey (3.5 million), Lebanon (1 million) or Iraq (650,000). Young men were prohibited from working, women were vulnerable to sexual exploitation in the camps, and families made prolonged journeys to and across Europe, all of which led to new and specific de- and rebordering discourses and policies.

In 2004 the EU states established the Frontex agency, designed to manage and coordinate the Union's external land and sea borders

(Neal, 2009). The agency ensures that key intelligence, for instance relating to human traffickers, is shared immediately with border authorities in all EU states. However, Frontex has not prevented official and informal camps and prisons in countries that border the Mediterranean from being occupied by a transient population of individuals from across Africa and the Middle East who were seeking to reach Europe. They have been joined by people from further afield, including Bangladeshis escaping unemployment and the low-wage economy who may have already spent years working in the Middle East or paid bogus employment agencies thousands of dollars to travel to Libya, with the intention of reaching Europe (Deardon, 2017).

Rebordering

As was widely discussed in the literature (e.g. Melin, 2016; Pisano, 2009; Casas-Cortes, Cobarrubias, and Pickles, 2013) and mentioned here in chapter 1, neoliberal globalisation has been accompanied not just by processes of debordering but also by processes of rebordering, outside and inside state territories. Much of this securitisation has been described as an outcome of 9/11 and the 'global war on terrorism'. However, as Huysmans (2000) observed, it started to develop even before that, as one of the outcomes of security forces' search for an alternative project after the end of the Cold War. The securitisation of bordering, as it has developed over the last decade, is characterised by growing reliance on sophisticated IT, which has been used in various surveillance techniques, from satellites to local CCTV cameras, as well as in the processing and production of huge and detailed data banks. These data banks have been used more and more in the international cooperation that grew in this area. This involved not only the establishment of international border securitisation forces such as Frontex, but also – as befits globalised neoliberalism – the use of private security companies with their own sophisticated equipment and border guards (van Steden and Sarre, 2007).

Paradoxically, however, much of IT virtual bordering technologies has been found wanting. This has been greatly highlighted in relation to the heated debate on the Northern Irish border after Brexit, in which the negotiating teams sought to find a solution to how the border might stay open to people, goods, and services and yet function as a bordering firewall between the European Union and the United Kingdom when the latter leaves the EU Customs Union (*Guardian*, 19 September 2018).

However, the contemporary paradox of debordering–rebordering is much wider than this, and to a certain extent more fundamental. We started this chapter by observing how bordering in antiquity, in China, in Rome, and elsewhere, has used walls as a defence against undesired invaders. Since 9/11, in spite of the securitisation technology industry, more than sixty bordering walls have been erected; and barbed wire fences separating various countries have been built internationally (some are still under construction) (Vallet, 2016; Hjelmgaard, 2018). Countries such as Israel, India, Hungary, Bulgaria, Norway, Turkey, Egypt, and Myanmar have built walls on their borders, all with a very similar aim in mind (Flores, 2017).

The Chinese wall was built when the most common mode of mobility was by foot. When we carried out our research during the migration crisis, we heard from many of the people we interviewed, as well as from narratives of other irregular migrants in the press and elsewhere, how they walked, often for weeks, months, and even years, in order to cross borders to where they wanted to arrive. This, in spite of the availability of sophisticated means of transport.

While the different walls serve a variety of specific local governance needs, they are all aimed at blocking irregular pedestrian border crossing outside formal border-crossing control points. Israel, which has been used as a securitisation model for many countries (Halpern, 2015), has built two major walls – one mainly of concrete and the other of steel – for different political purposes. The first wall was officially built after 2000, to prevent terrorists attacks from the West Bank. However, it was built so that the wall cut off thousands of Palestinians from their fields or from the rest of the Palestinian West Bank territory. The second wall was built in 2010–12 along the Egyptian border and the Sinai desert, to stop irregular African migrants from fleeing from war and famine in Africa. Later, when ISIS activism grew in the Sinai, the wall was used to stop infiltrations of Islamist terrorists.

India has also been building barrier fences along its borders with Pakistan and Bangladesh, to prevent border crossing from migrants and smugglers. However, where the local topography is not conducive to building such walls, India has developed 'laser walls' instead (Khajuria, 2017).

The barbed wire fence barrier in Hungary was built along that country's borders with Serbia and Croatia, as a direct response to the refugees crisis in 2015. It was intended to prevent asylum seekers from entering Hungary and to protest against what Hungary considered the very inefficient way the Union was handling that crisis. The combination of that fence and the EU agreement with Turkey, which followed shortly afterwards, radically cut the number of asylum seekers who passed through Hungary.

Perhaps the most outspoken proponent of border securitisation in recent years has been US President Donald Trump. Although the process of the militarisation and barrier building along the Mexican border started gradually after 9/11, Trump's anti-immigration stance and promise to build a border wall with Mexico made bordering a key campaign issue in the 2016 presidential elections. As president, Trump introduced an executive order titled Border Security and Immigration Enforcement Improvements (BSIEE) that directed the Department of Homeland Security (DHS) to plan for the construction of a wall on the 3,200-kilometre border between Mexico and the United States. In the first two months of Trump's presidency, arrests of 'removable' foreigners from the border numbered 21,400 (Kaur, 2018) which included cases of the forced separation of parents and children that was so widely reported in the media, contributing to Agamben's (1998) construction of border crossers as paradigms of 'bare lives'.

Elsewhere states have sought to build upon natural barriers, for example water barriers or seas, in order to disrupt flows of certain groups into their territories. This was prominent not only in Europe (e.g. Lesbos and Lampedusa) but also in Australia, which continues to use both the offshore, third-country processing of asylum seekers and neo-refoulement (Hyndman and Mountz, 2008) – that is, the return of asylum seekers to transit countries as part of the rebordering that emerges from securitisation. As Mountz (2011: 118) has argued, these practices turn an island into a kind of 'enforcement archipelago', as islands 'deflect migrants from the shores of sovereign territory'. The resulting phenomena of entrapment in grey zones and in-betweenness are explored in detail in chapter 5.

The barrier walls between Britain and the European Union have manifested themselves in the growing physical and virtual securitisation around the Eurotunnel's entrance into Calais and around the 'Jungle' nearby, which will be discussed in chapter 5. However, the logic of everyday bordering has permeated the entire British society, as the next two chapters will reveal. The most significant political outcome of this bordering discourse has been the Brexit referendum.

Brexit

The result of the 2016 Brexit referendum in the United Kingdom (52 per cent for and 48 per cent against) reflects the major divisions and contestations in Britain between liberal, pro-European, and inclusive discourses of social solidarity and discourses largely based on what Paul Gilroy (2004) has called postcolonial melancholia: a post-industrial sense of despair in sections of the population and a growing autochthonic political project of belonging (Yuval-Davis and Vieten, 2018).

As McCall (2018: 285) argues, the Brexit referendum campaign focused on the nexus between bordering and security. Its primary objective was to establish a hard security border regime in order to prevent the movement of unwanted outsiders to Britain, including ones coming from within the European Union, and thus to remove an 'existential threat' to British identity.

Those in the Brexit camp imagined that 'regaining control over our borders' will make Britain 'great again' (to paraphrase Trump's call for America), would stop mass immigration, resurrect a supportive, well-funded welfare state and health services (for those who 'belong'), and cleanse 'British culture and values' from undesirable others. As we shall see in the next three chapters on the basis of fieldwork that was carried out mostly before the Brexit referendum, this discourse has been growing for years in various sections of British society, and the technology of a 'hostile environment' for migrants' everyday bordering has been a governmental response both to the neoliberal governability crisis and to the autochthonic response that grew out of the neoliberal governmentality crisis.

Conclusion

In this chapter we have sought to challenge discourses about the 'inevitability' of the contemporary proliferation of bordering by identifying and contextualising some significant bordering processes, both historically and globally. The examples demonstrate both alternative forms of delimiting territorial control and, most significantly, past relationships between bordering processes and governance and belonging in premodern and modern contexts. We have shown how new bordering processes that have evolved during the period of expansion of neoliberal globalisation have both built on and transformed older bordering regimes.

Importantly, we have argued for the need to take an approach that decentres European or Westphalian perspectives, which often obfuscate the complexity of global bordering. We view these ongoing processes of bordering as embedded both in imperialism and in the rise of neoliberal globalised capitalism. For Dipesh Chakrabarty (2000), situating modernity within Europe not only had an enormous impact upon what constitutes social scientific knowledge, but means that nonwestern ideas from the 'periphery' must always be translated as they move towards the 'core'. Our approach to understanding the context of bordering recognises, but also problematises European thought as hegemon in this field. While it is clear that ideologies emerging from Europe have contributed greatly to the history of borders and borderings, it is also evident that they do not provide a total narrative. Not even those moments that are considered to be the most decisive – such as the treaties of Westphalia – have necessarily been as definitive or unambiguous as they may have appeared.

Through this approach we seek to contextualise and unpack the complexities of contemporary bordering scapes that are presented in the next three chapters. This attempt includes denaturalising the notion of national borders by foregrounding their creation and re-creation through specific historical and political contests. It encompasses understanding the contrasting imaginaries of those who try to cross or to control different borders. It involves exposing the always present relationship between bordering processes, governance, and belonging.

3

Firewall Bordering at State-Managed Border Control Points

Introduction

We're going to build a wall. It's going to be a great wall. And it's going to have big beautiful doors in it because we're going to have people coming into our country, but they're going to come into our country legally.

Trump, 2016

Trump's representation of the US–Mexico border wall has evolved since his 'SECURE THE BORDER! BUILD A WALL!' tweet in 2014 (Nixon and Qiu, 2018). The vertical and horizontal extensions of the US–Mexico wall – like the razor-wire fences around the train and ferry terminals in Calais or the 200-metre-wide canal planned by Saudi Arabia to separate itself from Qatar – are observable barriers that perform governmental rhetoric. The 'doors' in Trump's 'wall' are metaphoric filters controlled by policies that define who should be stopped or encouraged to enter the United States. Trump's bordering discourse, initially focused on preventing poor Central Americans from crossing the southern border and, later, directed at Muslims who were flying into the United States from specified countries, later changed position, as the president announced that those needed by his political project would be able to enter. The administration's exclusionary, nationalist discourse and policies exemplify the argument that we outlined in chapter 1 and contextualised historically in chapter 2, that, as borders and borderings move to the centre of political and social life, they redefine notions of citizenship, identity, and belonging for both hegemonic and racialised minorities. The filtering actions of Trump and his predecessors have encompassed increasing security at the territorial border with Mexico, suspension of visas or use of Advance Passenger Information (API) to prevent travel, and use of traffic offences to detain and deport long-term residents (Coleman, 2012; Jones, 2016). Rather than creating new divisions, these contemporary borderings work as mirrors, reflecting existing racial and economic hierarchies that govern transnational mobility for some while also reminding various populations of the state's capacity to dictate who has the right to belong (Parmar, 2018). Different technologies of bordering, at external and internal border control points and through everyday encounters, work as computer firewalls (Rumford, 2006) to perform an intelligent filtering of those who seek to cross borders. As it discriminates between people, the firewall obscures the border for those near the pinnacle, even as it makes it increasingly visible and dangerous for those placed lower down economic and racial hierarchies. An increasing array of bordering technologies regulate the categories of people allowed to enter a country, the length of their stay, and the civil and political rights they are able to claim. Bordering processes also filter the movement of finance, goods, and services. Practices range from the offshoring of financial operations to visas that enable the consumption of 'luxury' products by tourists and to the increasingly profitable businesses of human trafficking and smuggling, which has grown out of state investments in a privatised border security apparatus and in the offshoring of migrant detention centres (Urry, 2014; Andersson, 2014).

In the remainder of this introduction we summarise selected filtering technologies of contemporary firewall bordering at state-managed border control points that are central to political projects of governance and belonging. Such technologies contribute to the social inequalities that constitute the global context for the three illustrative UK bordering scapes to follow.

Firewall bordering at state-managed border control points in the contemporary global context

Filtering citizenship

Become a Global Citizen. Discover the power of second citizenship. Live the life you were destined to live.

Arton Capital, 2017

Mobility across borders and citizenship acquisition have always been easier for people with financial resources. Across the globe, governments have introduced bordering policies that support neoliberal economies by attracting capital and foreigners able to access it internationally. New types of visas and routes to residency encourage investment and consumption for high-earning and high-spending individuals who, in contrast to compatriots with fewer financial resources, are targeted by citizenship marketing campaigns such as that of Arton Capital.

In the United States the EB-5 visa has provided a route to citizenship through job creation investment since 1992. The scheme became important as a means to attract private foreign capital and plug financial gaps in the absence of domestic capital. In areas of high unemployment, a half-million-dollar investment and the creation of ten jobs formed a minimum requirement. By 2015 most EB-5 visas were being issued to Chinese citizens who used China as a wealth-gaining opportunity and the United States as a living environment, remaining in China to manage their businesses while acquiring residency rights for their offspring (Simons et al., 2015). After media disclosures such as of the use of the EB-5 visa to fund housing developments in wealthy neighbourhoods (Harney, 2017), the future of this preferential visa is debated. Many countries have investment routes to citizenship, the earliest examples being the Caribbean Island of St Kitts and Nevis (in 1984) and Canada (in 1986): a passport from the former gives visa-free access to the United Kingdom and all Schengen states, and a passport from the latter to 155 countries. Several European countries, including Hungary, Bulgaria, Cyprus, and Malta, have similar schemes. Frequently citizenship is acquired in order to obtain visa-free access to other countries. For example, Portugal's Golden Resident Permit Programme is taken up mostly by investors who use their visas to live abroad, including in other Schengen states (Pegg, 2017).

Global businesses match up individuals with investment opportunities who meet the initial visa and the later settlement and citizenship requirements, demonstrating the close relationship between the mobility of people and capital. Private companies offer services for passport acquisition, offshoring of banking, corporate tax avoidance, residency and investment capital – their agents making $100,000 per EB-5 client (Harney, 2017). Marketing focuses on enabling wealthy individuals to build new lives with a US company and declares its vision 'to play a small part in changing a person's destiny for the good' (Harney, 2017) by helping that person to obtain US residency. Qiaowai, a China-based company, offers comparisons between fifteen destinations in point of free education, healthcare, statutory holidays, and visa-free access to other countries (visit http://www.iqiaowai.com/he).

Filtering consumers

Business travel and leisure travel are worth trillions of dollars and employ millions of people directly and indirectly (UNWTO, 2016). In 2016 there were over 1,235 million international travellers made up of tourists, business people, pilgrims, and patients (UNWTO, 2016). Globally, Chinese tourists are the highest spending group, spending twice as much as the next group after them – US short-term visitors (UNWTO, 2016: 13).

The bordering policies of governments reflect the contests between corporate interests from the hospitality and transport sectors, which demand fast and accessible travel, and the interests of anti-immigration groups, which see tourism as a route to 'overstaying' and terrorism. In 2016, 58 per cent of the world's population required a tourist visa issued before departure while the rest could enter visa-free, with an eVisa, or on arrival. Emerging economies have increased their visa openness while advanced economies have become more discrimi-natory (UNWTO, 2016: 21). The United States uses an electronic visa waiver for people with biometric passports from wealthy countries – including EU countries, Japan, and Australia, which all have reciprocal programmes. However, issues of 'security' have been used to block visits by citizens of Eastern European Union countries who should have been entitled to reciprocal visa-free travel alongside citizens of specified Muslim-majority states (Morris, 2017).

Tourist visas are used as a means of entering in order to 'overstay', which leads to a tightening of the requirements for nationals of countries perceived to be at a higher risk of generating irregular migration. As in the case of investor visas, the growth of a middle class in China and elsewhere has facilitated the release of tourist visas across continents for wealthy citizens at the same time as access is closed to those suspected of being migrant workers.

Filtering labour

As explored in chapter 2, the regulation of migrant workers has been central to different bordering regimes. In the post-independence era, quota systems and lotteries, often racially based, were used to organise migration for the purpose of meeting the demands for labour. This was particularly the case in European settler colonies, including Australia and Canada. Since the 1990s, the quickly changing global labour market has led to the introduction of 'points-based' migration schemes that use the slippery concept of 'skills', aimed at letting in those who would 'benefit the economy' (Mezzadra and Neilson, 2013: 138–9). Politicians in the United States and United Kingdom, too, have been considering points-based systems. Other schemes, such as the Australian 457 visa (now Temporary Skill Shortage visa), rely on employers to sponsor skilled workers in places where the local residents are not available to do the work. In the first bordering scape we examine how UK working visas block the migration of labour likely to seek work in the ethnic enclave economy, while encouraging those likely to work in more established businesses or sectors of the economy.

Filtering families

Family reunification is the largest category of migration in the Global North and allowances for it have been central to immigration legis-lation globally. The proportions of men and women who migrate to join their relatives change as a result of differences in the types of family and in the immigration and emigration policies targeted at various categories of labour (Kofman and Meetoo, 2008). Labelling the reunification of extended families 'chain migration', the US president has repeatedly sought to limit the opportunities for this phenomenon, for example in his 2018 State of the Union address:

> The fourth and final pillar protects the nuclear family by ending chain migration. Under the current broken system, a single immigrant can bring in virtually unlimited numbers of distant relatives. Under our plan, we focus on the immediate family by limiting sponsorships to spouses and minor children. This vital reform is necessary, not just for our economy, but for our security, and for the future of America. (Trump, 2018)

American culture appears to be threatened by the extended and future families of immigrants – but not by the Slovenian parents of the First Lady, who became US citizens under family reunification rules in 2018. Marriage contracts and family visas have historically worked as filtering border technologies designed to exclude people of a specific gender and ethnicity and from lower socioeconomic groups (Charsley, 2012). Transnational marriages, whereby partners in a cross-border marriage become part of established transnational communities, have been the target of bordering legislation, which seeks to regulate the size of ethnic minority communities within states (Williams, 2012). In Denmark, regulations are aimed at restricting transnational marriages with would-be members of Turkish and Pakistani ethnic minorities and are interrelated with policy goals for integration (Jørgensen, 2012). In the United Kingdom marriage migrants must demonstrate their ability to communicate in English. Even if they fulfil the legal regulations, a 'culture of disbelief' – a starting point of extreme scepticism – frames how bureaucrats, politicians, and the media view marriage partners' retelling of their reasons for marrying. This moral economy of suspicion (D'Aoust, 2017; Fassin, 2005, 2009) is especially invasive when a 'genuine relationship' has to be demonstrated by displays of physical affection, over long periods, to border officials and their public informants. In Canada, until 2017, foreign partners of citizens had to live with their sponsor for two years in order to retain their permanent resident status. However, in response to arguments about domestic violence, the government removed the condition, stating that, 'while cases of marriage fraud exist, the majority of relationships are genuine and most spousal sponsorship applications are made in good faith' (Government of Canada, 2017).

In the remainder of this chapter we use three UK bordering scapes drawn from our empirical research in order to explore processes of firewall bordering at border control points. Adopting the situated intersectional methodology discussed in chapter 1, we seek to identify the specific and shifting permeabilities of borders, locate those whose everyday actions work as bordering processes that create and enact the filter at different scales, and observe how individuals' experiences of different levels and methods of filtering impact on their feelings of belonging.

Bordering scape 1: 'External' border control points: visas, airports, train stations, seaports

Order is maintained in the airport, train station, and seaport border through extraterritorial granting of entry clearance, diverse visas regimes, API, biometrics, and the growth of e-borders. These strategies regulate and block some categories of travellers while rendering border control points seamless for others, so that the UK border appears to be relatively invisible for those who have already been filtered either as Economic European Area (EEA) nationals or via varying visa regimes. The (b)ordering role of separate queues for non-EEA nationals is clear to the individuals who wait in them. Airline passengers can also observe the speed at which those with biometric e-passports are able to proceed through the border, or how first-class passengers 'fast-track' security and passport control. Encounters between passengers and border officials perform and re-create geopolitical configurations of inequality.

Fast-tracking to multiple citizenship and to belonging

In 2001 a government minister was accused of attempting to speed up the application for citizenship of one of the Indian Hinduja brothers after their million pound donation to the British government's Millennium Dome project. The minister was cleared of wrongdoing and both brothers became British citizens (White and Harding, 2001). In contrast, Mohamed Al-Fayed, the Egyptian businessman, had his applications for citizenship rejected by the Home Secretary in 1999, after the resignations of two MPs who had not declared the money he had paid them to ask questions on his behalf in parliament. Al-Fayed's response – 'I'm not desperate, I'm not leaving the country, I'm here forever – I'm staying' (Guardian Staff and Agencies, 1999) – reminded politicians that his wealth enables him to be wherever he chooses. The involvement, both clandestine and open, of politicians demonstrates the contingency of firewall bordering as global elites encounter the UK border.

For very wealthy individuals and their families from outside the EEA, visiting and gaining settlement in the United Kingdom is facilitated by the Tier 1 Investor and Entrepreneur migrant visas (UKVI, 2018a), which are part of border-filtering processes whereby government and the private apparatus work together to smooth the mobility of individuals involved for example in the 'offshoring' of finance in the City of London and other tax havens (Urry, 2014). The trillions of dollars held 'offshore', to avoid billions of dollars of taxation, have contributed to spatial inequalities that are evident in the United Kingdom, where the highest concentration of the super-rich is to be found in small enclaves in London (Burrows, 2013; Atkinson et al., 2017). The permeability of this bordering process is enabled by its invisibility. Anticorruption campaigners have highlighted the invisibility of the sources of wealth of 3,000 people who obtained investor migrant visas between 2008 and 2015, arguing that the Home Office and the banks both assumed each other to be carrying out checks (Pegg, 2017). They also contest the neoliberal political project of governance, in which belonging can be bought with vast wealth:

> This is an area where successive governments have allowed rich people to jump the queue. It's the sort of thing that tax havens do to encourage inward investment ... We have in effect been selling off British citizenship to the rich from often non-democratic countries who otherwise one would not regard as desirable immigrants. (Lord Wallace of Saltaire, quoted in Pegg, 2017)

One of the few known beneficiaries of the UK investor visa is Kazakhstan-born Madiyar Ablyazov, who obtained indefinite leave to remain in the United Kingdom in 2013. Knowledge of his visa only became public owing to a court case related to his father's alleged embezzlement of 3 billion pounds from a Kazakh bank and purchase of houses worth 35 million pounds in the United Kingdom. The case exposed a variety of strategies used by the wealthy to cross borders or to avoid being forced to cross them. Apart from the son's acquisition of an investor visa, the father had been granted asylum in the United Kingdom and the mother was using a passport from the Central African Republic to cross borders (Goodley, 2013; Neate, 2014; Pegg, 2017).

Since global elites easily acquire visas and residency rights even if they do not secure citizenship, they experience relatively frictionless borders – from obtaining the visa to crossing the border control points and, further, to buying property, education, and healthcare as well as political influence. They are almost invisible in political and media discourses about the United Kingdom's permeable borders, thanks to their categorisation as 'desired migrants', iterated as 'the brightest and the best' (Maidment, 2017).

Private businesses further facilitate border crossing for non-European elites that hold visas. The web page of one such bordering facilitator suggests that 'not being well known' (which in some settings can be interpreted as a euphemism for not being white) is a factor in problematic border crossing:

71

It is our mission to provide a seamless travel experience for our clients who are unaccustomed to waiting in long lines or enduring the crowds and chaos of today's airports. Many of our clients have a high profile in their own countries or within their companies. They often need extra attention when traveling overseas where they are not as well known. (Royal Airport Concierge, 2017)

Visa regimes work with private companies to enable the smooth global travel of the wealthy while creating barriers for others.

Differential visa-free travel to and from the United Kingdom

We interviewed professional 'high-flyers' who approach the border control point with the confidence that crossing international borders is their right. BB, a British white male who, as a business-class frequent flyer fast-tracked through security, does not usually require a visa, told us: 'I will just completely assume with all the places that I go to that are mainly Europe and the United States that it is my complete right to get through these annoying queues as quickly as possible and do not expect any problems at all.' Despite prominent notices ordering passengers not to use their phones to photograph the UK border at airports, he admitted that his sense of entitlement meant that he took pictures of queue-free control points to share his experience of fast tracking with us. However, his experiences, as he told us, were not shared by his work colleagues: 'I have travelled with members of my research group who have had Middle Eastern backgrounds and in the States they have taken two or three hours longer than me in being put to one side and it being obviously not as straightforward.' However, while he can be categorised as a member of the highly mobile global elite, BB was less confident in his encounters with officials at US border control points: 'The US is the closest one where you are feeling that you have to be careful of the power of the people sitting behind the desk. In those situations just occasionally I have sensed that you are at their mercy.'

Professional women (including ourselves), who otherwise experience smooth border crossings, are routinely questioned upon entering the United Kingdom when their surname does not match that of their child. This is exemplified in the report of a Labour MP, Tulip Siddiq, who was boarding the Eurostar in Paris with her daughter, who bears Siddiq's husband's surname. The UK border guard at the juxtaposed controls asked her: 'Who is this girl?'

I was really surprised by the question ... I said: 'This is my daughter,' and he asked why we don't have the same name. He also asked for my marriage certificate and my birth certificate ... my daughter was crying and saying 'mama, mama' but that didn't seem to be what would convince him. (Tulip Siddiq, quoted in Elgot, 2017)

Questioning adults travelling with children with different surnames is part of the United Kingdom's antitrafficking policy (Border Force, 2013). It is possible that, as a British Bangladeshi Muslim woman with a mixed-race child with an English surname, Siddiq was more likely to be questioned.

We interviewed AS, a British white male Muslim who spoke of 'a border in their minds' with reference to border officials' stereotyping him – 'a white convert who travelled frequently' – as a suspected terrorist. He told us that he ran a business in Belgium to which he used to travel weekly. In 2008 he was detained at Heathrow for eight hours upon returning from Pakistan, where he had children. Since then he has always been stopped at the Dover border, once being threatened with twenty-eight-day detention under the Terrorism Act. Since he could no longer rely on not being stopped at the border, he pulled out of the business. AS told us that, before this experience, 'borders were meaningless' for him as a white man. However, since then he worries about borders – not just when crossing them but in anticipation of doing it. He had also shaved his beard.

Anticipatory bordering is experienced by those who cannot change their perceived identity by shaving. We spoke with AM, a frequent flyer and an Indian citizen with a Muslim name. In his professional life he has worked in many countries, including the United Kingdom, and his passports contained numerous visas collected during his working life. However, he told us that he has never travelled to the United States and would not consider applying for a visa, as he knew he would have been denied one even before the Trump 'Muslim ban', despite not being from any of the listed countries.

Work-related visas: UK citizenship and belonging

Work-related visas are an example of how borders work as firewalls that filter those who seek to cross them. The required income levels and specific, 'skilled' employment categories are filters that appear to be easily altered according to the demands of the economy. Up to 15 per cent of London's top-end financial workforce consists of migrants recruited from a global labour market, concentrated in key financial centres. They follow complex patterns of short-term migration between those hubs and are filtered through selective bordering regimes that encourage their mobility (Mezzadra and Neilson, 2013: 113–14). In London, the financial workforce includes EEA citizens who benefit from free movement and citizens who require the Tier 2 general visa for skilled migrants, which discriminates between different categories of employment through salary levels and occupational criteria (Gov.UK, 2018; UKVI, 2018b).

The example of one of the listed 'shortage occupations' – chefs – demonstrates how the border is constructed by legislators so as to exclude specific categories of migrants and thereby prevent migration to racialised minority populations, and how this firewall bordering is contested by people from the populations targeted for exclusion. Uniquely among occupations, the category 'chef' comes with a list of requirements specifically worded to ensure the exclusion of those who work in businesses that make up the ethnic enclave economy, thus discouraging migration from nations in the Global South that already have established populations in the United Kingdom (Bloch and McKay, 2015 and 2016; Bloch, Kumarappan, and McKay, 2015). The government document specifies that skilled chefs who may be granted Tier 2 visas should have jobs where

> the pay is at least £29,570 per year after deductions for accommodation, meals etc.; and the job requires five or more years relevant experience in a role of at least equivalent status to the one they are entering; and the job is not in either a fast food outlet, a standard fare outlet, or an establishment which provides a take-away service. (Gov.UK, 2018)

This firewall blocks ethnic minority businesses from sponsoring chefs from former colonies and elsewhere in the Global South; and it does so through four specific requirements. First, the level of pay is too high for the sector; second, many chefs live and eat in accommodation above the restaurant, which makes the threshold even higher; third, whether or not they are highly skilled chefs, it is unlikely that chefs from the Global South would be able to obtain experience deemed 'equivalent' before arriving in the United Kingdom – besides, in the past chefs were trained in the job; finally, takeaway services are an economically necessary addition to most ethnic enclave economy restaurants. In 2014 we interviewed BR, an owner of several restaurants and a member of the Conservative Party. He reflected that, while staff shortages had always existed, immigration rules had meant that men could come over and be trained as successful chefs once they arrived:

> I always find that staff crisis in our industry ... But somehow we managed ... Those days when people came from Bangladesh for a job, the status was easier ... All the skilled workers, some of them are aging, because of the success there are not enough skilled people here. We cannot bring skilled people from European countries. In 2009 we did a survey, we needed 34,000 people then ... because of the shortage the average restaurant is losing about £19,000 per year.

In partnership with owners of Chinese and Turkish restaurants, BR lobbied parliament to allow chefs to migrate and to regularise undocumented migrants on whom the business owners depended:

> Our lobbying is very strong and actually a lot of our MPs agree and they say you are lobbying very successfully and we sympathize with you but unfortunately it is not happening because of the world of immigration issues!

> ... Regularise them, then they can work properly, pay the tax and national insurance, in the end they can have a work permit or something and then they can go back. This is the way you can identify how much [sic] undocumented workers there are ... If you want to sort out the immigration problem in this country then they should do this.

In 2016, industry owners lobbied to leave the EU in the belief that a new 'points-based system' would enable them to sponsor chefs from outside Europe. This has not happened and the 2016 Immigration Act extended the continuum of firewall bordering still further, into the everyday lives of restaurant workers. We will return to explore this issue in chapter 4.

Tourists: short-term consumers

Like other wealthy states, the United Kingdom seeks to attract high-spending foreign tourists while preventing those on short-term visitor visas from overstaying and working illegally. Inbound tourism was worth more than 24 billion pounds to the British economy in 2013 (Deloitte, 2013). While people from a range of relatively wealthy countries do not need visitor visas, people from countries whose citizens have historically been excluded from settling in the United Kingdom, for example India and China, do.

Visitors from the Global South are routinely denied visas on the basis of the assumption that the visits would be used as a route to 'illegal settlement'. This culture of disbelief permeates bordering encounters at every level, as exemplified by RR, a middle-class Indian woman we interviewed who wanted to catch up with old friends in London, where she had previously studied. She had to second-guess every assumption that a border official might make; so, from her visa application to the time she spent in the United Kingdom, there was not one stage of the journey that she could envision with confidence and a sense of entitlement:

> I had to prove to them that I had roots in India and I would come back ... then you have to tell them your plans, you have to give them an itinerary or something, and I just put down 'everyday life'. I said I want to have breakfast here. I want to take a walk here. I want to go see a film here. Because that is what for me is London. It is not about tourism.

She was careful not to appear to be enjoying the types of pastimes assumed to be for those who 'belong' in the United Kingdom rather than the activities designed for tourists. She and her friends felt compelled to prove that the visit would not be interpreted wrongly:

> And then they said if you have email conversations with friends then print them out, about what you are going to do. So I told my friends I am going to make an email which I'm going to print out and give. So let's talk about holiday plans there ... so they came back with things they thought would be nice, like travel, and then I printed that and gave that ... I went through emails deleting things, like from my friends saying things like 'maybe we can do some art here' ... Because I had heard of someone who had come and been sent back at the border because she had emails about a performance.

Before RR left India, the bordering had extended to her friends' lives: 'The uncomfortable bit was that I had to get details from my hosts. Their passports, their council tax, their rent agreement, their bank account statements.' After submitting her biometric data, she received a visa she felt had depended on the whiteness and marital status of her friends rather than on any trust in her: 'I have a feeling, because my friends are white, and they are not family, so I will come back and not stay, and they are a couple, not a single man so I won't get married!'

At Mumbai airport she hadn't felt prepared for further questioning before being allowed on her flight:

> The man from [airline], it wasn't even at the desk, it was just before the queue starts, he was taking down details, was like 'why are you going to the UK?' So I was thrown back. I wasn't ready for it. Holiday? Friends? And suddenly I was like, I really need to get myself together for when the questions start coming.

When she landed at Heathrow she encountered the ordered border but perceived a test of her genuineness in the seemingly friendly questioning:

> I landed at Heathrow and I got the most wonderful border officer [laughs]. It was so pleasant. It was amazing. So he was like 'what do you do?' and I was like 'I do photography' and he said 'it is your first visit?' and ... It was like small chat but trying to know whether I am really who I am claiming to be.

Her experience contrasts with those of people of similar socioeconomic background who travel in organised groups, where the power of consumers ensures relatively 'frictionless' border encounters. An Indian cruise passenger reported on his experience of no visible immigration control in Southampton:

> The other passengers being all British or American, there were no landing cards, fingerprinting machines or computers to call up history. No wonder the immigration official looked uncomfortable. As unprepared for us as Britain is about leaving the EU, he had to accept what we said and let us through ... Our driver had a pragmatic explanation. Immigration knows only the rich go on cruises. So they take it easy in Southampton. (Datta-Ray, 2016)

Pressures from businesses hoping to profit from the mobile middle classes have led to changes in the UK visa regime exclusively for Chinese visitors who travel in high-spending organised groups (Gov.UK, 2015). In 2016 a new two-year visitor visa and streamlined application process was introduced, in a move to attract to the United Kingdom the estimated billions of pounds that Chinese tourists would otherwise spend elsewhere, while visiting European countries only on a Schengen visa (Bickell, 2016). The manager of a shopping centre in Kent told us that, since Chinese tourists spent more per head than any others and since they could spend only a week in Europe, retail outlets aimed to get on tour itineraries before the visitors left home. They therefore targeted international tourists who arrived through London, while overall business came mostly from EU visitors who travelled on the Shuttle or arrived through Dover Port. In Dover we spoke with employees in the retail and tourist industries who regretted that high-spending tourists from cruise ships spent their money on trips inland. These employees were trying to negotiate with cruise companies to encourage passengers to spend in Dover.

Border guarding at the territorial borders

Government immigration enforcement teams and private transport carriers partner up to manage the border at official border-crossing points. Their overlapping bordering roles include stopping people who can give no proof of their legal right to cross the border and identifying forged documents. Immigration enforcement teams also focus on identifying those who they believe intend to overstay their visas. These teams' perspective on (il)legality extends bordering matters into the discourse on national belonging.

We interviewed border officials who had previously been employed in decision-making in high commissions and worked in immigration enforcement within the United Kingdom, for private airlines and security companies, and for the government agency at border control points in seaports and airports and at the juxtaposed controls at the Eurostar terminal in Paris. Their perspective on the UK border changed over time, as they moved from one site of border control to another and their view of their professional bordering role became more complex as a result. AD, a female officer who had moved from searching lorries at a seaport to carrying out raids in London, was surprised to find that the border was more permeable than she had imagined: 'At the port we found people in the back of lorries. We thought we were doing a good job finding people there but it is surprising how many more have got through and are here.'

Immigration enforcers' discourse constructed a clear binary between being a 'legal' and being an 'illegal' border crosser; this enabled them to manage the contradictions of asylum and refugee law that they encountered. KD, a senior female officer, explained:

Migrants have different identities all at the same time. Immigration offence is step one. The person is illegal. When they are an asylum seeker they are still an illegal immigrant. Once they are accepted as a refugee they are no longer an illegal immigrant.

The legal–illegal binary enabled her to manage her enforcement team's work with those whom they prevented from entering, those whom they arrested or detained, and those whom they deported from the United Kingdom: 'We must implement legislation, but I tell my team that you must never forget that you have a person. I say "put yourself in that person's shoes and think how they are feeling".'

The border guards also shared views about how legal and illegal border crossers dress. We spoke with BD, an off-duty Border Force officer who had been taught how to make a counterfeit passport in order to be able to spot one. He said that, although he can identify a fake passport quickly, he wouldn't look at the passport. He would 'look at the person': 'With illegals they will have been briefed to remember their date of birth etc. and react differently. They are also likely to be more dressed up than legal travellers.'

He spoke of 'immigration clothes and immigration shoes' as identifiers, but did not explain. However, his references shared much with the descriptions of suspect airline passengers by authors who worked as immigration officers, for instance in Saint's (2003) novel *Refusal Shoes* or in Clarke's (2016) memoir subtitled *Stirring Tales of UK Border Control*. Unsurprisingly, the shared discourse of those books and the off-duty officer contrasted with those of our official interviews.

Transport industry employees are required to carry out bordering roles as an adjunct to their primary employment. We spoke to FS, a British employee in a cross-channel ferry company who crossed the border several times a day. He told us that his colleagues recognised individual migrants who were repeatedly found on board and returned to France. When we told him that we had spoken to employees of Eurotunnel about their attempts to stop undocumented migrants from using the rail tunnel in order to reach the United Kingdom, he quickly responded: 'We bring them back raw, they bring them back cooked.'

What sounded like a frequently repeated joke was a chilling reference to unknown numbers of people electrocuted or crushed by trains – an example of the violently dehumanising discourses that are used in constructing exclusive nationalisms, common to many contexts (Wemyss, 2009).

Migrant smuggling and trafficking networks become more complex and profitable as they respond to the tightening bordering policies of

Turkey and European states (Triandafyllidou and Maroukis, 2012; Andersson 2014). One government response to media discourses about these networks is to incorporate border-guarding roles into the lives of inhabitants of border areas. At the end of 2017, the Home Office announced a plan to use volunteers to 'bolster' Border Force staffing levels in small sea harbours and airports, as a result of reports that half of the unmanned ports on the east coast were not regularly attended by Border Force officers, that the number of 'clandestine migrants' detected in such ports doubled, reaching 400 in a year (Bolt, 2016), and that small ports would be used by terrorists (D. Anderson, 2016). Unsurprisingly, the volunteer border-guarding plan was opposed by unions and politicians with constituents in border-related employment (BBC News, 2017). While politicians from both the left and the right opposed volunteer border guards at territorial borders, in chapter 4 we focus on how increasing numbers of citizens are becoming obliged to take on border-guarding responsibilities with no remuneration and with the threat of fines and prison sentences for non-compliance.

Bordering scape 2: Firewall bordering at the 'internal' border control point of registry offices

Transnational marriages between naturalised, racialised British citizens and people from their country of birth have long been seen as a threat to British immigration control, marriages between individuals from areas of the former empire being labelled 'sham' and therefore illegitimate if they lead to the acquisition of settlement rights in the United Kingdom (D'Aoust, 2013; Wray, 2016). The border between Britain and its former colonies has always been multiply located, as bordering activities of filtering take place overseas in high commissions, villages, airports, and domestic registry offices (Charsley, 2012; Williams, 2012; and Wray, 2011, 2012, 2016). (B)ordering is evident in the separation of visible 'onshore' and hidden 'offshore' state bordering practices that distance official government policy from accusations of racial discrimination. Chaotic scenes in UK airports led to the introduction of entry clearance requirements that have to be satisfied before travelling. Disputed marriage migration decisions can then be made at high commissions, ensuring that the airport border regained its 'orderly character' (Wray, 2012: 48). Levels of rejection remain highest for intraethnic marriages that enable migration. Spouses who are citizens of Somalia and

Bangladesh have high refusal rates, whereas spouses who are citizens of white settler former colonies have low refusal rates (Charsley, 2012: 200–4).

UK citizens from lower socioeconomic groups are unable to be joined by non-EEA spouses, owing to the requirement that a minimum income be demonstrated by citizens who intend to sponsor foreign spouses and dependants (Gower and McGuiness, 2017). While this bordering regulation is familiar to targeted transnational racialised groups, it only becomes visible in the media when white British citizens are affected, as demonstrated by the tone of the report below, which involved a British student and his partner from the United States, both white:

> The little-known rule means not only does he need a job, he also needs to prove he has earnt at least £18,600 in the past year. But he said the requirement made it virtually impossible for any British full-time student to marry a non-EU student and get them permission to stay. He said: 'It's cruel – it gives the impression foreign spouses are some kind of luxury good.' (Phil Green, quoted in Belger, 2017)

However, EU legislation that overrides domestic law has meant that the internal UK border at registry offices and churches became more visible as a site of state bordering, represented as threatened by 'sham marriages'. The 2004 EU Free Movement Directive ensured that, if an EEA national has the right to stay in the United Kingdom, the same rights extend, without the minimum income requirement, to family members who are not EEA nationals. Consequently EEA and non-EEA national marriages were identified by the Home Office as open to abuse 'by people who falsely claim to be, or be related to, an EEA national' (Vine, 2014b: 3.19). John Vine, the independent chief inspector of borders in 2014, was concerned about the EU Free Movement rights extending to four generations of dependants:

> The reason people are going through sham marriage is to circumvent immigration laws that require a much more onerous burden of proof. So someone married to an EEA national acquires the same Treaty rights as the EEA national, can reside in the UK indefinitely and bring in dependent children and grandchildren and dependent parents and grandparents. (Vine, 2014a)

His anxiety was especially focused on naturalised EEA citizens from Britain's former colonies:

There is a higher refusal rate for EEA nationals who are naturalised from other countries and are sponsoring resident permits for partnerships from their own country of origin. Those particular countries are Nigeria, Ghana and Pakistan. (Vine, 2014a)

He perceived registrars and 'the public' as the frontline of the UK internal border, threatened by the nexus of citizenship laws of EEA countries, the EU Free Movement Directive, and 'chain' migration. Successive governments have securitised this internal border by strengthening the partnership between marriage registrars and the Home Office Immigration, Compliance and Enforcement (ICE) teams and by drawing various media and the public into active bordering roles. The Immigration Act 2014 compelled registrars to refer all notices of marriage or civil partnership that involve a non-EEA national where 'a person could gain an immigration advantage' to the Home Office and extended the power of ICE teams to surveil the lives of couples before and after marriage through home visits and the monitoring of social media accounts (Vine, 2014b: 6.37).

Enforcement performances and public reporting

I was shocked to see there is an allegation of sham marriage at the rate of one every sixty minutes ...The public last year made almost 7,000 reports of sham marriages and registrars 2100 up from 900 four years ago ... Only 90 were deported. (Vaz, 2014)

This statement by the then chair of the Home Affairs Committee (HAC) signalled the significance of the unpaid, untrained border-guarding role of the 'public', in contrast with the patchy bordering work of paid registrars who, before the 2014 Immigration Act, used their own initiative in deciding which marriages were 'suspicious'. As the Act was being implemented, the Home Office worked with media outlets: first, to alert 'the public' to its role in reporting sham marriages; second, to warn prospective 'couples' that they are suspect; and, third, to publicise new legislation demonstrating that the Home Office is carrying out its job of combating illegal immigration. The immigration minister and marriage registrars were interviewed on mainstream shows, which exposed 'sham marriages' as the new regulations were coming into force (BBC One, 2014; Channel Five, 2014). Both programmes encouraged members of the 'wider public' to act as border guards by reporting suspicious marriages, while racialised couples were forced to perform and justify their relationships not only in front of those who conducted the marriage ceremony, but also in their everyday lives (see Wemyss et al., 2018).

Perspectives from secular and religious registrars

Secular and religious registrars experienced the transformation of the process of marriage registration from a celebration into a security interrogation. The narratives of registrars demonstrate how their work contexts, individual experiences, and conceptions of a 'genuine marriage' influenced how they managed their bordering roles in their everyday work. The assumed underreporting of 'suspicions of sham marriages' by many registrars before the 2014 Immigration Act reflected their awareness of the nuances of the situation and their emotional engagement. A registrar interviewed by the HAC disliked carrying out more rigorous interviews and gave the following reason:

> We are also dealing with a lot of genuine couples, many of whom will be foreign nationals, and for them the experience we want them to have is not of an immigration interview ... Also some characteristics that registrars are supposed to look out for can apply to genuine marriages. (Registrar 2)

Echoing an official list compiled for registrars, he said that his suspicions would be raised if there was 'little interaction' and 'no common language' between the two, or if a 'third party' was in control of what's going on with the couple (Charsley and Benson, 2012: 16). He added that he had a 'gut feeling about genuine responses' and had to assess what is 'natural nerves'. Another registrar expanded on the subjectivity of 'hidden indicators' that she looked out for but that might be ignored by her fellow registrars in the half-hour interviews with couples:

> As soon as you go out to call a couple you are making that first impression 'how do they look in the waiting area? ... sometimes they are all over each other saying 'we are in a relationship, we are so in love' whereas in reality they would probably be sitting with their mobile [laughs] ... or when you ask a question 'what name are you known by?' and they will try to put everything in the answer ... because they will be saying 'look how much I know about this person!' (Registrar 3)

For her, less suspicion is raised by EEA or non-EEA couples from the same ethnic backgrounds:

> If a Congolese is marrying a Congolese, then their cultures are similar, their language is similar, it's likely their families, their elders, so again you would look more favourably at that as a marriage than at someone who is [from] a totally different culture, a totally different system. So, Pakistanis marrying Lithuanians, Latvians, Hungarians! (Registrar 3)

However her view that those with similar cultures may be looked on more favourably conflicts with Vine's evidence that there were more refusals of marriages between naturalised EEA citizens born in Ghana, Nigeria, and Pakistan and partners from their countries of birth.

Registrar 3 showed us a tally she was keeping of the variety of recent EEA/non-EEA marriage combinations that invited suspicion. She pointed out Afghan male and Romanian female partnerships, saying that they are 'very culturally different'. The suspicion that surrounds Eastern European women who marry Muslim, Asian, or African men echoed those articulated in the inspection reports produced by Vine (2014b). However, the one-dimensional view that unions involving different cultures should invite suspicion contrasts with the more complex understandings of those who inhabit transnational spaces in their work and leisure. An interviewee told us of his Bangladeshi friend who had married a Romanian fellow student. He was surprised that a British registrar would be unable to see shared cultural characteristics. Moreover, research among Slovakian au pairs in London has shown that women actively sought non-Slovakian and non-English men:

> relationships in London were ... most common with men of Albanian/ Kosovan, Pakistani, Ukrainian and Moroccan origin ... Sometimes the attraction is precisely the history and depth of that culture as an antidote to feelings of transience and alienation. (Burikova and Miller, 2010: 145)

Narratives of romantic encounters via shared social and work spaces were reiterated by two Kurdish British interviewees who had married women from Eastern Europe. One couple had met at a nightclub and the other at a factory.

Until the 2014 Immigration Act, the Anglican Church gave notice of marriages independently from registry offices. Now, for marriages with a non-EEA partner, notice interviews have to take place at a registry office four weeks before the priest conducts the wedding ceremony. Priests from different denominations spoke to us about the conflicts they negotiate at the intersection of their religious values and state bordering obligations, which have increased since the 1999 Immigration and Asylum Act introduced the duty to report 'sham marriages'. FA, a Church of England priest, reflected on the dilemmas that existed for him since 1999:

> You don't have to profess a faith at all to be married in the Church and that raises lots of issues. It becomes clear in issues of immigration where over the last ten years we have increasingly been asked to behave as immigration officers as well as [as] parish priests. It is difficult enough to identify why people are getting married in church while on top of that deciding whether they are doing it for real.

MM, a Methodist minister, told us:

> When a couple come to be married your first question should be 'congratulations, I'm here to help' but now there is no congratulations, it's immediately down to the business of 'Are you legally allowed to be in the country?'.

He was aware of the complexity of couples' situations and of the subjectivity of those who evaluate the validity of relationships. He gave the following example, which illustrates both his moral dilemma and his willingness to believe the couples:

> It is fundamental to the theology of the church, and how we regard human beings and our job is not to police. A struggle can be that a couple want a marriage for convenience which puts the minister up against legislation and for us that feels wrong to put foremost the law rather than the integrity of the situation. It is possible that an authorised church minister could feel obliged to assist both inadvertently and deliberately. Most ministers understand the law and therefore become immigration officers.

Both men negotiated their state bordering obligations and moral responsibilities, including their commitment to the continuation and expansion of their congregations, in a conflicted ethical situation that they had not chosen when they first joined their ministries.

Perspectives from the targets of marriage-bordering regulations

The moral gatekeeping of bordering professionals and of the media, which construct who should be considered an appropriate marriage partner, is a manifestation of the racialised, exclusionary–inclusionary boundaries of belonging. Many of those we interviewed felt that their embodiment of the border made them objects of the amplification of 'sham marriage' stories in the media, so that they would have to second-guess how their behaviour would be interpreted by the people they encounter in every sphere of their lives.

The fact that border enforcement professionals categorise marriages between naturalised EEA citizens who were born in Europe's former empires as 'sham' aimed at 'circumventing immigration laws' denies the transnational social spaces of postcolonial diasporas (Pries, 2001). People from the former colonies have been relocating to the United Kingdom from EU countries under the EU Free Movement Directive for various reasons, including reasons related to English language and established community resources. Somalis, many of whom have migrated from the Netherlands to the United Kingdom, continue to have the highest refusal rates for spouse visas (Charsley, 2012: 204). We interviewed Bangladesh-born Italian citizens who moved to the United Kingdom and who perceived bringing a partner or a dependant from Bangladesh as a family reunion, not as legal manipulation.

We also interviewed people for whom internal state bordering continued well beyond the marriage itself and into the intimate lives of others. A European Union nanny, married to a man from an African country, experienced hostility from the Home Office as the latter asked for additional evidence to prove the legal nature of her residence in the United Kingdom when she applied for her husband's residence permit. As part of this process, she had to produce the marriage certificate of her white British employers, because they had different surnames; that had been a cause of suspicion, as one had signed the contract and the other the payslip. She was upset that the Home Office suspected her of dishonesty and embarrassed to have to ask her employers for the document. Her employers told us that they were not embarrassed and barely remembered the incident, indicating how internal bordering can remain invisible to those who are not its targets.

We also spoke to people who gained no 'UK immigration advantage' from marriage but continued to be an object of suspicion. During the notice-giving interview, BF, a Bangladesh national student who was marrying a Bangladeshi American citizen, experienced irrelevant questioning from the registrar about their intentions even though no 'immigration advantage' was to be gained from their marriage: 'The registry worker thinks we get married for passport or something – but that is not the UK passport at all.' Such practices have stretched even further into the lives of couples after they get married and into the private lives of others. BJ, a British Bangladeshi man, told us that the bordering practices and publicity surrounding sham marriages extended temporally and spatially beyond the immediate family:

> After 22 years a [transnational] family has arranged a marriage and the whole family is subject to the suspicion of the UKBA [border enforcement] agency. They cannot share this with their counterpart in the marriage. This puts them in a difficult situation. They have to invite hundreds of people, they have to book venues and you cannot arrange anything until you get permission from the authority, so it is eating up people's lives.

He argued that the government was 'harassing' families by amplifying suspicions about 'sham marriage' as part of its policy to reduce immigration. As with the minimum salary required for supporting a non-EEA spouse, the aim was to force young British Bangladeshi people to marry British rather than Bangladesh nationals: 'It is not that they are stopping illegal immigration, but, *in the name of it*, they are stopping legal immigration.'

Following the increased marriage-related bordering regulations, individuals who lived in the United Kingdom since childhood but were unaware that they were not British citizens have been threatened with deportation. Cynsha Best was called for an interview with the Home Office after giving notice of marriage to her Barbadian partner. She assumed that the interview was due to suspicions about her partner's gaining an immigration advantage, but it happened because the Home Office had identified her as an 'illegal immigrant'. She had a British birth certificate but, because she was born after 1983 and her parents were not British at the time, she was not automatically British:

> I was more worried about him than myself, and then it all turned on me. He was fine because he was still within his six months [visitor visa] … and then it all just flipped on me. They were like, 'You're the one who's got no status.' … The chief immigration officer was ready to [send me to Barbados]. It was so emotional. I was meant to be going about the marriage and they just sprung all of this at me. (Dugan, 2017)

She was thrown into a state of precariousness and was unable to work, claim benefits, or be certain of the future. In 2018 the international media exposed what became known as 'the Windrush scandal', grown out of the 2014 and 2016 Immigration Acts and 'hostile environment policy' that has caused the loss of employment and homes and the deportation of people with parents from former colonies who were unable to prove their British citizenship or right to remain. We explore this further in chapter 4.

Bordering scape 3: Firewall bordering, 'external' and 'internal' bordering encounters experienced by Eastern European Roma and Nepali Army families

The third bordering scape is that experienced by Nepali and East European Roma populations resident in the United Kingdom, as they cross border control points and in their everyday lives. These experiences are illustrative of the continuum of firewall bordering – from the visas and territorial border control points that we have focused on in this chapter to everyday bordering encounters that we expand on in chapter 4. While all visible resident minority groups experience bordering at the edges of territories and internally, we discuss these examples for four reasons. First, both Nepali and Roma have been the direct or indirect focus of legislation that has worked to deny them rights granted to their differently situated peers or compatriots. Bordering mechanisms related to pay, pensions, and residency rights introduced during colonial times prevented low-paid Nepali soldiers employed by the British Army and their dependants from settling in the United Kingdom, while in the twenty-first century new bordering mechanisms worked to prevent EU citizens from lower socioeconomic groups, including Roma, from settling in the United Kingdom. Secondly, Roma and Nepali residents are part of transnational communities, working across (and thus crossing) international borders quite often and maintaining kinship and financial bonds in their countries of birth. Thirdly, a dominant political and media discourse that includes key themes of 'loyalty' and 'criminality' places Nepalis and Roma in the opposite categories of 'good migrant' and 'bad migrant', contributing to constructions of local, national, and transnational hierarchies of belonging. Finally, this discourse was drawn on by people whom we interviewed in the border towns of Dover and Folkestone two years before the EU Brexit referendum, and the interaction between the discourse and bordering legislation exemplifies the complexities of and contestations over firewall bordering. In this section we begin by illustrating the discourse, then we focus on Nepali and Roma bordering encounters.

The bordering discourse on loyalty and criminality

SP, a Kent police officer, made the following remark about a local anti-migrant discourse that groups diverse minorities into the single, confusing category labelled 'Slovak':

> There is this general generic term called 'Slovak', which relates basically to anyone who is Eastern European. But whether they would differentiate between an asylum seeker, any other sort of migrant, an EU Roma, pretty well not. ... The other day we had a crime report of a guy who verbally abused a Roma. And he said, 'You bloody Slovaks, why don't you go back to Pakistan?!' and that just sums it up really.

While the police officer pointed out that the term 'Slovak' was used to abuse very diverse minority groups, Nepalis were excluded from this discourse, so long as they were seen as being associated with Gurkha regiments of the British Army. Referring to complaints about migrants putting pressure on welfare services, he continued:

> Retired Gurkhas, now they are regarded very positively, they fight and die with us, you know, if they are good enough to die fighting for us they are good enough to live with us, all that sort of attitude, that most of us agree with. They don't cause a lot of problems, they are respectful. There are some issues, in that community, but the Roma community bring their own issues with the perception that they are gypsies when all is said and done, there is a antipathy internationally towards gypsies anyway.

Young white men we interviewed used the same binary construction:

> GW: So when you say immigration, who do you mean? Who are you talking about?
> JS: Eastern Europeans. Mostly Eastern Europeans.
> GW: So for example here you have quite a lot of people from Nepal? ...
> JS: And they're really nice.
> NK: And they serve our country. Whereas Czechs and Slovakians [referring to Roma] just ...
> DN: Come over here and bum around and stuff.

Below we consider how this discourse links with past and present bordering practices so as to make 'loyalty' or citizenship insufficient to ensure belonging for Nepalis and Roma respectively.

Nepali

The Nepali population in Kent is predominantly made up of serving and retired soldiers and their dependants. Gurkha regiments commanded by white officers are rooted in early nineteenth-century colonial wars and in the 'martial race' theory that structured the recruitment into the British Indian Army of racialised communities from Nepal and other places on the subcontinent – communities seen as physically powerful and 'loyal' to the British Empire (Rand and Wagner, 2012). This history has contributed to the representation of Nepali people in the British media as being loyal to the United Kingdom and 'valued for their fearlessness, physical endurance and courage' (Ware, 2012: 25). However, until 2009, despite being employed by the British Army around the globe, Nepali soldiers and their families experienced discrimination in relation to their employment conditions, pensions, and residency rights in the United Kingdom. The British border was embodied in the army hierarchies and in the terms and conditions that affected every part of the soldiers' lives. Veterans and their supporters ran a successful campaign against the lower pay and pensions of former soldiers and their families and against their deportation from the United Kingdom, winning for them the same terms and conditions of pay and the same pensions and benefits as their British colleagues enjoyed (Ware, 2012: 17–19). The campaign drew on the discourses of 'good migrants' and 'bad migrants' and on the 'perceived value of military service' (Ware, 2012: 19), as exemplified by a former Conservative Party minister who supported the Gurkha's demands:

> Whenever the Gurkhas appeared in civic parades they earned a huge round of applause and Britain did not understand why they were treated so badly ... I had been battling with ministers for years to give them something better than a P45 and a one way ticket to Nepal at the end of 15 years' service when anybody coming into Britain on the back of a lorry got better treatment. (Widdecombe, 2014: 397)

While discourses of loyalty dominated the media campaign for equal rights, interviews with retired Gurkha soldiers demonstrated the centrality of economic reasons to enlistings in the army and the strategies that families used – for example, educating children abroad – to make sure that members of the next generation were not compelled to become soldiers. Many had transnational families because they had not been allowed to settle in the United Kingdom. Here is for example JN, a soldier who retired after a career that reached back to the 1982:

> My country is troubled. I like peace, I like quiet so I like to stay in England ... Been to working as soldier fighting ... [lists] many places, Falkland islands ... Children studying in Nepal and Australia and sometime come to visit us. They don't want to go in army, they want education. In my time there was no school over there so I needed to join the army but they don't need to join the army.

Retired before 1997, JN was from a generation that, until 2009, had been denied equal access to benefits or residency and depended on support from his extended family, which had not acquired the right to reside in the United Kingdom. SN – who belongs in the generation of JN's children and is married to a soldier about to be made redundant after eighteen years' service – told us that it was very difficult for retired soldiers to survive on the pension alone. Despite years of training, they did not have the language skills required for employment. She spoke of pensioners who were not entitled to bring adult children into the United Kingdom, yet were looking for strategies to bring them over in order to be supported by them: 'They have to support their parents! Cos that is the right thing, it is for their rights, they were doing such big things.'

SN's husbands' pay and pensions were now equal to those of British soldiers; and the family knew that it would not be deported at the end of his service. They planned to stay in the United Kingdom for their children's education, to 'make their time easier'. They had already bought a house in Canterbury that she said would enable her children to attend grammar schools and university. However, SN also spoke of the bordering they continued to encounter as Nepali nationals. While their documents show them to be part of the British Army, her family was treated differently from those of her colleagues when crossing the border into the United Kingdom:

> When we are in the queue they filter us, [those with] European citizenship, can easily pass immigration without saying lots of things, verification, but for us everything is legal, [we have] legal documents

but still they are asking us lots of questions ... I don't know why they are doing like this as our Nepalese Gurkha people they support a lot here, in other countries and elsewhere, they have to trust us.

This couple's experiences of firewall bordering, which divided their family in the tense context of airport security, echoes those of other people we spoke to who had moved to the United Kingdom from the Global South:

Both children already have British citizenship and are travelling with British passport[s]. On that time, it feels so bad, you know me and my husband have to stand in a different line and they ask my children to go on this side. It is very bad at that time because they are children, children have to be protected by their parents, it is really hard at that time... They checked our passport and then they separated us like that. That's not fair.

Because of her Nepali passport she had difficulties obtaining a Schengen visa and was unable to cross the Channel:

My children ask in the holiday time ... 'mum, let's go somewhere for holiday', my friends went, and I want to go but the main reason is my passport, there will be a problem. Anyway, I was thinking for my children, maybe I am going to apply for a British passport, but not with my willing.

She said that, when her husband is made redundant, they will apply for British passports for convenience; however, their ultimate aim was to settle in Nepal. Hence, apart from working in a local factory while her children attended primary school, SN was working transnationally, running a business in Nepal via the Internet and annual visits.

Roma

Unlike Nepali migrants, Czech and Slovak Roma have the legal right to visa-free travel, work, and residence the United Kingdom, in their status as EU citizens. However, their mobility across borders, before and during the EU Free Movement legislation, has been curtailed by different EU states (van Baar, 2017; Tervonen and Enache, 2017; Yildiz and de Genova, 2017; Yuval-Davis, Varjú et al., 2017). Roma from the Czech Republic and Slovakia first arrived as asylum seekers in Dover after the breakup of Czechoslovakia in 1993. Some lost their asylum claims and were deported, while others stayed and were later joined by family members. After the 2004 EU enlargement to eight countries (known as A8), including Slovakia and the Czech Republic, some of those previously deported returned and others came and settled in Dover, many working in a local factory and as cleaners. In 2007, when Romania and Bulgaria (referred to as A2) joined the European Union, the British government put transitional controls in place, limiting labour market engagement, residence rights, and welfare benefits for A2 nationals for seven years. The transitional controls were responding to the political campaigns and media discourses against the perceived effects on jobs, housing, and welfare of the migration of A8 nationals and of changes in border securitisation since the 1990s – a decade that has seen the enforcement of the United Kingdom's border beyond border-crossing points, into the everyday lives of people across Britain, thereby 'maximising the benefits of labour migration without incurring its costs' (Poole and Adamson, 2008: 33). In addition to the differentiated categories of EU nationals created by transitional controls, their impact is filtered through the actions of administrators. These bordering processes are experienced differently by various citizens of A8 and A2 countries, including Roma and people from the Global South who have settled across Europe and moved to the United Kingdom.

As A8 citizens, Czech and Slovak Roma were not subject to the transitional controls. However, they experienced bordering via associated discourses and practices aimed at preventing poor migrants from Bulgaria and Romania from living and working in the United Kingdom after the end of transitional controls in January 2014. Discourses about potential A2 migration extended the border more deeply into the everyday lives of EU migrants and most intrusively into the lives of Roma residents. On the day when transitional controls ended, the leader of the Kent County Council was quoted in the local media making direct references to Roma as a 'problem' and drawing on the discourse of Roma criminality referred to above:

> Politicians and councillors in Kent have expressed concern that increased migration will only stretch the demand on local government services and could create 'township ghettos' in some towns like Maidstone. [Council leader] added: 'I think more people looking to work here will only put added pressures on education, health and sadly crime. A significant amount of criminality is being carried out in parts of Kent by people from Eastern Europe. Everyone's seen the Roma issues in

Boston and in Sheffield, in those places it's putting significant additional burdens on those local authorities and we have a significant problem in East Kent.' (KentOnline, 2014)

While there was no evidence that Romanian and Bulgarian Roma intended to settle in Kent, the council leader used the local media to link local Roma with discourses of criminality and pressures on welfare elsewhere in Britain. GN, a teenage Slovak Roma student, told us about local people's reactions to negative media discourses on Romanian Roma:

> They don't care where you are from, they don't care whether you are Romanian, they are just racist to anyone and when they see something on the news that is why it affects us as well. It doesn't matter if it is about Romanian people because they think it is us as well and they say to us 'you are getting our money' so it does affect us.

During a discussion among Slovak Roma women living in Kent, TH reflected on the impact of similar media reports about presumed criminality:

> We feel that store detectives are suspecting us and following us around the shops and it is very unpleasant, and the second thing is the people think that Romanians and Roma are the same people because we look similar, but it is far from the case.

Another woman, KZ, suggested that negative media attention affects the ability of Roma to gain work through a particular employment agency: 'They also have more strict criteria about who and when to register to the agency for employment … I know that they are now more fussy about the people they register there.'

Several Roma women told us of their hopes for their children in the United Kingdom and of the links they maintained with their families in Slovakia. Some said they had built houses and kept family ties in Slovakia but preferred to live in the United Kingdom because of the racism the suffered from the public and authorities in Slovakia; and one reason why they lived close to the border in Dover was being able more quickly to drive 'back home' every summer. GN told us that she felt that, although they were EU citizens, they were targeted by officials at the borders. This happened in Slovakia because they were identifiably Roma driving GB registered vehicles where she said the police collected bribes for alleged traffic offences; and in Dover where they were suspected of drug smuggling.

The bordering encounters experienced by Roma were not tempered by the discourses of loyalty that contributed to improved rights for Nepali soldiers. However, despite the apparent positivity shown towards army families, Nepali as well as Roma residents spoke of negative experiences of bordering at external airport and seaport border control points and on UK territory, demonstrating that bordering works in ways that mean that 'loyalty', residency rights, and citizenship are not enough to ensure equality of belonging.

Conclusion

In this chapter we have explored the shifting permeabilities of firewall borderings from the differently situated perspectives of a range of people in contrasting bordering scapes. These are part of a bordering continuum that stretches from encounters at visa offices abroad to intimate questionings in local registry offices that transform convivial experiences of travel or marriages of racialised citizens from celebrations into issues of border security. Discourses on 'overstaying', 'sham marriage', and 'Roma criminality', together with associated enforcement practices, work as technologies of governmentality (Foucault, 2007; Yuval-Davis, 2012) that delimit individuals' rights to belong and impact adversely on the whole society. Different experiences of bordering encounters are illustrative of how firewall bordering produces and regulates national hierarchies of belonging, as the social and racialised stratification of border crossing becomes more formalised. Those who feel an entitlement to belong to national collectivities organise to pressurise governments into enlisting further bordering techniques so as to restrict the access of others, further increasing inequalities.

These examples, which involve men and women from a wide range of socioeconomic backgrounds, nation-states, and racialised minorities, demonstrate the historical and geopolitical contingency of firewall bordering as well as its complexities, as legislation is created through historical precedents and contemporary struggles in the context of neoliberal globalisation. Political and economic contests re-create bordering regimes that increase permeabilities for some while tightening them for others. For example, in 2017, US border regulations shifted as pressure groups campaigned for and against a border wall and visas for nationals of specific Muslim countries. In the United Kingdom, businesses wanting to attract Chinese tourists won visa concessions, and Gurkha soldiers won equal rights. The unsuccessful lobbying of ethnic minority restaurant owners to recruit cooks from outside the EAA pushed them to vote for rebordering via Brexit.

This exploration of the first three bordering scapes demonstrates that firewall bordering at border-crossing control points cannot be analysed in isolation from the histories summarised in chapter 2, or from the contemporary media amplification of sensational stories about migrants. In chapter 4 we develop this argument further, by examining bordering encounters as the firewall bordering continuum reaches deep into peoples' everyday lives via their employment, accommodation, and education.

4

Everyday Bordering, Citizenship, and Belonging

Introduction

Each Windrush story is the hostile environment policy personified and writ large. Each case is directly linked to a policy that ignores the principle of *habeas corpus* by imprisoning innocent people without reference to a judge, jury or evidence of guilt. It is this policy that barred British citizens from accessing the public services and benefits that they themselves built with their own hands, staffed and paid for.
David Lammy MP, *Guardian*, 30 April 2018

In chapter 3 we focused on bordering at or beyond the imagined national territorial border, from its outward extensions to distant visa offices and airport check-ins to the internal scrutiny of prospective travellers and marriage partners. In this chapter we examine how this 'firewall' bordering constitutes part of a continuum of legislation and practices manifested through everyday bordering processes that are moving further away from border-crossing points into everyday encounters between all residents, differentially affecting individual citizenship duties and solidarities. While the hostile environment created by these everyday state bordering processes is targeted at 'illegal workers' or 'bogus asylum seekers', the Windrush scandal has exposed how it has caused loss of livelihood and homes, and even detention and deportation, for British citizens from former colonies – memorably described in David Lammy MP's 2018 *Guardian* article. We show how everyday encounters with ordinary people who carry out state bordering duties impact most significantly on the lives of migrants and racialised minorities identified as suspected illegal border crossers. We demonstrate that those who may be prosecuted and fined for not carrying out the work of unpaid and untrained border guards are also likely to be racialised minorities.

Everyday bordering in the contemporary global context

In the final decades of the twentieth century, in nations of the West, variations of equality legislation and multicultural policies have influenced access and entitlements to employment, education, housing, health, and social care for people in very different positions in society. We are arguing that, during the same period, a range of bordering policies and practices have become increasingly significant as ordering mechanisms that work to construct, maintain, and control the social and political order, both within states and transnationally. Since 9/11, bordering discourses and practices have proliferated, especially when contiguous with those of securitisation (Guild, 2009; Maguire et al., 2014). However, we argue that these discourses also extend beyond the reach of counterterrorism, territorial border control, and frontline policing. Bordering delimits the area in which equality legislation and policies extend equal rights to specific categories of people; and it does so on the basis of their citizenship and immigration status as they intersect with racialised and gendered identities, for example (Yuval-Davis, 2006; Wilson, 2013). This ensures that, in the always shifting national hierarchies of belonging, some categories of people remain in a low place. At the same time, by determining who has the right to cross borders, firewall bordering ensures that those higher up in that hierarchy retain or improve their relative positions, as they are able to belong to different national collectivities.

The contemporary outsourcing of bordering duties to ordinary citizens is part of the dynamics of contemporary mobile borders, which involves de- and rebordering processes (Newman and Paasi, 1998; Popescu, 2012; Szary and Giraut, 2015). Below we summarise a few selected global examples of everyday bordering technologies; these contextualise the three illustrative bordering scapes related to everyday state bordering in the United Kingdom that make up the remainder of this chapter. They combine to demonstrate the global pattern of the deterritorialisation of borders from fixed border zones and the relocation of border checkpoints in a multiplicity of spaces, throughout civil society (Balibar, 2004; Vaughan-Williams, 2008).

Everyday bordering via public reporting

Authoritarian and liberal political systems alike have encouraged the collection of 'intelligence' via individuals reporting on each other. While not always targeted at perceived foreigners, it is often related to the reporting of non-border-related activities, such as claiming welfare benefits. The history of contemporary 'denunciatory atmospheres' can be traced back to the accusations encouraged in imperial Russia, in revolutionary France, in Spain under the Inquisition, in Nazi Germany, and in the Soviet Union and its satellites (Dzenovska, 2017: 285). During the British colonial period, members of the public were encouraged to report escaped enslaved Africans and Asian seafarers who had 'jumped ship' (Fryer, 1984; Visram, 2002). The notion of the 'good citizen' who reports his or her suspicions has become a normalised instrument of governance whereby policing, surveillance, and bordering are shared between state institutions, private organisations, and ordinary people. Enlisting the public in migration policing instils a sense of civic responsibility, created by mobilising exclusionary aspects of citizenship (Aliverti, 2014: 216). While the intention may be to re-create a version of social cohesion in a fragmented society, states also recognise that individuals will report one another to resolve personal grievances rather than out of a sense of fulfilling the role of 'good citizen'. While in the Soviet Union everyone was considered suspicious, newly independent states, such as Latvia, have adopted reporting as part of their post-Soviet migration control. This rebordering focuses public suspicion on those perceived as foreigners or 'failed citizens' (Dzenovska, 2017). Citizen reporters in Latvia, border vigilantes on the US–Mexico border such as those involved in the Minuteman Project (Stewart et al., 2015), white residents in French suburbs (Fassin, 2013), and those residents who phone crime, terror, and immigration hotlines after 'fly on the wall' TV programmes such as *Border Wars* in America and *UK Border Force* in England (Philo et al., 2013; R. Jones, 2014; Jones et al., 2017) produce what state institutions refer to as 'intelligence'. Bridget Anderson (2013) suggests that the state's intention may be that those in marginal situations (rather than 'good citizens') report others, effectively policing themselves.

Everyday bordering via police and street-level bureaucrats

Globally there has been a growth in police powers designated to check the immigration status of individuals and to detain them, and also a growth in the number of 'street-level bureaucrats' (Lipsky, 1980, 2010) who administer various states' internal borders. In the United States, state, county, and city employees cooperate with state and local police in interior immigration enforcement. The 1996 Welfare Act forced the administrators of temporary assistance and housing to report to the immigration authorities the use of their facilities by 'undocumented aliens'. Legislation known as Section 287(g) permitted local police to make criminal immigration arrests. These were not widely taken up until after 9/11; however, since then, most arrests leading to immigration detention and deportation have been for minor traffic and other non-serious offences in everyday situations, racialised minorities facing disproportionate immigration checks when in custody (Capps et al., 2011; Coleman, 2012: 428–31). The Secure Communities (S-Comm) programme launched in 2008 allowed law and immigration enforcement agencies to share databases so that the police could use biometric data to check the immigration status of those arrested but not charged. This has led to the large-scale detention and deportation of racialised immigrants without a criminal background (Valdez et al., 2017). The everyday actions of those who implement Section 287(g) and S-Comm enforcement may challenge the legislation, create new actions, or lead to changes in the approach of other actors.

European welfare states, including the Netherlands and Norway, have increasingly been contracting bordering responsibilities to health and social workers who filter those entitled to use the services (van der Leun, 2006; Ryymin and Ludvigsen, 2013). As in the United States, everyday encounters with such workers are contributing to new experiences of bordering and to further extensions of the border into everyday life. In Finland, municipal workers and the local police work to restrict, through direct and indirect bordering techniques, the access of Eastern European Roma migrants to social provision. In 2011 the Helsinki Social Board paid money to Roma to return to their country of origin after they had been evicted from illegal camps. The return-home scheme was seen as a failure as many immediately came back to Finland from their home countries. Those who returned to Helsinki continued to face everyday bordering practices: for example, minors were barred from entering primary education if their parents lacked residence rights (Tervonen and Enache, 2017). Bordering encounters include the struggles between Finnish counter-staff, whose members attempt to deny access through requests for documentation, and Finnish volunteers, who advocate for migrants' rights. Like the youth workers in the French suburbs who argue on behalf of racialised young people (Fassin, 2013) or volunteers who leave water on routes near the US–Mexico border (Kamalizad, 2017), Finnish NGO volunteers working to provide or access emergency welfare support for Roma EU citizens experience the hostility of everyday bordering from state or municipal employees. Fassin (2015) has demonstrated that state agents, including the police and social workers, mobilise specific values and emotions as they interact with clients, implementing laws and regulations that result in practices that appear to contradict each other. The involvement of increasing numbers of differently positioned employees of state education and of health and welfare institutions along with ordinary citizens in everyday bordering is making the resulting encounters and practices complex and dissonant.

Everyday bordering via ID documents

Within the European Economic Area (EEA), some countries have compulsory national ID cards for all citizens from as young as the age of twelve. Others have a non-compulsory national ID card alongside a requirement that citizens possess other official forms of identity documentation, such as a passport or driving licence. The remainder, including the United Kingdom and Denmark, have no national ID cards, photo IDs such as driving licences and passports being demanded in different situations. Just like passports, national identity verification systems in both the Global North and the Global South are updated through biometric technologies. India's Aadhaar ID system is currently the world's largest biometric ID system; in it every adult legally resident is required to submit biometric information. In order to exclude 'illegal migrants', the reach of the ID system has expanded from welfare services to the submission of tax returns. Civil rights groups oppose it on the grounds that, in the name of 'national security', it gives government access to increasing amounts of data about residents who have no protection against state monitoring. The Aadhaar Act was challenged in the Supreme Court in 2017 owing to concerns around surveillance, privacy, and the exclusion of eligible beneficiaries from welfare schemes (Datta, 2017). As the legal challenges continued, activists reported massive data breaches (Khaira, 2017) and women dying of starvation after being denied their pensions or rations, as administrators siphoned off resources for themselves (Kamayani, 2017). There are frequent media reports of 'illegal' immigrants using forged documents to

101

obtain Aadhaar numbers. These have led, in the states of Jammu and Kashmir and Assam, to renewed actions designed to list suspected 'illegal immigrants', especially Muslims from Bangladesh and Myanmar, which further contributed to the precarity of resident minority communities (Manhotra, 2016; *Hindu* 2017). The evolving practices of the Aadhaar system exemplify how the interplay between federal and state-level legislation and the encounters between administrators and residents work to extend the reach of the internal border in ways that increase the existing inequalities and assert more rigid hierarchies of belonging.

All the examples above suggest that everyday bordering encounters, both when taken individually and as they overlap and combine (e.g. when street-level bureaucrats demand identity documents that are not required by law), are more dynamic and create more complex borderings than would be accounted for if ordinary people were merely acting out the requirements of legislation produced by politicians. In the United Kingdom, bordering legislation, discourses, and everyday practices have combined to construct the hostile environment policy and the Windrush scandal.

Everyday bordering in Britain: Constructing the 'hostile environment'

The policy of extending everyday bordering practices so that their combination synthesises into something that is more than their individual roles was clarified in 2012, in an interview with the then Home Secretary Theresa May, who confirmed that the aim of immigration legislation 'is to create a hostile environment for illegal immigration' (Kirkup and Winnett, 2012). The subsequent bordering legislation, discourses, and practices are transforming relationships and everyday life for everyone, not just for the 'illegal workers' at whom it is targeted. In the final part of this introduction we summarise some of the recent legislative and historical background that has created and strengthened this hostile environment; and we do so in order to contextualise the UK bordering scapes of everyday employment, accommodation, and education that follow. The internal reach of the UK border has been extending in complex ways since World War II, through the interplay of immigration policy, privatisation, and deregulation of state roles and the British welfare system. The 1971 Immigration Act required captains of ships and aircraft to declare the names and citizenship of all passengers and to detain and return those who were refused entry. The 1987 Immigration (Carrier's Liability) Act imposed penalties for non-compliance (Scholten, 2015: 72–6).

The Conservative government's 1996 Immigration, Asylum and Nationality Act and subsequent amendments imposed fines of up to £5,000 on employers who took on migrants not authorised to work. Subsequent legislation passed by Labour governments successively strengthened and widened the reach of everyday bordering. The 1999 Act introduced fines of £2,000 per illegal passenger on vehicles coming into Britain and increased restrictions on marriage for immigration purposes; the 2006 Act required employers to carry out more rigorous document checks of employees, increased fines to £10,000 per irregular worker, and made it a custodial offence to employ them knowingly. Earlier laws were rarely enforced until after the 2006 Act (Webber, 2012: 156).

After 2010, the coalition government identified the category of most 'irregular' migrants with people who had overstayed their visas. Parliamentary debates focused on discouraging 'overstayers' by inhibiting their ability to work and live in the United Kingdom. The 2014 Immigration Act achieved that by subcontracting and extending border-guard roles beyond employers, to employees of private and public organisations such as banks, the Driving and Vehicle Licensing Agency (DVLA), and hospitals as well as to private landlords, so that undocumented migrants would find it harder to work, rest, drive, or access bank accounts, healthcare, and education. Successful legal challenges to border-related laws have led to tighter legislation. The Conservative government, elected in 2015, responded to criticisms of the 2014 Act with the 2016 Immigration Act, which made the environment even more hostile, for example by doubling the civil penalty to £20,000, by introducing criminal sanctions for employers, and by categorising the wages of 'illegal' workers as 'proceeds of crime'. The Act also introduced custodial sentences for private landlords who consistently rented properties to illegal migrants and gave them the right to evict tenants without a court order. Human rights, migrant, and antiracist groups monitor the reach of the hostile environment legislation and continue to put pressure on government to push it back (Liberty, 2018).

Media coverage of enforcement operations aimed at encouraging public reporting and threatening those who work illegally contributes to the conscious extension of the border. In 2008 the Home Office paid £400,000 to help fund the Sky television programme *UK Border Force* (Philo et al., 2013: 167). *Sky* returned the money because of a controversy about the government funding of advertising-funded programmes (ibid.). However, it would not have been possible for the programmes to be made without the Home Office giving access to a selected range of diverse Border Force activities and premises. The programmes show arrests and attempted arrests at territorial and internal borders and narratives of Border Force frustration with the limitations of the law, for example by how the Human Rights Act prevents them from immediately deporting suspects. Although only eighteen of these programmes were made, they continue to be repeated on television and online.

Up until it was abolished in 2013, the UK Border Agency publicised raids and arrests across the country via its website and press releases that included requests to the public to report suspected immigration crimes (Wemyss, 2015a). The latter continue via the Home Office Immigration Enforcement section. In 2013, as the 2014 Immigration Act was being drafted, the Home Office launched Operation Vaken, in which two vans displaying large posters that asked those 'in the United Kingdom illegally' to 'go home or face arrest' and gave them a number where they may text 'for advice and help with travel documents' circled the streets of six ethnically diverse neighbourhoods in London. At the same time, immigration enforcement checks were being carried out at transport hubs where officials were accused of the racial profiling of commuters. Civil society organisations and individuals protested against the racism of these actions and used social media to ridicule the vans, which were soon withdrawn (Jones et al., 2017: 11–13). The message and the placing of the vans in the context of the other highly publicised immigration enforcement operations focused on racialised minorities further poisoned the already denunciatory atmosphere by emphasising residents' duty not only to report those whom they suspect but even to hand themselves in. The 'political performance' (Rai, 2015) of strong borders, which were aimed at reassuring some 'good citizens' while making others fearful, was continued during June 2014 via Operation Centurion, in which immigration enforcement partnered with food safety and trading standards agencies and with the police in conducting raids on workplaces that employed people of specific nationalities (H. Jones, 2014).

The hostile environment spread to health and education, where political and media discourses added fears about 'health tourism' and 'education tourism' to the already familiar 'benefit tourism'. In 2013, signs were displayed in hospitals stating that 'NHS hospital treatment is not free for everyone'. In their study of the effects of the performance of immigration enforcement in everyday spaces, Jones and colleagues found that, as in other public performances of enforcement, the signs were experienced differently by differently situated people. Some felt 'reassured' that the government was taking action against 'illegal immigration' while others 'felt concerned that some people were treated with unnecessary suspicion in everyday situations' (Jones et al., 2017: 46). In the past, hospitals had discretion in charging 'overseas visitors'. However, the 2014 and 2016 Immigration Acts compelled NHS employees to carry out ID checks to identify migrants not entitled to free healthcare. Further and higher education institutions already had stringent responsibilities for monitoring and reporting on overseas students that had begun to transform the relationship between educators and students.

In the following sections of this chapter we focus on three illustrative UK bordering scapes in the areas of employment, accommodation, and education, showing how separate bordering regulations work – both in tandem and in combination with the 'denunciatory atmosphere' – to expand the 'hostile environment' beyond its target group of 'illegal workers', to other members of the society who are coerced into bordering practices within their roles as employers, landlords, and educators. Our interviews took place during the period 2013–15, when the hostile environment legislation was being debated in parliament and in the media.

Bordering scape 4: Employment

Operation Skybreaker

The Home Office followed Operations Vaken and Centurion with Operation Skybreaker in 2014. Its aim was to deport 'illegal workers' and prosecute businesses that employed migrants without permission to work in areas of London with high numbers of irregular workers. Skybreaker started with a well-publicised 'community engagement' strategy whereby Immigration and Customs Enforcement (ICE) officers visited every business in the designated wards. The visits were ostensibly designed to explain the legislation to the owners and to inspect the files that employers are required to keep updated with the immigration status of employees. This 'community engagement' worked to alert 'good citizens' to submit 'intelligence', to warn employers to dismiss employees with an irregular status, and to encourage voluntary repatriation. When ICE teams were suspicious they followed engagement visits with immigration raids. We interviewed people as Skybreaker and the publicity surrounding it unfolded. We found, however, that it largely impacted on those in the ethnic enclave economy; others we interviewed were often unaware of it.

Perspectives of border enforcement professionals

As well as speaking to ordinary people co-opted for the role of everyday border guards, we interviewed professional border enforcement officers during the period of Operation Skybreaker. KD and AD, both white English female border enforcement officers, worked for the ICE team in London. They said that contestations to the 'go home' vans of Operation Vaken had come from inside as well as from outside the Border Force, contributing to the more targeted bordering processes of Operation Skybreaker. They considered the 'go home' vans' campaign as an ineffective 'macho' gesture politics, in contrast to Skybreaker's community engagement strategy. In contrast to the huge mobile posters of Vaken, they showed us visiting cards, which their team gave out to employers on 'engagement' visits as part of a more subtle performance of immigration enforcement where, as well as checking files, they noted whether their visit created 'panic'. If so, they would tell their ICE team colleagues to return and carry out an 'enforcement operation' leading to the detention of suspected illegal workers.

In contrast to the expressed view of their more senior colleagues, BD, an Asian, and LD, a white junior enforcement officer, with whom we spoke during a 'community engagement' operation, viewed the outsourcing of border work to employers and the ICE teams' resultant 'engagement work' as a cost-cutting exercise, ineffective because in their view it gave 'illegals' the opportunity to 'escape' by warning them about future raids.

While Home Office operations indicate that raids target businesses in ethnic minority neighbourhoods, giving rise to the claim that this immigration policy is racist, the Border Force officers we interviewed did not see it as such. BD referred to his positioning as a member of a religious minority, oppressed in many parts of the world, and gave us the example of how his family was protected by the United Kingdom's anti-discrimination laws. He said he believed in enforcing the UK border against people who want to deny the right of his community to belong in his ancestral country and in the United

Kingdom. He emphasised that an 'acceptance of diversity is different to an acceptance of when people are here illegally'. KD told us that, while she enjoyed living in pluralist multicultural London, 'everyone should prove their right to work'.

ICE teams also carried out 'engagement' activities in partnership with large businesses, which can avoid penalties by reporting 'illegal workers'. In 2016, managers from the upmarket burger chain Byron, owned mainly by an investment firm that used tax havens to reduce the tax bills of its investors, liaised with enforcement teams to detain their employees. In several branches across London managers required staff to attend apparently work-related meetings where many were detained and thirty-five arrested (O'Carroll, 2016; Corporate Watch, 2016).

While border officers at different levels had a range of views on everyday bordering and varying insights into the heterogeneity of minority communities, they shared a discourse that made a solid and simple differentiation between the 'legal' and the 'illegal', identifying the former with those who were allowed to belong and the latter with those who were not. While some might have regarded this as an ineffective measure, they saw no problem in requiring every-one's identity documents to be checked by employers in places of employment and, as we show in the following bordering scape, by landlords.

Perspectives from ethnic minority employers and employees

Employers and employees from ethnic minority backgrounds experi-enced the everyday border as confused and as having destructive consequences for people's lives. Recruitment and employee relations in London's ethnic enclave economy present complexities related to social networks, kinship obligations, and language and cultural knowledge (Bloch and McKay, 2015 and 2016; Bloch, Kumarappan, and McKay, 2015). As the informality of recruitment processes, including the casual employment of kin and conationals without permission to work, has been challenged by the increased employer penalties, social ties and practical needs of the business mean that many continue to risk large fines, while others refuse employment to legal workers. Those we interviewed found it unfair and impossible to distinguish the migrants with a right to work from those with false papers. DC, a South Asian grocery shop owner, would not recruit a person if he was not sure about his or her status:

I was going to employ a European guy who comes from Italy but he had no passport, he had his ID card and his medical card, he showed me this and I refused him as I had no idea about it because [I thought] he has to have a passport with a visa ... so many countries' people coming here, so how do I know who has the right to work?

Although an EU identity card is sufficient for employment purposes, experiences of the devastating effect of the raids on businesses led to ethnic minority employers feeling targeted. BR, a British Bangladeshi, owner of several restaurants, complained about the enforcement raids:

[Home Office people] are making life hell for all the owners of the businesses as they are targeting the owners. I find that they do not really want illegal immigrants' problem to be sorted out. They are actually targeting all the owners so that if they find anyone there, they can fine them. It is a kind of revenue collection, which is not true Britishness.

He, like others we interviewed, pointed out the destructive effect on businesses of these raids:

They raided on the Friday night. Friday and Saturday evening are the busiest in the whole week. They actually target your restaurant, they don't care about your reputation or damage to business ... they just lock the door and they always treat everybody like a criminal ... You build a reputation for years and years, that way your thirty years of work, your twenty years of work is down the drain.

And, as DC pointed out, 'if any customer goes into a shop and faces any trouble by the police or immigration officer, will they come again in the shop? Never!'

Relationships between employers and employees, too, are being damaged by raids and the denunciatory atmosphere they encourage, as BJ, another British Bangladeshi businessman reflects:

It is creating divisions in the society. Not only between the white indigenous people and the immigrant people, it could just be one of my friends who has fallen out with me. If he knows that I somehow employ one person, just to harass me ... so the Home Office are trying their best not to make a cohesive society although they preach for this ... they are trying to employ people as police against each other they are creating a situation of chaos in this society.

Employees from racialised minority backgrounds can also feel themselves under suspicion when they are employed by businesses that operate outside the ethnic enclave economy. BF, a betting shop manager legally employed by a large chain and working across several branches, was confined with customers in one of the shops while his status was checked:

> It was a raid ... We are the employees and all documents are at head office ... I said 'contact this address, call them up' ... They stayed in front of my door and if anyone was on the footpath they checked their ID. On the road ... it's shameful ... it is not the right thing. If someone checks me I feel bad. What kind of thing that they can check everywhere?

He felt threatened because copies of his papers were kept at a central office, not at the different outlets where he worked. IC, a British taxi driver from a Middle Eastern background, told us that, while he is often asked about his nationality by curious or hostile passengers, during the period of media amplification about illegal migration in the run-up to the Immigration Act in 2014, a customer demanded to see his passport: he had to prove to this customer that he had the right to work.

Everyday employment bordering can have a greater impact on women. JK, a British Chinese woman, reflects here on the exploitation she observed as a result of immigration policies:

> If you don't have your papers you can't do anything. Obviously there is a black market but it is getting increasingly hard now while there are always employers who are willing to take people on for cash in hand – the type of job – the type of salary ... we were chatting to a Bangladeshi waitress and she gets £40 a day for a 12 hour day, and you have very little rights and I think that instead of [the law] protecting, it is ensuring you don't have the right to work. If you are here, you still need a roof over your head.

She was referring to the vulnerability to economic and sexual exploitation that we have encountered in other interviews, especially in relation to the accommodation border discussed in our fifth bordering scape.

Perspectives from EU employees

Migrants from the margins of the EU often feel helpless in the face of immigration legislation complexity. Often the only way employees can prove their right to work legally is by using support networks of family and friends who have had similar experiences. TB, a student from Bulgaria, explained that one of her mother's friends, married to a British national, had encountered problems with her employer due to confusion surrounding the rules on Bulgarian and Romanian (A2) nationals living and working in the United Kingdom before they were given the rights of free movement in 2014:

> When she started working, the people in the office upstairs were asking for her blue card [worker registration certificate giving the right to work in the United Kingdom]. But you don't have to get a blue card. ... And she said it is taking a long time to get an appointment. She comes to my mum asking her what to do ... I went to the government website and I printed the information for her and she took her marriage certificate and passport to the office. ... But I had to tell them the rules! Then maybe one year later, she calls my mother again and tells her that there is a new boss and they are asking again for blue card!

Employers choose the easy route of demanding official papers that are not required. The intervention of TB proves the importance of informal ethnic networks in facilitating successful border crossings.

The rules surrounding work in the United Kingdom also placed stresses on A2 workers concerned about not complying. MR, a seamstress from Romania who had lived in London since 2008, held a yellow registration certificate (which is restrictive, but accords some rights to work in the United Kingdom) but felt she lacked understanding of what was required of her: 'When I worked for the agency and [her husband], he lost his [driving] licence, I was frightened about the authorities. I was frightened about the tax and not doing something correctly.' She had grounds for fear. LB is a Czech citizen and her non-EEA national husband was refused leave to remain because there had been a short period when the Home Office mistakenly accused her of not having the private health insurance required for non-working partners. Such confusion is often exploited by agencies, which force their workers into precarious work under the minimum wage, and this affects everyone in the workplace. PB, a white British branch manager in a FTSE-250 company with a typically diverse workforce, told us of his frustration with his company's use of an employment agency that was paying workers below the minimum wage:

> Why do you think I have spent the last few months trying to get us out of this contract with him? I know what he does and I know that

if we were found to be involved in this we would be in trouble. This is a legacy that I inherited and I'm trying to resolve it with the help of head office, but it has been difficult and I have had to fight for my own job in this.

Many of the agency workers had worked at the branch for a year or more, and PB wanted to employ them directly, in order to reduce his wage bill. He later found out that a senior manager had received kickbacks from the agency owner and was using the legislation to prevent workers from being employed directly. The senior employee was able to exploit the demands of immigration legislation to defraud his own company and to ensure that many workers with the right to live and work in the United Kingdom were denied direct employment.

The immigration regulations have spread a sense of anxiety and precarity far beyond the realm of low-paid agency workers or people with questionable rights to work. The volume and complexity of paperwork can put off people in professional employment from applying. For example, although LB was an experienced teacher and entitled to British citizenship in 2014, she said she would not apply until she has been working for a single employer for five years, because it is 'exhausting getting together so many pieces of paper to prove employment and residence' for the application. Until she acquires her British passport she feels she is in a precarious position.

Perspectives from metropolitan professionals

We heard shocked reactions from employees of an academic institution in London that amalgamated with another, when they were required to have their passports checked by their new employer. All employees, with no regard to seniority or length of employment, had to show their passports in order to prove that they are legally working in the United Kingdom. Similarly, academics employed on permanent contracts in one university have to prove their legal right to work in the United Kingdom before they can be paid as guest lecturers or external examiners in another UK university. Similar practices exist in all other fields of professional employment. The effect of such policies in a global metropolitan city has been to sensitise people to who carries a British passport and who does not. In this way, citizenship status became a salient feature of ascribed identity, making those who do not carry such passports potentially guilty of

111

working illegally until otherwise proven and generally making the racialised boundaries between those who 'belong' and those who 'do not' a more central feature of everyday life. The immigration legislation requirements thus have a general effect on the economy and on society. NL, a member of London First, a lobby group aimed at promoting London's business interests, told us: 'Many businesses in the City find it hard to attract talented global people to come and work here because of the visa requirements. There has been damage done. I've seen it on the ground.'

Owning £200,000 in investment funds is enough to gain the right to work in your own business in the United Kingdom. As we found when interviewing City employees, even for people with smaller financial resources the path to legal employment, long-term residency, and citizenship is being smoothed out if they have the ability to hire the right legal expert. Thus, although the impact of bordering is not limited to lower-paid workers and to workers in specific sectors, individuals with higher incomes can pay for legal services to ensure that they remain in employment. Here is for example OB, a professional woman from a non-EU former Soviet republic who had moved to London as a student in 2002:

> Yes ... I became British about 2–3 years ago, after I spent 10 years in the country. I think I've been in every single working visa available in the UK for sure. Because at the time I was getting my passport, my immigration lawyer, he was taking out my file and he said, '[OB,] you actually have eight cases with me and I've never had eight cases on [one] individual ever before. It's usually companies.'

But the fact that one may be able to manage the path to legal residency does not mean that everyday bordering has not affected the lives of all migrants and of the rest of population.

Bordering scape 5: Accommodation

A key technology in consolidating the hostile environment is the right to rent scheme introduced via the 2014 and 2016 Immigration Acts. This scheme requires private landlords to check the immigration status of all adults who rent their properties or live in them and to evict those without the status of legal resident. Local authority housing officers and those from housing associations already had the bordering role of checking residency documents. However, since most rental accommodation in England is private (DCLG, 2016), the new legislation significantly increased both the numbers of individuals who have the legal obligation to check immigration status and the numbers of individuals compelled to prove their right of residence.

The 2014 Act imposed fines on landlords of up to £3,000 per 'illegal' tenant and the 2016 Act introduced custodial sentences of up to five years for landlords who 'repeatedly' fail to comply with the right-to-rent rules. In order to carry out the checks, landlords have to examine, copy, and retain the tenants' and other adult occupiers' passports or residency documents. They have to record the date of visa expiry and evict tenants who overstay their visas. Since a quarter of the number of landlords are 'accidental' landlords (in that they did not plan to become landlords) and most of them let out only one property (Shelter, 2016), they do tend to subcontract these tasks to lettings agencies. The increased income that letting agencies can make from this service was predicted as a 'benefit' before the 2014 Act was passed (Home Office, 2013a).

Even before the scheme was rolled out nationally, there was evidence of racial discrimination by landlords – including against the 17 per cent of British citizens who do not have passports (see ONS, 2013). The housing campaigner Sue Lukes and the women's group Southall Black Sisters told us in 2014 that landlords were already refusing to offer properties to people whose immigration status they did not understand, or who may 'look foreign'; or they were taking advantage of people's perceived vulnerability. Research by The Joint Council for the Welfare of Immigrants (JCWI) found evidence of such discrimination by landlords:

> 42% of landlords said that the Right to Rent requirements have made them less likely to consider someone who does not have a British passport. 27% are reluctant to engage with those with foreign accents or names. Checks are not being undertaken uniformly for all tenants, but are instead directed at individuals who appear 'foreign'. (Grant and Peel, 2015: 38)

EU and non-EU tenants face different levels of discrimination: '51% said that it [sc. the legislation] would make them less likely to consider letting properties to foreign nationals from outside the EU, 18% were less likely to rent to EU nationals' (Patel and Peel, 2017: 34).

The everyday bordering carried out by landlords contributes to the discrimination against British non-passport holders from all ethnic backgrounds. This discrimination included the evictions from their homes of British citizens of Caribbean descent – evictions exposed in 2018 as 'the Windrush scandal'.

Perspectives from landlords

Research by Shelter (2016) and JCWI (Patel and Peel, 2017) have detailed extensive evidence of discrimination against different categories of people caused by making landlords into border guards. JCWI's mystery shopping exercise found that British racialised minorities without passports were significantly more likely to be refused accommodation than a white British citizen without a passport (Patel and Peel, 2017: 35). The perspectives and actions of landlords depend on their specific situations. Before the passing of the 2014 Act, we attended a local stakeholders' meeting where a white representative of a landlords' association voiced her fears about the forthcoming legislation, saying that, while her organisation 'broadly supported' the right-to-rent checks, she was concerned 'about the integrity of landlords who were not affiliated' to her organisation. She was referring, specifically, to the possibility that 'rogue' landlords would be complicit in identity theft since they have access to documentation and to the impact that negative publicity might have on members of her organisation.

A landlord surveyed by JCWI indicated that, in choosing tenants, landlords would follow the path least complicated for themselves:

> [M]y requirements would be influenced by the fact that one tenant will be more difficult to check out than another. In this area I can afford to be very fussy about who I let to and going for an easy life is a factor. (Quoted in Patel and Peel, 2017: 26)

Some landlords resented being obliged to act as border guards. Such was JK, a landlord of three properties who had come from Hong Kong to the United Kingdom as a child and faced homelessness herself. These experiences contributed to her views on monitoring tenants and she sensed a threat to the conviviality of the part of London where she has lived for thirty years:

> I think it is a big brother thing creeping in. I don't think it is right to ask for that sort of information from tenants. The bottom line is that you want to make sure your tenant is creditworthy and they have the means

114

to pay. I think it is a horrible situation because if someone doesn't have the right to stay, you are not allowing them to occupy your property so where are they supposed to go? They are going to go to unscrupulous landlords who ask a lot of money and give them substandard accommodation. It is not socially responsible. By law I am not going to be able to [rent the flat to a vulnerable tenant] and I think that is an infringement of my rights.

She saw that her rights over whom she was entitled to let property to were being violated and was worried about the fate of vulnerable tenants; even more, she also voiced the pressure of proving one's right to belong that is felt by racialised minorities, including herself and her family:

Even though everything is legitimate with them they still experience a lot of things you don't expect. Even if you have the right paperwork it doesn't exempt you from having to prove your right to be here. ... I have been here since I was 8 and I do feel part of the fabric of the country and I feel British, I know I don't look it but when you hear about these things sometimes you do feel like you have two hats. I will never be British born and bred but yet I feel part of the country and everything of the values, so I don't agree with how we are doing things really.

SF, an 'accidental' British landlord who rented out her London flat while living abroad, also focused on the border-policing relationship that was forced on her: 'I feel very strongly about this and I very much resent the idea of being put in a policing role in regards to people who are coming to live in my flat.'

She made parallels with her parents' experiences of racism when they were trying to find accommodation in the 1950s:

My mother who is white/Irish would be told the place was available and that she and her husband could move in. Then when my father, whose heritage is originally from India, turned up, the place would be 'gone' again ... to think that some landlords wouldn't resort to racial profiling again is naïve ... I'm concerned that the role and powers of the immigration system are being devolved to those who have no expertise in this area and are not accountable in the way that government departments are.

The perspectives of differently positioned landlords differ, but none of them indicated that they were willing to break the new law and handed the legal responsibilities of making the checks to lettings managers. One agent, MS, told us before the legislation came into force that agencies planned to pass the charges for checking the paperwork onto the tenants:

> They were preparing a service for landlords to check immigration status. As far as I know this was going to be widespread throughout the industry. But as with other checks, most felt that the cost should be passed onto the tenants and not the landlords ... Given that the London lettings market is so competitive and that tenants are used to these high costs, most felt that this would be possible.

Through their actions and interpretations, landlords and letting agencies, charged as they are with the responsibility of everyday bordering, may extend the border beyond the stated aim of the law, forcing those with the right to live in the United Kingdom to negotiate and even pay for the administration of the border. The resentment shown by some landlords about being forced into border-guard roles demonstrate how the landlord–tenant relationship becomes a site for negotiating belonging, drawing on histories of colonial relationships and twentieth century racism.

Perspectives from tenants

Before landlords were forced to take on border-guarding roles, the everyday border reached into people's lives through those not directly involved in the landlord–tenant relationship. At a meeting we attended, a firefighter informed colleagues that, when he gives advice to householders about fire safety, he is able to gather information about possible migrants who live illegally. Reports from professionals and anonymous members of the public, as well as leads collected from raids on businesses, provide intelligence for immigration enforcement raids in private accommodation. BF told us about his experience of being raided while he was a student and staying in his aunt's family's house, of which the enforcement officers had been 'given information that there are illegal people living here' (as they told him). He was convinced that the 'information' came from a neighbour who bore a grudge. The false report led to a frightening experience for the family:

> They came at 5 o'clock ... Everybody was sleeping ... they were banging the door, they got in, they just say 'we came from the UK

Border Agency'. They go where every single one was asleep, they enter the door, they don't knock ... They were very rude ... They asked for residence card and checked them all, and didn't get anything because we are not illegal in this country.

By the time of the 2014 Act, BF was renting privately and told us that the checks would give landlords further reason to discriminate:

When you get to any landlord they are not going to give to foreign people, they are treating very badly when they actually get higher rent, that is the reason they give the flat to student or foreign people and they think you are not going to say anything.

The right-to-rent scheme allows landlords to evict without a court order; all occupants are disqualified from obtaining legal tenancies. For those with complex immigration status, the threat of this possibility can increase the fear and vulnerability to other oppressive situations. Before the scheme was in place, DB, a refugee, told us her experience:

It's like you are always afraid that maybe one day you will be thrown out on the street. Some landlords use it to intimidate you into sexual activities ... I am an example. There has been a situation where the landlord was telling me that it would be much better for me to accept his sexual advances in order to stay in the house. It's true. It's one of the things that led me to leave that place but you leave it to an even worse situation.

Many migrants in London already faced significant difficulties in accessing housing in the capital. MR explained that, owing to the irregularity of agency work and the intimidating character of the London housing market, she was living with other Romanian families, in accommodation supplied by her (ethnic Romanian) employer. This left them open to exploitation by the agency owner, as another Romanian, AR – a young man in his twenties who worked for the same agency – explained:

[The agency owner] makes a note in his diary when people can't pay their rent. Then, in the summer, for example, when there is lots of work, he phones them all the time to go to shifts. Then, on the day he pays their money into the bank he phones them and tells them he is coming round for the rent and they need to get the cash out for him.

Such situations are often easier for the wealthier migrants we interviewed, who are able to purchase their own property or live in university accommodation during their studies.

In what follows we examine everyday bordering in the context of homelessness.

Everyday bordering and homeless people

The hostile environment policy has extended the border beyond private accommodation and onto the streets at night. Since 2009 some charities have worked with the Home Office Immigration enforcement team to identify homeless EAA citizens who they argue are not exercising their treaty rights (i.e. are not working). Since 2014 access to benefits for EU citizens has been restricted, and since May 2016 those found sleeping rough can be detained and deported. Charities collect information about homeless individuals and report to the local authority and to ICE teams:

> St Mungo's would assess any rough sleeper met in the borough. If there was a query over their immigration status they would refer to our in-house legal team for advice. If that offer was not taken up and they did not engage with our service St Mungo's would then refer to ICE/Home Office. (Islington Council response to FOI request, quoted in Corporate Watch, 2017)

Charities have justified their bordering role by claiming to give people who have fallen on hard times in the United Kingdom the means to return home through 'voluntary reconnection'. However, the words of an Eastern European man who has worked in the United Kingdom demonstrate a combined Home Office and charity focus on prioritising deportation over accessing support, which indicates that these 'reconnections' are not always voluntary:

> I had been sleeping near Charing Cross on my own for about a month. I was never contacted by any outreach workers before the Immigration Officers came, they arrested me on the spot and took me to detention. I told them I was working for 18 months before, but it didn't matter. Now I am in detention, they say they are going to deport me back to [an Eastern European country]. I have nowhere to live there. (Quoted in Corporate Watch, 2017)

Other organisations choose not to partner with immigration enforcement. We interviewed GS, a black British male who worked with street homeless people in London and observed the recent rise of Eastern European males who had lost their jobs and sometimes their passports and were living rough. He told us that he would not inform immigration enforcement and that this did not stop him from helping people to return to their countries of origin if they requested, as he had been involved in directly contacting family and voluntary organisations at the homeless person's request, to facilitate his or her return. He reported on the frequency of homeless people losing passports:

> I have helped people buy their passports. On many occasions I have said to people on the street [local charity] has a safe deposit, cos they are valuable and people are losing their passports all the time … passports are powerful, important documents but on their person, on the street they are a target and vulnerable. I can't remember the numbers of guys who have had their passports stolen or lost or misplaced.

Increased everyday bordering is leading to the exclusion of homeless people from health services as a result of new demands for ID documents to access healthcare introduced by the 2016 Immigration Act, as outlined by a health professional:

> We work with homeless people who have chaotic lives and are often coping with years of trauma. Many of our patients, including those who are UK nationals, simply don't have ID documents … These kinds of rules simply create layers of difficulty and red tape for medics, while making patients' lives miserable. (Samantha Dorney-Smith, London Network of Nurses and Midwives Homelessness Group, quoted in Gayle, 2017)

The vulnerability of rough sleepers and tenants to identity theft grows as bordering legislation increases the demand for stolen and forged identity documents. This was exposed by an undercover investigation into the growing market for passports and residency documents for the purposes of obtaining tenancies. The reporter paid £500 for a counterfeit Indian passport and a biometric residency card that would fool landlords, but not 'a proper immigration officer'. A lettings agency accepted the documents during a right-to-rent check (Adesina and Brennan, 2017).

119

Bordering scape 6: Education

In this UK bordering scape we explore different types of everyday bordering in the contexts of contrasting further and higher education institutions and private and state schools. UK visa regimes for students are aimed at preventing those with lower incomes from remaining in the United Kingdom. However, individuals from lower socioeconomic groups are in demand as customers or in education institutions and experience a varied range of everyday bordering, which combines with bordering processes in employment and accommodation to limit the possibility of a long-term residence in the United Kingdom.

During the era of the British Empire, relatively small numbers of colonial subjects crossed borders to enroll at metropolitan educational institutions. Those who did were monitored by government agencies, in view of colonial anxieties about students campaigning for independence and local racism focused on their presence in the United Kingdom (Visram, 2002; Kushner, 2012; Holmes, 2015). In the context of neoliberal globalisation, the marketisation of education, practices of international benchmarking, and comparisons such as 'world rankings' constitute increasingly entangled layers of governance that cross national borders. In responding to the demands of global capitalism, education has become an increasingly important element of global trade (Rivzi and Lingar, 2010). There is huge variation in the levels and types of education marketed and in the reasons for their consumption. Elites seek to enhance their educational capital via international mobility so that they can confidently operate as part of a global, multicultural community (Brooks and Waters, 2015). Private schools, public and private universities across the world have recognised the strategic and economic importance of recruiting students from abroad (Brooks and Waters, 2011). Non-elite families migrate in order to educate their children in state schools in wealthier parts of the world or pay to send their children as students to less expensive further and higher education institutions abroad. In the United Kingdom at the turn of the twenty-first century, the Labour government enabled an expansion of private colleges aimed at recruiting overseas students. Since student visas allowed twenty hours of work per week, many students from the Global South supported themselves by working in a range of jobs, including in the ethnic enclave economy. Concurrently education professionals found themselves co-opted into carrying out border-guard duties such as checking attendance and the number of hours

120

worked, and this fundamentally changed their relationships with students.

Perspectives from further and higher education

The government monitoring of non-EEA students shifted from Home Office employees to administrators and teachers in universities and colleges from around 2005 on. Home Office staff had previously been responsible for checking on attendance, progress, or excess of paid work in the context of considering applications from students for visa extensions. After 2009 the 'end-to-end' recruitment and border policing of students was outsourced to private and state-funded education providers, who were issued a licence to sponsor and monitor non-EEA students 'from arrival to departure'. Since the introduction, in 2010, of the 'highly trusted sponsor' status for providers with the most robust monitoring systems, the checks and computer systems required by colleges and universities to retain their licences have become increasingly complex and costly, with the result that many 'overcomply' in order not to risk losing their licence (Webber, 2012: 152–5). A significant element in the hostile environment discourses of both politicians and the media focuses on non-EEA overseas students in private colleges who overstay their visas and become 'illegal workers' or initiate 'sham marriages' with the aim of settling in the United Kingdom. The Conservative partners in the coalition government pledged to cut the numbers of overseas students by tens of thousands. In 2012 a university had its 'highly trusted sponsor' removed on the grounds that it was seen as not complying with immigration monitoring requirements (Grove, 2012), and between 2010 and 2015 over 700 colleges had their licences to sponsor students revoked (UKVI, 2015a), which led to thousands of students losing their right to live, study, and work in the United Kingdom (Shepherd, 2012).

In both private and state-funded colleges, managers are responsible for ensuring that they admit only students who have the right to study in the United Kingdom and, in partnership with the teaching staff, for monitoring their attendance and informing the Home Office of absences. While DS, the British Serbian manager of a private college in a prosperous London suburb, experienced her bordering role as straightforward, HA, her British Bangladeshi counterpart working in a state-funded college in inner London, experienced his bordering role as a threat to his own security. At the private college,

121

most students were from non-EEA non-Commonwealth countries and had their fees paid for by relatively wealthy families, or were sponsored by governments or private companies. DS emphasised how few issues this raised:

> We have random checks from Home Office, to just check on our Tier 4 students, so they just make sure that everything's done properly. ... I mean couple of times we did have phone call from border from airport and stuff saying you know, 'so and so is 16 and he's coming over'. Purely because they're minors ... and the immigration's just checking will they be studying there, are they going to so and so address and once it's confirmed it's fine.

HA had a contrasting experience, informed by his ethnicity as well as by the location of the college. In a tone that echoes that of the church minister required to be alert to sham marriages in our second bordering scape (see chapter 3, p. 85), HA regretted the shift in his role from education advisor to border administrator:

> Now, before someone enrols or even applies, if they are a non-British passport holder, whereas what it used to be was 'what do you want to study?' now it is 'What is your immigration status?' because, depending on your answer, we advise you accordingly.

If the documentation was not straightforward HA would refuse to accept the student, as

> the consequences of making mistakes are too grave [for me]. ... Because we have a spate of dodgy colleges around here, that hasn't helped us at all. The Home Office don't [sic] seem to distinguish between us and the private colleges. Why would we even risk such a thing?

He saw his state-funded college being targeted as a potential immigration law transgressor by the Home Office because it was located in an area where private colleges that flourished by sponsoring students from the Indian subcontinent had been closed down in the aftermath of Home Office investigations. Despite being a British citizen and legally employed in the United Kingdom, HA felt that he had to demonstrate his own right to be trusted in the role of border administrator:

> When I became an authorized officer I had to provide a photocopy of my passport so they could check I was legit ... if I make an offer and it

122

is a dodgy student, the college could be in trouble and they could lose their licence … I could also be prosecuted or interviewed by the Home Office on the basis that I did not take responsible actions.

DS, on the other hand, whose students are mostly from wealthy backgrounds, does not demonstrate such concern or discomfort in performing this role. When asked about their approach, DS explains how much is up to the judgement of the individual at the college, on the basis of a Skype interview they carry out:

It's up to us to decide whether we want to issue a pass or not for them. I mean we often say no, if there's concerns. But luckily we didn't have to have that many and we haven't had any refusals, which is great because we really try and kind of judge.

HA admitted to 'overcomplying' with monitoring, as he was fearful that if he did not he would lose his job. Others in less precarious situations have been able to opt out of college employment actively in order to escape from state bordering obligations. A white male English language teacher told us that he left his job in a college after observing the willingness of colleagues to comply with monitoring and witnessing the dismissal of students with complex immigration status.

Similar contrasts in carrying out everyday bordering were experienced by workers in different higher education institutions. NL, the manager responsible for student compliance at a London-based new university, reflected on the fact that she had not seen her career in border enforcement when she started working in education: 'My route into the job was not that I chose to be working for the border force. I worked as a counsellor and advisor … Being an advocate for students and working within legal parameters and legal guidelines.' As new monitoring requirements came into the university, she moved into working with their new immigration compliance team, where she felt that the pressure from the Home Office's 'culture of disbelief' caused her team to spend an excessive amount of time sorting out cases:

If a student in the past was working 22 hours instead of 20 hours they would ask them to regularize it, now if they find that out they have to shop them. A recent case was complicated and confused, involving holiday hours as well, and they managed to work with that student who was actually within the regulations.

123

She told of other legitimate cases that could not be sorted out in time and where this led to the university losing the students. From her experience of working with other institutions, she felt that new universities such as hers had to demonstrate that their systems and processes of compliance are excellent in ways that elite universities do not have to.

However, although the level of Home Office scrutiny may be felt less in elite universities, the atmosphere of suspicion seeped into the education-focused relationship between supervisors and students, as the former were required to include bordering tasks as part of their academic supervisory role. BB, a white male professor at a Russell Group university, was surprised to be asked to fill in forms about PhD students' 'engagement' without explanation as to their purpose:

> [questions on the form were asking,] are these students 'engaging' which seems to be a completely parallel process to the processes to check that they are doing well or not well. The university hierarchy sends them round and they get asked to do them and what is interesting about them as opposed to other forms is that there is no interest in any remedial action. This is not for the student's benefit. There is a real sense of whether or not that the course that they are on is a *device*.

BB and his colleagues filled in the forms in spite of being concerned about the atmosphere of suspicion regarding the students' motives that they created. Each of the examples selected from further and higher education demonstrate how the interests of education and student–teacher and advisor relationships are threatened by the responsibilities for border monitoring forced on educational institutions and how the threat of job losses and of sanctions against universities – threats made to those who carry out everyday bordering – extend the border far beyond those at whom the corresponding legislation is ostensibly targeted.

For overseas students, the long process of negotiating the education border – from identifying bona fide colleges through being recruited and obtaining visas abroad to adapting to the complex and changing regulations once they are in the United Kingdom – is expensive and exhausting and has led to some students travelling elsewhere or being deported. Overseas students from non-elite backgrounds recounted to us their experiences of being recruited abroad by 'dodgy' colleges and, after wasting up to two years engaged in work for some valueless certificate, having to reapply and pay for properly accredited courses. Some had their colleges closed down while they were still registered; others were forced into illegal work as they lost their employment rights.

In 2017 a report from the Office of National Statistics challenged the government's discourse about the threats posed by students 'overstaying' their visas. It stated that 'there is no evidence of a major issue of non-EU students overstaying their entitlement to stay'; and another report based on exit checks carried out on people who left the country found that, of those non-EEA students whose visas expired in 2016/17, over 97 per cent departed in time (UKCISA, 2017).

Perspectives from schools

The international super-rich who invest hundreds of thousands of pounds in obtaining citizenship, who use tax havens, and who purchase property in exclusive neighbourhoods are significant consumers of elite British schools and universities. Especially after the 2008 recession, overseas pupils have become a sought-after income source for Britain's elite and less prestigious private schools (Brooks and Waters, 2015). While elites encounter everyday bordering in accessing education, their experience is one of rather invisible, seamless, or frictionless borders.

Children under sixteen can only obtain student visas for the United Kingdom if they are studying at fee-paying schools. Approximately 750 fee-paying schools are registered with the immigration authorities (UKVI) as sponsors of children from outside the EEA; they sponsor 15,000 pupils annually on Tier 4 (child) visas. Once the initial visa is obtained, monitoring proceeds via class registers, alongside the monitoring of all children. While the UKVI carries out compliance checks, the only revocations for non-compliance have been from less prestigious schools (UKVI, 2015b). However, in the aftermath of the Brexit vote, the head teacher of a private school expressed a fear that, if EU students had to face the visa entry requirements experienced by non-EEA pupils from the Global South, they would look elsewhere:

> it is a possibility that the uncertainty caused by Brexit and the additional hurdles – like more stringent visa entry regimes – needed to be overcome could lead families to look elsewhere for private schooling, seeking countries that appear to be the easier and more reliable choice. (Norton, 2016)

125

During the period of our research, English state schools could not refuse admission on the basis of suspicions about the immigration status of a child and, unlike independent schools, state schools did not have a role in checking visas. A state school could advise parents and alert the Home Office, but could not then act on behalf of the Home Office to exclude the child. However, a Freedom of Information (FOI) request found an agreement, in place since 2015, between the Home Office and the Department for Education to share the details of up to 1,500 schoolchildren a month, specifically in order to 'create a hostile environment' in schools:

Where it is suspected that an [immigration offence] has been, or is being committed, the DfE will [share] their data with the HO [Home Office] to assist in the process of identifying potential new contact details (including addresses) for the individual(s) and their family members. (Gayle, 2016)

Later on the agreement adds that the 'strategic aims' of data sharing include re-establishing contact with families the Home Office has lost contact with, reducing the population of illegal migrants, and 'creat[ing] a hostile environment for those who seek to benefit from the abuse of immigration control' (Gayle, 2016). The Department for Education response to the FOI request showed that over a four-year period individual details of children on the national pupil database had been passed to the Home Office's absconder tracing team, which was searching for parents who had been told that they faced deportation or for unaccompanied asylum-seeking children who had disappeared (Travis and Gayle, 2016).

In 2015, amid media discourses about 'education tourism', the education secretary ordered a review designed to 'investigate how much of a "pull factor" state schools are for immigrants with families who decide to move to the UK' (Ross, 2015). The increase in the numbers of EU nationals in English state schools became one of the rallying cries of the Brexit campaigners. Six weeks before the EU referendum, the *Telegraph* reported on government (ONS) statistics about children of EU citizens legally attending British state schools:

Schools are under 'huge and unsustainable pressure' from a dramatic rise in the number of children from European migrants' families ... Almost 700,000 school-aged [*sic*] children – one in 15 pupils nationally – have a parent who is a citizen of another European country. The number has more than doubled since 2007. (Ross, 2016)

126

After the EU referendum, the government introduced additional requirements to the annual National School Census, demanding that state schools in England collect information about children's countries of birth and nationalities. The government document framed the data collection in terms of improving education planning in the context of immigration (DfE, 2017); however, since 2015 data have been shared with the Home Office for immigration enforcement purposes. Against Borders for Children campaigned successfully against the bordering duty (Against Borders for Children, 2016). Legal pressure from campaign groups forced the withdrawal of a similar data-sharing agreement between the NHS data service and the Home Office (Liberty, 2018; Wemyss, 2018). However, even if these requirements were withdrawn, data sharing extends to other arenas, including the police sharing information about victims and witnesses of crimes with immigration enforcement (Townsend, 2018b).

Conclusion

In this chapter we have analysed three bordering scapes, exposing the continuum of firewall bordering that has been moving beyond the border crossing points into everyday encounters between citizens and residents of different status – including other citizens. We have shown that everyday bordering processes are multilayered and overlapping and are experienced at work, at home, and in educational institutions, so that at different times an individual may be a border guard or may be the subject of the border work of employers, landlords, educators, and others. We have argued that these everyday state bordering processes affect everyone in different ways and to different degrees; and we have shown that the unevenness of these experiences contributes to increasing inequalities and shifts in hierarchies of belonging.

In education, foreign students who attend elite universities and private colleges and have a wealth of social and economic capital to support them do not encounter the difficulties experienced by students from poorer backgrounds. This places a differential burden on contrasting institutions of education that are obliged to manage the border. Administrators encounter students from particular, racialised minority populations and from less privileged positions who feel that they have to overcomply in carrying out monitoring duties. Non-EEA migrants with short-term visas and EEA migrants in precarious employment experience difficulties with accommodation because landlords are overzealous about their bordering roles, out of fear of prosecution or in order to exploit the vulnerabilities of tenants. The costs for these groups rise further, as letting agencies pass on fees for right-to-rent checks carried out on all tenants. This extension of the UK border into everyday life has created business opportunities for letting and employment agencies as well as for arms-length businesses such as those involved in the collection of digital data about individuals. Employers face difficulties in checking the rights of migrants to work; this contributes to the fact that some miss out on equal access to the labour market. Small business owners in the ethnic enclave economy feel targeted and their businesses suffer from immigration raids and from large corporations' attempts to avoid penalties through close ties with the Home Office. British non-passport holders from all ethnic backgrounds are likely to come from lower socioeconomic categories; but, as the Windrush scandal made clear, racialised minorities without passports and vulnerable people who have lost them are more likely to face problems in accessing employment, accommodation, and welfare services and may face deportation.

We separated out the bordering scapes as an analytic tool that allowed us to disentangle the complexities of the bordering encounters of differently situated individuals. However, our examples of bordering scapes in chapter 3 combine with those in this chapter to demonstrate how the expanding social, economic, and political inequalities are constructed through the multiscalar continuum of firewall bordering. This is illustrated through our discussion of the external and internal bordering encounters of British Bangladeshi business owners, who campaign for changes in working visa rules and are also subject to immigration enforcement raids carried out on their premises as a result of Home Office suspicions that they continue to employ chefs illegally. The economic damage of these raids – together with the violence of immigration raids at home, or the feelings of humiliation experienced when spouse and short-term visitor visas are refused – is evidence of how firewall bordering constructs the unequal, racialised hierarchies of citizenship and belonging.

By contrast, we have shown that the UK border can appear to be relatively invisible and 'frictionless' to those wealthy enough to invest in the United Kingdom, to purchase property, to pay private school fees, or to afford the services of private companies and lawyers who can smooth their path to residency, citizenship, and a feeling of belonging. However, the bordering scapes also expose feelings of dissonance for more wealthy individuals, for example the white professional who experienced crossing borders as 'a right' but was angry that his racialised colleagues were stopped at the border. Evident throughout is the divisive nature of firewall bordering processes as they permeate through border crossing points into everyday encounters. They create obstacles both for those who find themselves unable to access education, housing, or employment and for those educators, landlords, and employers who feel uncertain about the border-guard role that is punitively being forced upon them.

5

Bordering and Grey Zones

Introduction

'We're stuck here. We can't go on and we can't go back,' said Hikmat, a Syrian farmer driven from his land by war, now living in [a] tent outside a shopping centre in Lebanon with his wife and young children. 'My children need to go to school, they need a future.'

UNHCR, 2016c

In this chapter we examine bordering grey zones, which have been expanding all over the world during the past couple of decades, mainly in the Global South but also in the Global North. The boundaries of these grey zones are always constructed by different political projects of governance and belonging. Grey zones differ in the extent to which states, international agencies, and civil society impose law and order, supply services and other forms of aid, and also attack and harass their inhabitants.

In her book *Expulsions*, Saskia Sassen (2014) analyses some of the devastating global impacts of neoliberal globalisation that she calls radical expulsions. She argues: 'The past two decades have seen a sharp growth in the number of people, enterprises and places expelled from the core social and economic orders of our times' (Sassen, 2014: 1).

In this, Sassen continues the work of Zygmunt Bauman in *Wasted Lives* (2004: 5), who argued that 'the planet is [sociologically and politically] full' and that not all the growing populations of the world are useful for this global social, political, and economic system. The radical expulsions that take place under neoliberal globalisation have major economic, political, social, and ecological effects, and in chapters 1 and

2 we have related to some of them. In this chapter we focus on the ways in which processes of bordering are being used to create and contain the 'grey zones' or 'limbo spaces' for those expelled, who are thus stuck in lives of permanent temporariness (Kimmerling and Migdal, 1993: 279): they, like Hikmat and his family, are indeed 'caught in territorial, spatial, and bureaucratic limbo' (Dona, 2015: 68).

Grey zones in the contemporary global context

Firewalls and everyday bordering have created a situation in which increasing numbers of people across the world are being 'suspended' in grey zones – spaces outside the protection of contemporary states. Grey zones are sometimes within, but also beyond, the territory of particular nation-states. For example they can be located within metropolitan cities, straddling national territories, or on remote islands. In this chapter we present three key processes that contribute to the production of grey zones across the world; these processes contextualise three illustrative bordering scapes related to the United Kingdom that we examine next. The first process concerns the seeming gaps between the rights guaranteed by international law to forced migrants and the ways in which national laws and the functioning of nation-states often prevent such rights from being implemented swiftly, if at all. Hyndman and Giles (2011: 361) discuss how waiting for any kind of settled legal status has become the rule among refugees, not the exception. As the numbers of forced migrants continues to rise globally (UNHCR, 2017), so too the numbers of people stuck in these grey zones also increase.

Secondly, states in the Global North have introduced a wide range of policies that have sought to externalise or 'offshore' their borders onto the territories of other nation-states, often exploiting economic inequalities of neighbouring countries to do so. The need for such measures arises from discourses of antismuggling or antitrafficking as well as of border securitisation (Huysmans, 2000). These spaces of extraterritorial 'camps' constitute microsocial, microeconomic, and micropolitical worlds in which migrants, international organisations, and civic society volunteers interact to create their own – precarious – alternative 'normality'. This normality can disappear or change swiftly as a result of alterations in the political projects of governance and belonging that have created it.

Finally, grey zones, emanating as they do from various impacts of neoliberal globalisation, are neither socially nor spatially neutral.

Grey zones are more likely to be occupied by specific groups and are found in particular places more than in others. Border towns have been especially impacted by these restructurings, as the latter often coincided with debordering processes from improved infrastructures that moved the traditional functions of the border (and the forms of employment related to them) to other locations (Cassidy et al., 2018a).

While the discussion in this chapter focuses on the lives of those who inhabit grey zones, we should not lose sight of how many actually lose their lives in these grey zones or in the attempt to get away from them. For example, in the deserts between Mexico and the United States, more than 6,000 'human remains' have been found since 1994, when the American Border Patrol decided to impose the strategy of 'prevention through deterrence' in order to stop easy urban crossing between Mexico and the United States, which was the traditional pattern of seasonal Mexican workers. In the Mediterranean, thousands of irregular migrants trying to reach European coasts die every year (IOM, 2018a).

Grey zones: Gaps between different constructions of 'migrants' in national and international discourses

In 2015, according to UNHCR's definition, nearly 6.7 million refugees were considered to be in a 'protracted displacement situation' – without a permanent solution to their displacement for five years. The legal framework that shapes the ways in which forced migrants are processed, by both the UNHCR and by nation-states, is based upon the 1951 Geneva Convention and the 1961 Protocol. The legislation states: 'No Contracting State shall expel or return [*refouler*] a refugee in any manner whatsoever to the frontiers of territories where his life or freedom would be threatened on account of his race, religion, nationality, membership of a particular social group or political opinion' (Article 33(1)). However, the burden to prove the existence of threat to their life or freedom is falling increasingly upon the forced migrants themselves. Those who apply for protection but whose claim has not yet been determined, in other words asylum seekers, find that state policies across the world often undermine the principles of the Convention.

In addition to asylum seekers and refugees contained in these grey zones, there are many other groups whose status may not afford them protection under international law. These include internally displaced persons (IDPs), modern slaves, and the stateless.

132

A recent global report on modern slavery that incorporates both forced labour and forced marriage suggests that 40.3 million people were victims of modern slavery in 2016 (International Labour Organisation and Walk Free Foundation, 2017). In the context of the Global North, clear links have been made between migrants and exploitation in the labour market, which has been defined as hyperprecarity (Lewis et al., 2015). While some people are trafficked directly into forced labour, others have more complex journeys into slavery (Craig, 2010). The lack of routes for legal migration into the United States, 'Fortress Europe', and other wealthy nations and the difficulties involved in obtaining asylum often leave migrants indebted to smugglers or without income or status in the country, making them vulnerable to mistreatment (Andersson 2014; Craig, 2010).

As Dona (2015) has argued, the term 'protracted refugee situations' fails to capture the numerous occasions on which forced migrants find themselves living in uncertainty for long periods of time. She suggests replacing it with 'prolonged displacement' in order to include others, such as asylum seekers, undocumented migrants, and people with a temporary status. For those who have been displaced, basic rights to work and mobility are suspended. As Agamben (1995, 1998) has argued, the camp has become a state of (non-)exception. However, as Bakewell (2008) notes, not all refugees in the Global South are in refugee camps. In Africa, for example, many thousands of refugees are living outside the formal camps and settlements and are unassisted by UNHCR. Ramadan (2013: 68) has also highlighted that the state of exception is too generalised to capture the 'complex sovereignties of refugee camps'.

Nonetheless, as Hyndman and Giles (2011) argue, refugees who remain in the camps and other spaces of the Global South are constructed as 'genuine', unlike the mobile migrants who try to travel to the Global North and become threatening. In consequence, there is an interest in keeping forced migrants in camp-like spaces in the Global South, where they remain unthreatening. The example of Palestinian refugees as the oldest unsettled refugee population in the world gives us some insights into the complexities of why and how certain groups might find themselves subject to prolonged displacement and how they can gain a different legal status and different entitlements (Agier, 2011: 188).

Grey zones built on legal loopholes and gaps between international and national law and the functioning of nation-states also exist on the inside of the borders that refugees seek to cross. The experience of permanent temporariness therefore continues even when the state border has been crossed successfully. While states differ in the ease, speed, and clarity with which they process requests for refugee status, for settlement, and for naturalisation, the sense of precarity is widely diffused across metropolitan cities in the Global North – and also across the 'tiger economies' of the South, which attract migrants who flee their countries for fear of losing their own and their families' lives or livelihoods and are now seeking to establish better and safer lives. The second bordering scape in this chapter explores what happens to those who do not have full citizenship, or at least full settled residency.

Grey zones: Offshoring processes

As mentioned above, the operation of international law is often in conflict with nation-state legislative frameworks when it comes to rights of movement and the status of refugees.

> Is there still a right to seek asylum in a globalised world? Migration control has increasingly moved to the high seas or the territory of transit and origin countries and is now commonly outsourced to private actors. (Gammeltoft-Hansen, 2011: i)

Nation-states in the Global North have increasingly sought to 'manage' migration flows outside their own territories – a wider trend of what has been described as 'neo-refoulement' or the externalisation of asylum (Hyndman and Mountz, 2008). In this context, the contemporary situation echoes the one described by Arendt after the Second World War: 'Not the loss of specific rights, then, but the loss of a community willing and able to guarantee any rights whatsoever, has been the calamity that has befallen ever-increasing numbers of people' (Arendt, 1973: 291–2).

In March 2016, the EU finalised an agreement with Turkey, a neighbouring and formally an accession country. The agreement was set to address one of the facets of the 'refugee crisis': the entry of migrants to Europe through the Greek–Turkish border. Although Greece had been a point of entry to the EU for third-country nationals since the 1990s, from around 2005 the Greek–Turkish border became a point of focus for irregular migrants, including people from Iraq, Afghanistan, Pakistan, Bangladesh, and sub-Saharan Africa (Angeli et al., 2014). However, in the summer of 2015 and into early 2016, the number of migrants increased rapidly, mainly as a result of the ongoing war in Syria; more than 800,000 migrants passed through Greece, primarily via the small island of Lesvos (see Afouxenidis et al., 2017). Public pressure within the EU grew after the dissemination of an image of the body of three-year-old Aylan Kurdi, who had died on a beach in Turkey after a failed attempt to cross with his family to the Greek island of Kos. The terms of the deal were that the EU (Greece) would be able to return all the new irregular migrants to Turkey; in exchange, the EU agreed to settle more refugees from Turkey (supposedly one for every refugee returned, up to an annual cap of 72,000), accelerate visa liberalisation for Turkish nationals, and offer further support to refugees in Turkey (Collett, 2016). In 2016–17 this support was said to be €3 billion (European Commission, 2017). Yet, while twelve months later the EU proudly announced a 97 per cent reduction in irregular migration through the Greek–Turkish border (European Commission, 2017), the agreement itself was subject to widespread criticism. One of the key critiques focused on whether it was in breach of the Geneva Convention and, particularly, in breach of guarantees against refoulement, as described above. The basis for this suspicion was the fact that Turkish law does not offer Syrians a secure status and has no safeguards against refoulement; it only grants Syrians temporary protection (Rygiel et al., 2016).

In addition to agreements to 'disperse' to other territories humanitarian obligations incurred under the Geneva Convention, countries in the Global North have also been engaging in a number of other extraterritorial border enforcement processes. Alison Mountz (2011: 118) has argued that islands have become key sites of these extraterritorial controls, as nation-states 'exploit legal ambiguity, economic dependency, and partial forms of citizenship and political status on islands to advance security agendas'. Islands and other sites beyond the territory of nation-states have become de facto new locations for the material borders and borderlands of these nation-states. These 'interstitial' states, in which more and more migrants are forced to seek asylum, are often not signed up to the Geneva Convention, which would guarantee the rights of these people (Mountz, 2011), and thus the migrants find themselves in between not only in terms of material location but also legally, because of the high level of ambiguity that such arrangements entail. One of the most prominent examples in recent years has been Australia's approach to border policing and its use of Papua New Guinea (PNG) and Nauru as sites or centres for the detention and 'processing' of migrants. The 2013

Regional Settlement Arrangement (RSA) between Australia and PNG ensured that all asylum seekers arriving in Australia by boat would be transferred to PNG, where, if the asylum claim was successful, they would be granted leave to remain and settle in PNG (Grewcock, 2014). More recent resettlement agreements have extended the relocation of refugees living on Manus Island (part of PNG) to Cambodia (2015) and to the United States (2017). These processes of 'offshoring' bordering processes or 'transferring' responsibilities assumed under the Geneva Convention via agreements with other countries not only lead to increasing stuckness but also extend the dispersal of borders away from their traditional location at the edge of nation-states.

These global examples of extraterritorial bordering and offshoring of migrant camps form the backdrop for the juxtaposed border controls that construct the grey-zone bordering scape of Calais, which we examine as our eighth bordering scape.

Grey zones: Historical trajectories of de and rebordering processes

Grey zones of post-borderlands affect people who formally have full citizenship rights. Border towns have historically occupied a privileged position for informal 'arbitrage' opportunities (Cassidy, 2013), as well as for the formal opportunities of the 'border as resource'. Debordering in the EU has largely been based upon creating a shared economic space, with the underlying logic that borders present barriers to trade (van Houtum and van Naerssen, 2002). But in the processes of debordering border towns lose, for the most part, their dominant 'industry', a key source of employment, and this has a major impact on the local economy. Havlíček et al. (2018) have detailed how the debordering and the rebordering that have occurred as a result of the fall of the Iron Curtain in 1989, the accession of Central and Eastern European states to the EU in 2004, and their joining of Schengen in 2007 have had complex and uneven impacts on old and new border towns, as free movement within the Schengen area contributed to the decline of some towns and a 'Euro-curtain' at the edges of the Schengen area affected others. On the island of Ireland, since the debordering instituted through the peace agreement between the Republic and the United Kingdom and despite the growth in the Irish economy, there has been a decline in the local economies and employment opportunities of counties in the border region, owing to neglected infrastructure and uncertainties about the post-Brexit border (*Irish Examiner*, 2018). Our ninth bordering scape will focus on Dover as a post-borderland town, a grey zone on the historical border between the United Kingdom and France.

Bordering scape 7: The Jungle in Calais

Our seventh bordering scape focuses on the border zone between France and Britain – more specifically, on the grey zone that has been created around the French town of Calais – the infamous Jungle. The location of this grey zone is a result of several political projects of governance – of the United Kingdom, of the EU, of France, and of the regional and local authorities. At the same time, the growth and intensification of the Jungle on the political agenda of both the United Kingdom and France has been a reflection of contesting political projects of belonging that have emerged as a result of the social, political, and economic developments in the area.

The border between France and the United Kingdom passes through the Channel, which is narrowest between Calais and Dover. While the United Kingdom is (still) a member of the EU, it has never joined the 1985 Schengen agreement, which initially established that fourteen states of the EU would have no borders between them. Although, as a member of the EU, the United Kingdom has allowed free movement of goods, services, and people within the EU, it did not trust the bordering agencies of other EU states on the points of first entry, establishing its own regime of visas for anyone who is not a citizen of the EU. As a result, Calais has become a major bordering point in-between the rest of the EU and the United Kingdom.

Until twenty-five years ago, movements between Calais and Dover took place via ferries, which carried both people and goods. Since the Channel Tunnel was opened in 1994, trains have added considerably to the volume of what is carried through from one side of the border to the other. The Sangatte Protocol, signed by the United Kingdom and France in 1991, introduced 'juxtaposed controls', whereby border checkpoints operated by French enforcers were set up at the English end of the Tunnel and by the British at the French end. In 2000 juxtaposed immigration checks were extended to Eurostar terminals in Paris, in London, and, later, in Brussels. The Le Touquet agreement of 2003 introduced juxtaposed controls to the

Channel ferry ports, shifting the controls from Dover to Calais and Dunkirk. Since then, given the growing migrant problem in northern France that is focused on the trains and ferries leaving Calais, there have been new agreements, the latest of them in 2018, in which the United Kingdom continues to pay France to securitise the border at the Eurotunnel site and in the port of Calais, as well as to make the processing of all passengers more efficient. Operating as a firewall (as discussed in chapter 3), British border enforcers based at bordering points near Calais filter tourists, shoppers, workers, and documented migrants on a daily basis.

For more than two decades, irregular migrants have been gathering around Calais, attempting to cross the borders illegally, in lorries, train, ferries, small boats, and sometimes even by foot along the Channel Tunnel. The number of these people varies depending on political and militarised conflicts in the Global South, especially in the Middle East and Africa, as well as depending on the bordering policies and technologies of the EU, France, and the United Kingdom. It is this group of people, caught in the grey zones between France and the United Kingdom, that is the focus of this bordering scape.

Since the Calais grey zone evolved, there has been a cyclical policy towards irregular migrants, moving from being gathered all in one major camp to being dispersed throughout France. The first large camp was initiated by the French government and run by the Red Cross at Sangatte for three years from 1999. It was closed down at the promise of the British government to accept and give work permits to 80 per cent of the mainly Kurdish and Afghan refugees; the remainder were to be given residence permits in France. Since 2002, migrants who have continued to travel to Calais slept in squats, small camps, and abandoned warehouses in the town and outside Calais, in camps in the woods, and in dunes known as 'jungles'. These places were repeatedly raided or bulldozed by police before being moved elsewhere. Many of them were inhabited by members of the same ethnic communities, who were often on antagonistic terms as a result of relations with competing *passeurs*, 'smugglers', on whom they depended for the facilitation of border crossing to the United Kingdom. They were largely dependent also on charities (funded partially by the French national and local government), which provided food, clothes, and washing facilities. During the day, parks in the centre of the town would be used by young men as places for meeting and sleeping. This was the situation when we started our fieldwork in Calais in 2013.

The 2015 Jungle camp

By April 2015, over 1,000 men were building an open-air shanty town known as 'the new jungle' (the last one was bulldozed in 2009). With the escalation of the European refugee crisis and the polarisation of attitudes towards those seeking to settle in Europe in general and in the United Kingdom in particular, the Jungle grew quickly and, by the time it was closed down by the French authorities in October 2016, it was inhabited by about 10,000 migrants from various countries, mainly Middle Eastern and African. Most of the inhabitants were dispersed to refugee centres all over France, often in isolated areas with few services. Some managed to cross the border to the United Kingdom.

We visited the camp in May 2016 and were shown around by a local charity worker whom we had first met two years earlier, when he was supporting migrants within the city. He told us that sometimes, in order to reduce the number of people in the camps, the French police would ignore attempts by residents to slow lorries down, break into them, and hide in them so that they would be able to cross the border into the United Kingdom clandestinely. He also said that the United Kingdom has allowed informally the crossing of some families with women and children, as well as the crossing of some of the unaccompanied minors officially agreed upon. After the destruction of the camp, some people despaired of crossing the border to the United Kingdom and applied for asylum in France or Germany; many came back to dwell in the woods and dunes along the coast. This happened in spite of the UK government's investments in razor-wired fences around the port, the train station, the Tunnel entrance, and parts of the motorway and in other technologies of securitisation, which made it much more difficult for anyone to cross the border clandestinely.

The number of migrants around Calais continuously fluctuates. In January 2018, British Prime Minister May and French President Macron announced a new treaty, which would include improvements to speed up the asylum process (Willsher, 2018). Just a couple of weeks later, there was a 25 per cent increase in the number of migrants in and around the port town and, as often happened, especially at times of dispersal and scarce provisions, violence erupted between Afghan and Eritrean nationals.

Our bordering scape concentrates mainly on the Jungle because that camp became emblematic. It is infamous worldwide and a political embarrassment for the two governments, French and British, as well as a major point of contestation between national governments, local authorities, and the EU. It also became the focus of many of civic society activists who wanted to protest against bordering in the EU, and especially in the United Kingdom. As a result, while in many ways the life in the Jungle has been typical of the stuckness of living in the grey zone, it also benefited from the help of many volunteering individuals and organisations, which contributed necessary items for survival, from clothes to tents to food, thus complementing the limited resources that the French government was pressurised to supply. Most importantly, the Jungle is a good example of the agency, perseverance, courage, and creativity that people in grey zones deploy in their everyday lives.

The Jungle was organised around three main sections. The Jules Ferry Centre, which offered meals and showers as well as accommodation to women and children (but not to the women's husbands), was controlled by an NGO that worked with the French government and had a health centre that worked in coordination with the hospital in Calais and with medical NGOs such as Médecins sans Frontiers and Médecins du Monde. Another section, behind security fences with gates operated through palm recognition, included over one hundred shipping containers, each with twelve beds to be used overnight. During the day residents had to remain outside the containers. The bulk of the camp, however, consisted of tents and caravans brought by migrants or donated by charities, as well as of self-made sheds and other habitation structures. More than a dozen shops, self-financed and sometimes helped by charities, were also opened to offer various services, from clothes and food to hairdressing and dentistry. The most popular places were the restaurants, which offered cheap food and drinks to those who could afford them, as well as free phone charging and social space. There were also a church, mosques, and a library, which was also used as a centre for a variety of educational courses for adults and children, including English and French language courses. Volunteers facilitated Western Union transfers for migrants. After going to a tribunal, the local authority fixed water outlets throughout the camp and generators supplied electricity to public locations.

Campzenship

Sigona (2015: 12), joining others in challenging Agamben's (1995) view of camps as states of exception, introduced the concept of *campzenship*, a 'situated form of membership produced by the camp'. Membership of the camp was negotiated in dialogue not only with authorities from France, Britain, and Europe – whose attempts to govern their claimed territories were shaping the limboscapes of Calais – but also with the migrants themselves.

A significant source of understanding the ways in which the different inhabitants of the Jungle have experienced and practised their campzenship can be found in the fascinating narratives in *Voices from the 'Jungle'*, a book edited by colleagues at the University of East London who ran a short, university-accredited course on life narratives. One of them described thus the feelings of camp belonging:

> I have been here for three months in this wonderful world, the 'Jungle'. Really it is wonderful. Because of the people inside, they are wonderful. You can see many nations, saying 'Hi, hello', in different languages. You can see in their eyes that they respect you … if I go to Calais to take rest, one or two hours later I will miss the 'Jungle' and come back here. Because I think I belong to this place. (Godin et al., 2017: 155–7)

This, of course, does not mean that there have not been tensions and frustrations due to the hard conditions of living in the Jungle, but our guide emphasised how much less conflictual the relations were at that time than before, when different ethnicities occupied different squats and camps in the city or woods. Nor does any of this mean that individuals did not seek and receive help mainly from people from the same ethnic group. As Muhammad, a doctor escaping the war in Syria described it, camp residents who seemed frightening strangers when he first set eyes on them later on became close friends in the camp, or were sometimes recognised as old acquaintances (Godin et al., 2017: 112–15).

Of course, their families of origin continue to be of vital importance – both the ones left behind and those already in Europe. The first thing that many migrants look for when they arrive in the Jungle is a place where they can charge their phones, in order to be able to reassure their families (sometimes, in order not to worry them, they report that they are already in the United Kingdom, as some admitted doing) and establish contacts for moving on.

Everyday lives in the grey zone

Mike Featherstone (1992) described 'everyday lives' as the opposite to 'heroic lives'. The Calais Jungle is a good example of how, in real lives, the two (if we include in our definition of 'heroic' any exceptional behaviour that requires uncommon physical and mental courage) can be intimately co-constituted. People in the Jungle developed their own everyday routines. They spent their days getting food from voluntary services and from enterprising individuals who opened shops; they sat in makeshift cafes, visited medical services and each other, attended community and religious centres, attended language and other classes offered on the camp. These activities took place in dirt, in mud, in temporary structures that ranged from tents to campers; but in many ways they were everyday routines, similar to those of the citizens of Calais. However, at night, many campers were absent from their tents, as they would engage in repeated attempts to find a way to cross the Channel to the United Kingdom, be it by lorry, ferry, or train.

We met people who would try to cross the border most nights, as part of their routine. They would fail, they would be arrested by the police for hours and days, then they would get back to the camp, take care of their injuries, rest, and continue to try – sometimes for many months, even years. In other words, their everyday lives encompassed what in action movies or folklore tales would be described as heroic actions. The stoic nature of the mental attitude required for leading such lives – life as a permanent temporary migrant – without giving up was well articulated by Muhammad from Syria: 'I realised that there is always one thing harder than whatever you have seen. And this was the worst thing I had seen until now. But maybe there is something worse than that worst thing too' (Godin et al., 2017: 113–14).

But we also met migrants who had been in Calais since we visited in 2014. When we spoke to them in 2016, half of the Jungle had just been bulldozed and the other half was to follow a few months later. Some despaired of ever crossing the border successfully into the United Kingdom and had asked a local charity to help them to seek asylum in France or some other European country such as Germany.

Of course, crossing the border can be much easier or more difficult, depending on people's physical and monetary resources and on the kind of *passeurs* they paid in order to get help from them. JC, an NGO worker, reflected on the fact that different national groupings in Calais also often paid different prices to cross:

Yeah, it depends on money. We know that Sudanese people have less money than others, organise themselves to get across, it's the same for some Afghanis. Syrian people are known, I don't know if it is a fact or not, to be richer, so they pay smugglers and they pay a higher price than other communities.

Thus some migrants, because of their situated positioning, were more 'stuck', that is, less able to cross the border than others.

KI is a Kurdish man from Iran who had passed through Calais on his journey to the United Kingdom, which is where we met him. He told us how his experience as a lorry driver in Iran, where he had crossed the borders of Iraq, Pakistan, and Afghanistan, gave him skills that helped him to imitate a lorry driver, to eat, shower, and hide in the lorry park and to make it to the United Kingdom independently.

Another asylum seeker, AI, whom we also met in London, had come through Calais in 2013 and, as he showed us, the scars on his hands, which had been lacerated by razor wire on security fencing, emphasised that women and children had fewer options for crossing the Channel than single men. 'Woman? No. This is for young men. For woman it is impossible because they cannot jump like a man, they cannot run. I have never seen a woman.'

Women were, however, living in squats and camps before the creation of the Jungle. Fears of sexual abuse and trafficking were significant reasons for a separate accommodation for women and children in the Jules Ferry Centre. However, many chose to live in caravans or tents in the main camp in order not to be separated from their husbands.

In a life of repeated attempts at crossing the border, the actual moment of crossing is often unexpected and shocking. As Mani from Iran described:

> On that last night, when our trafficker put me in the lorry with 15 other people, I had no idea that this time would be the time I was successful. I just thought to myself that this try would be like all of the other times ... I didn't want to let myself believe it. (Godin et al., 2017: 211–12)

And, once they were sure they were in the United Kingdom and celebrating, they almost died from the lack of oxygen in the container. 'What a stupid fate!' he thought. Luckily, eventually the police opened the doors of the container and they could start the next stage of their precarious lives in the grey zones after claiming asylum in the United Kingdom – which is the focus of the next bordering scape.

Bordering scape 8: Grey zones in Britain

The stuckness of asylum seekers is not over when they manage, often after years of repeated failed attempts, to arrive to the United Kingdom. It is directly related not only to the complexities of immigration law and to poor decision-making on the part of the Home Office, but also to the extreme poverty and isolation that structure these people's lives as a result of the ways in which the United Kingdom approaches asylum accommodation and support.

In the previous chapter we examined the United Kingdom's legislation and policies, which create differential experiences of everyday bordering. In this bordering scape we focus on those who have been forced to live in the resulting limboscapes.

Irregular migrants' legal status

In 2016, asylum seekers were 6 per cent of the immigrants to the United Kingdom, the majority of the initial asylum applications (66 per cent in 2016) failing, although 41 per cent of those had been overturned by courts (Hawkins, 2018). Applications for asylum in the United Kingdom are well below the levels of applications for asylum in many other EU countries: in 2016 there were six asylum applications per 10,000 people resident in the United Kingdom, by comparison to an EU average of twenty-five (Refugee Council, 2017), and this made the United Kingdom's share in EU asylum applications in 2016 only 3 per cent (Blinder, 2017).

Although the Home Office has a six-month target for reaching an initial decision on an asylum application and in spite of a 21 per cent reduction in the number of cases in 2017, about half of the applications waited longer in that year. Two of those we interviewed waited more than twenty-five years for their legal status to be settled. Most difficult, people's status, once granted, can often be revoked, being limited to five years or until the government decides that the country of origin is now 'safe' to return (Yuval-Davis and Kaptani, 2009; Conlon, 2011).

Since the 1999 Immigration and Asylum Act, asylum seekers have been placed on an accommodation system with a 'no choice' basis (Darling, 2011), which predominantly means dispersal away from London into areas of low housing cost, where these people have no connections and 'often meet a hostile reception' (Hynes and Sales, 2010: 39). In 2010, the provision of asylum accommodation moved from public to private providers (Darling, 2016b). The introduction of this for-profit component, alongside the reduction in support services, generated greater uncertainties for asylum seekers (Darling, 2016a) and made it difficult for local councils to intervene in cases of abuse (Grayson, 2016).

While awaiting the outcome of asylum applications, asylum seekers in the United Kingdom are not able to access either the labour market or social security payments. They are entitled to accommodation, healthcare, children's education and some cash support (less than 50 per cent to that given for daily living expenses to British unemployed). Those on immigration bail, whose applications had been refused, are issued with an electronic payment card with which only food, clothing and toiletries can be purchased. After a year, if considered not to be responsible for the delay to their decision, asylum seekers may get permission to work in jobs on the government's shortage occupations list (Home Office, 2018).

Limboscapes of life in the United Kingdom

> I feel so suffocated all the time ... I'm not allowed to work; I'm not allowed to do anything. I'm just sitting at home. And no money, no money for medication and every time I'm thinking it's better to die rather than living this kind of horrible life.

This quotation from NI, a female asylum seeker who lost her status in the country after leaving behind a violent partner, contains a number of key elements of what we call stuckness: being stuck at 'home', being unable to work, and being trapped through lack of resources or poverty. Underlying these narratives is an inability to 'move on' with one's life – the result of a political project that intentionally situate asylum seekers and undocumented migrants outside most structures of social inclusion by denying them the right to a safe home, to a decent standard of living, and to physical and mental health and family life and by continuously controlling their movements through various technologies of everyday bordering.

The 'no choice' accommodation and dispersal system can cause extreme hardships to asylum seekers. KI, the Kurdish lorry driver from Iran who had come to the United Kingdom through Calais, was eventually dispersed to the north-west of England. He described how, after his asylum claim was refused, he came to depend on charities for his accommodation: 'There was a charity run by churches, so

145

there were seven churches for seven days a week, so we had to move between churches every night.' Later on he was sent to a large homeless shelter in Salford, while the charity kitchen he could eat in was in Moss Side:

> We walked four miles from Salford to Moss Side every day to get food and then again walked back to the shelter ... I was four months there and really bad mentality, I was crazy, I was thinking about stopping my life, many times actually and then I decided to sign a voluntary return.

Despite the pressure of the 'hostile environment' policy, KI did not sign and did not return to Iran.

Many asylum seekers have to attend a reporting centre while their applications are being processed. AB, a woman in the queue at such a centre in London, echoed what others had told us: 'Each time I come here, I never know whether I'll be able to return home, will get arrested or just be taken directly to deportation. I feel frightened all the time.'

Many of those with a failed claim or on appeal live in the United Kingdom on immigration bail, in constant fear of being 'raided' (Wemyss, 2015a) or picked up by the authorities and detained. Fear of detention and deportation, as experienced day by day by many of the people we interviewed, affects one's sense of stability; here is MI:

> They raided in the morning six o'clock, and it was so scary. My son started crying when they came, and he was so scared. He was thinking, what going to happen next? What gonna happen to my mum? So, what gonna happen to my dad? They are so scared.

Temporary accommodation, detention, and the threat of deportation are part of the high level of anxiety and uncertainty of being stuck in the grey zones of Britain. As we argued in chapter 1, belonging has often been seen to relate to feeling comfortable and 'at home', as well as 'safe' (Ignatieff, 2001). In the United Kingdom's approach to asylum accommodation, we find a political project that attempts to exclude; asylum seekers are housed with one another in places where integration is very difficult (Hynes and Sales, 2009).

Restricted access to state support makes many migrants without status in the United Kingdom depend on a third sector, which can be food banks for their everyday needs, or prompts them to work illegally in big cities. KI and MI tried to survive working in the informal economy:

146

Some of them … knew I haven't papers and they wanted to give me a job … to work 7 days a week just to pay rent, all that stress was for nothing. Just roof and a little food. (KI)

Sometimes you go to an employer to just get a job in a restaurant or whatever, in the shops. They say, 'It's a training period for one week.' And after one week, they say, 'We don't like your work.' And this way they just get the new people all the time so that they don't have to give them salary. So these things they just degrade, they demoralise people. (MI)

Giving asylum seekers rights to work after six months if there is no decision on their claim has been a focal campaigning point for NGOs, trade unions, and politicians for several years (Mayblin, 2014). By working without permission to do so, asylum seekers also put in jeopardy their claim to remain in the United Kingdom.

In 2013 almost all immigration cases apart from asylum ones became ineligible for legal aid (Wilding, 2017). Consequently, many providers of legal support and advice to migrants were forced to close down. Even for asylum seekers who do have the right to legal aid, obtaining legal representation has become extremely difficult (Wilding, 2017). Recent victims of the Windrush scandal (discussed in chapter 4) – people who had been living and working in the United Kingdom for decades but were unable to prove their legal status after the consolidation of the hostile environment – were affected by cuts to legal aid and became dependent on pro bono representation, just like recent migrants. In some cases, financial constraints are a reason for their failure to apply for leave to remain. In 2017, charges on immigration and nationality applications increased by 18 per cent, taking the cost of applying for indefinite leave to remain to £2,297 per person, while the actual cost of processing an application is £252 for the Home Office (Yeo, 2017). This approach reflects firewall bordering (discussed in chapter 3), which clearly favours those with more abundant economic means.

Living in the grey zones has serious implications for people's health. Prior to the 2014 Immigration Act's implementation, entitlement to free NHS treatment was based on being 'ordinarily resident' in the United Kingdom, that is, living there lawfully. The 2014 Act defined 'ordinarily resident' as having lived lawfully in the United Kingdom for at least five years. Health services were also required by the Home Office to submit the personal details of all those they treated.

Given problems of access, language, and life hardships, migrants' health has been found to be worse than that of the general British

147

public (Potter, 2018; Potter and Milner, 2018). However, stories of 'health tourism' from politicians and in the media have encouraged the government – which is dealing with a growing crisis in the NHS – to scapegoat migrants by extending the health surcharge linked to visas; patients are obliged to provide identification in order to access healthcare, and charging for hospital services is very strictly monitored. Health workers working with migrants strongly deny that there is any health tourism in the vast majority of cases. They argue that the extra charges and the media-fuelled 'perceived threat of charging' for free services (such as for TB) prove ineffective for the NHS budget (Potter and Milner, 2018). A maternity advice service has evidenced how NHS charging deters women from accessing maternity care; many avoid it owing to fears of being charged and of the Home Office being notified (Feldman, 2018).

PM, a health worker who ran a clinic for undocumented migrants, told us that people often accessed NHS services only through the free A&E services once their condition was more serious, thus creating significantly greater costs for the health system: 'We're not saving resources if we all are just pushing people towards using already stretched accident and emergency services.' Others point out that avoiding medical care because of fear of deportation has a detrimental effect on the physical and mental health of the asylum seekers and can contribute to the increase in contagious diseases (Grayson, 2016, 2017). In 2018, after public pressure grown out of the Windrush scandal, the government suspended the legal obligation of health providers to pass on to the Home Office the data related to their patients. However, access to the health system may not much improve, as migrants told us that they could not afford the cost of health services for non-residents. One such experience was recounted by a student from West Africa who was diagnosed as suffering from breast cancer during her studentship. She started radiation treatments, then her student visa expired before they ended. Her health condition prevented her from leaving the country; she was not allowed to work; and she had to pay thousands of pounds for the continuation of her cancer treatment as a private patient, which she could not afford.

SB, another health worker working with migrants, pointed out some of the implications of these policies:

The GP–patient relationship should be based on trust, privacy, and it should be productive. It should be a conversation. You can't have a conversation if you're worried that the person you're talking to might be telling the border police about you or your immigration status. That fundamentally breaks the doctor–patient relationship.

Moreover,

> The broader impact on society is that you start to have tiers of society who have different levels of access to public services and this is fundamentally wrong, particularly when this starts to happen on a migration basis ... people who are not white British or European face significantly more questions that other people are not asked.

Griffiths (2017: 156) argues that the UK immigration system is gendered, racialised, and class-based – as well as harmful to families. In particular, this is reflected in the double bind in which those who try to remain in the United Kingdom as a parent to a British citizen find themselves in. As 90 per cent of those in immigration detention are men, this invariably relates to the ways in which men are expected to demonstrate ties to their UK-born children. The system expects them to perform the role of a parent, but then actively prevents them from doing so through dispersal to other parts of the country, detention, and no access to the labour market. Inability to participate in family life fully is another key experience of living in the grey zones. While the asylum seeker in Griffiths' paper had started a family, AI saw his lack of status in the United Kingdom as an inhibitor to establish one. He described having 'been trapped since 2007, unable to progress in life'. For him, to 'have a life' involved getting married.

In addition to being unable to settle and start a family in the United Kingdom, the person caught or 'stuck' in this state is also unable to be part of and contribute to transnational family life. As we have seen in the camp in Calais, regular contact with family members, even just by phone, is what grounds individuals in life and gives hope. ZL, a former refugee and now a British citizen, told us of the impact that the incapacity to leave the United Kingdom to be with the family at a time of grief and mourning had on asylum seekers:

> I think the most difficult thing I have seen about people within borders is when a family member dies ... to not be able ... four or five years later to go there when your mother died. I think it's psychological damage.

In this bordering scape we have examined key areas in which migrants living in grey zones experience in-betweenness in their

149

everyday lives – in their abilities to make themselves 'at home', to maintain and create familial relationships and to support themselves.

The experience of living in a grey zone has a long-term effect on the situated gazes of all those who go through it, even if they manage to obtain some formal status. For some, such as AI, it just left a bitter taste in the mouth and a sense of powerlessness and of being excluded by the British state:

> The immigration law is strange. Everybody has [a] different law, it is not the same for everybody. Sometimes they deport you, sometimes they don't deport you ... Even if you spend 100 years in the United Kingdom you never understand what the immigration are doing. I felt it. Never, never ...

For others, however, such as KI or JC, stuckness or, indeed, the process of waiting (Conlon, 2011) has been an opportunity for self-reflection, enhancement of personal agency, and politicisation:

> My life changed to different thinking. I grew up in the last two years actually. Reading, I used the Internet on my phone, because I was homeless I couldn't use a computer. All I had was my phone. It gives me a lot of information. The things on the Internet are not 100 per cent true, but I could read and think about it, what is true and not true. I talked with a lot of people... When I came here, actually I never before think about politics. When I came here I became atheist, I became a politician... I became involved with Kurdish people. (KI)

> Working here [in a migrants volunteer organisation], I learned so many things. I learned to cook. I learned to manage a kitchen and now that I finally have my work permit I could get a job in this. But mostly, I met so many wonderful people and learned how it is to be part of a community of people from so many countries and help each other. (JC)

In this bordering scape we have explored the grey zones of life in Britain for people with uncertain migration status. We have shown that they experience different kinds of stuckness, owing to the mechanisms of internal control and to internal bordering regimes. It is not possible to capture all the complexity of these spaces, but we have highlighted some of those that emerged most frequently during our research. What is clear is that the structural factors, which often leave people feeling stuck and unable to move on with their lives, are also those that are frequently used to exclude them from becoming part of British society. There are many organisations and individuals who try and support migrants with uncertain status. Many migrants, especially from earlier waves of migration, have managed to formally settle in the United Kingdom. However, the technology of the 'hostile environment' detailed in chapter 4, dominates the lives of those who live in the grey zone of Britain's metropolitan city and beyond and inflicts suffering and additional hardships on those who want to settle in the United Kingdom and escape from their grey zones.

Bordering scape 9: Post-borderland Dover

As we discussed in chapters 1 and 2, the rise of everyday bordering and improvements in transport infrastructure across the world have moved much of the administrative and economic functions of borders away from traditional border towns to other places, such as airports – and, as we saw in chapter 4, also to employers, landlords, and other citizens. We have argued that these traditional borderlands can be understood as post-borderland borderscapes (Cassidy et al., 2018a) – spaces that remain embedded in their border(land) past, in spite of a complex array of de- and rebordering processes that have transformed social, economic, and political relations.

In this final bordering scape of our book we analyse the ways in which Dover has come to be left behind and stuck as the result of overall British deindustrialisation and economic decline, as well as of debordering processes that have moved bordering functions outside the town. In Dover, debordering has contributed to a reduction in employment in occupations traditionally associated with the 'industry' typical of the border, for example in the port. With the construction of the Channel Tunnel, whose entrance for vehicles is based in nearby Folkestone, and with the introduction of frequent Eurostar train services, which now connect London with cities on the continent, the border has literally moved elsewhere. It is now located at the Eurostar terminals in Paris, London, and Brussels, at the Coquelles and Folkestone ends of the Eurotunnel, and within the security fences of the Calais port – as a result of the United Kingdom–French agreements on juxtaposed controls discussed earlier.

These local processes were accompanied by an increasing internalisation of (de)bordering (discussed in chapter 4), which moved borders, in material terms, away from the margins and into everyday life. So, while the port remains one of the busiest in Europe, the town of Dover became increasingly disconnected from it. Disconnection is one of the key themes in this bordering scape. Passengers travelling through the port rarely stop in the town.

Debordering in and of Dover can be linked more widely to historical changes in travel and tourism. However, the key date for the town was the opening of the Channel Tunnel in 1994. The Tunnel was a topic of policy debates since the 1950s; an initial proposal in 1963 led to a false start in 1973, then to a relaunch in 1981. The Tunnel was seen to be a means to remove what was widely considered a final barrier to the single market of the European Economic Area, namely direct road and rail links to the continent (Fayman et al., 1995). The so-called bottleneck caused by ferry transportation at Dover was to be bypassed by a rail connection from nearby Folkestone to Coquelles in France. Unlike in France, where plans for the Tunnel involved collaboration between central, regional, and local government, planning on the British side was very much undertaken in Westminster (Dundon-Smith and Gibb, 1994).

At the same time as the Channel Tunnel was completed, the port of Dover was directly connected to the new M20 motorway via a dual carriageway extension to the A20. By providing an efficient route for lorries from the continent, the road separated the town from the port, and hence from its major industry. Dover remains the United Kingdom's busiest port, carrying over 12 million international ferry passengers; however, this figure was 20 per cent lower than ten years earlier. International sea passenger journeys for all ports have been in decline since the Channel Tunnel opened (Department for Transport, 2013).

So, while there has been a reduction of traffic through the port overall, it is clear that passenger traffic is the one most acutely impacted, and this has particularly (re)bordering effects upon Dover. There are therefore, we argue, three key axes upon which Dover's stuckness is based, and these relate to unemployment and worklessness, immobilities, and disconnection. In a border town such as Dover, all these forms of decline are inseparable from debordering and subsequent rebordering processes.

Stuckness in unemployment

Research has revealed a strong link between rising and now multi-generational worklessness (Simmons et al., 2014) and increases in poverty in Britain since 1979 (Nickell, 2004). In 2015, 12 per cent of the population of Dover district aged between sixteen and sixty-four was claiming out-of-work benefits, by comparison to 7 per cent in the south-east region (Dover District Council, 2015). Median gross weekly earnings were 6 per cent below the average for the south-east. However, in Dover town and in particular wards there were even higher levels of deprivation. St Radigund's ward in Dover is one of the top 5 per cent most deprived areas, 40 per cent of the population being defined as income-deprived.

Asylum seekers and other migrants who were denied permission to remain in the United Kingdom would sometimes end up in Dover at the Immigration Removal Centre, which formally closed in 2015. The centre was located so as to overlook the town, in the Western Heights, on a site that had for centuries been home to fortifications that protected England from potential hostile forces arriving from the continent. This site was taken over by the prison service in 1957 and became an immigration removal centre (IRC) in 2002. At the time when we started fieldwork there in 2013, the centre was one of the few remaining elements that connected Dover as a town to the border. It was also one of the few remaining local employers in town.

The levels of deprivation in the town and the way they had shifted over time were key themes in our interviews with local professionals. FD is a local woman who has grown up in this town and is frustrated by the attitudes of some local people.

> In spite of the port, in spite of the fact that they might be working on ferries with French nationals and this sort of thing, no, no, no. Dover is for Dover people ... There is a lot of poverty in Dover, which leads to high unemployment and low education, so all of that is going to breed animosity and ignorance towards migrants.

NB, a local minister whom we met in 2013, mentioned the traditional industries and the ways in which their decline had led to 'lack of ambition and aspiration, particularly in the Buckland [area of the town] community and especially among teenagers'. He explained that the low-paid monotonous work that was available in a couple of the local factories failed to hold young people; it was not just the monotony of the work itself, but the fact that opportunities for progression were very few. He noted that, while opportunities in the port were much reduced, it was still a major employer in the town, alongside the Channel Tunnel and care work with the elderly, which was also poorly paid. He claimed that EU migrants were filling the gaps in the local job market. He was also concerned about the ability of younger generations to leave the town through education.

Local people cannot afford to go to university and are wary of taking on the debt. Young people see graduates working in casual, part-time jobs with degrees, which also puts them off. Some young people do move away, but the older youths who stay don't have much aspiration. They are caught in the cycle and there is nothing to encourage them to try and break this and to no longer be on benefits or out of work.

This suggests patterns of worklessness similar to those observed by Nickell (2004) in other deindustrialised areas. The stuckness in Dover was embedded in decline and unemployment, linked to a wider restructuring of the national and global economy. One local police officer told us that only the most deprived of the migrants stayed in the town. This was evidenced by an element of growing diversity among the town's homeless population. A dispersal zone had recently been introduced on account of problems with town drinkers, which in recent years had come to include more foreign nationals. Just like GS, the worker we interviewed in London who supported street homeless threatened with deportation, the police officer noted that many among the diverse street homeless had lost their IDs and possessed no documents.

Stuckness in immobility

In addition to unemployment and worklessness, there was also a growing sense that people in the town have become less mobile over recent decades. For FD, growing up in Dover was marked by the uniqueness of the town's continental connections, which were not only the preserve of the middle classes. Ordinary working-class people would go to France for day trips. Rather than giving a sense of stuckness, these mobilities and the accessibility of France shaped local understandings of Dover, where the border was a resource and opportunity for travel:

> Yeah yeah, we'd spend time in Calais and it was always quite exotic, because as ten–eleven-year-olds and being able to say *bonjour*, being able to practice French that you're learning in school [*sic*]. So actually I hadn't thought about it for a long time, but it was really nice – it's like, I've got relatives who live up in Nottingham and I would feel that they were quite jealous at the fact that we were able to go to another country with[in] an hour and a half.

154

The ferry companies offered a range of specialist services that seemed to be based on the idea that mobility in and of itself, even without a destination, was to be celebrated and enjoyed:

> well it used to be a pound, but as we got older, about eighteen–nineteen, a group of us, of me and my friends used to do the 'dance to France' on the ferries and you don't get off. Yeah they used to just have a disco, so you would treat yourself every couple of months, and go on there and get your duty free at eighteen–nineteen and just do a 'dance to France'. It used to be very popular back then.

Mobility to France across the Channel was part of belonging in Dover; locally, people negotiated their positionality in the United Kingdom in relation to Dover's role as a border town, and one neighbouring France. But when costs began to rise for foot passengers, after the opening of the Tunnel, Doverians became increasingly less likely to make the regular trip to France. MJ, a local professional who had moved to Dover a couple of decades before we interviewed him, highlights that this had made things difficult for working across the border, too:

> What's important to know … is that things are becoming more difficult rather than less difficult for cross-channel work. In the days when I started to live in Dover nearly twenty-five years ago now, you could cross the channel for a pound, two pounds, nowadays it is considerably more expensive to travel, and that does affect the way that you do things. We used to go for our team Christmas lunch to Boulogne. We can't do that anymore; it is too expensive. It doesn't work properly, so actually prices is [sic] very important … and that does effect [sic] parts of Dover.

As FD also emphasised, it was not just the mobility and the benefits for work and leisure that were leading to stuckness, but also the pride that people felt in this very specific location, which framed their imaginaries of the town.

> I think it's something that Dover is quite proud of … you hear it a lot; people saying it's only twenty-one miles to France. London gosh! That's seventy miles away. You could say people feel more – not affiliated, but more connected to France than London. I know more people who went to France more often than to London, when I was young. It's different now, high-speed rail links and so on, but as a child, it was often the case that you had some sort of relative who was working on the ferries, so you would always go.

The mobilities of border crossing had also shaped Dover's position-ality and its distinctive links to other parts of the United Kingdom, particularly to the north-west; AS, a white man who had grown up in a hotel in Dover in the 1960s and 1970s, remembered people staying there who were involved in smuggling cheaper cigarettes (and other non-specified goods) through the port. He also echoed FD by reminiscing that many of those who came to Dover from Liverpool and Manchester stayed on and settled in the town, getting married and starting families. An older middle-class woman we spoke to during a visit to the town in 2013 associated some of the contemporary social issues with these groups. She was critical of the high numbers of drug addicts, who, she believed, were not local people but had come from Liverpool and other places and were linked to the cross-border trade. Just as the opportunities for formal work had diminished, so had the possibilities for this type of trade as well. However, the comments above also highlight the connectivity of Dover to other places in the United Kingdom, thanks to the border. It is the opposite feature – the disconnection that emerges now in the town – that we explore as our final aspect of stuckness.

Stuckness in disconnection

While Dover became less connected to Calais and France, it was also going through (re)bordering processes that opened up disparities between the rapidly globalising centres, particularly London, and other parts of the United Kingdom, as the limits of neoliberalism (Kingfisher and Maskovsky, 2008) and its crises of governability and governmentality (Yuval-Davis, 2012) have become apparent. Many people in Dover felt acutely the impact of the loss of connections to the border and sought to challenge the multiculturalist political project of belonging that promoted diversity – a project initially connected to large cities. Dover is, on the whole, less diverse than the surrounding areas. According to the 2011 census, Dover has the lowest number and proportion of residents from black and minority ethnicity (BAME) groups in Kent: just 3,708 people – a little over 3 per cent of Dover's population – were from a BAME group.

For some Doverians, this showed that Dover was 'stuck' in the past and was increasingly adrift from more cosmopolitan urban centres. Hence they were often keen to include migrants and other minorities that moved to the town. However, these views were contested and led to increasing isolation for some of the town's residents. FD described how her openness to increasing diversity had caused conflict with her friends from school.

> So for me personally ... I think that is probably one of the best things that ever happened to Dover because it dragged Dover from being out of touch with the rest of the world, it dragged Dover into the twenty-first century where the reality is multicultural, multiracial and multiethnic and a town like Dover, being a passenger port, if it cannot deal with multiethnicity, multiculturalism, different people, then how will it ever be successful as a port?

She and some of the other public sector workers in town whom we spoke to saw diversity as a symbol of progress, a way in which Dover was becoming more closely aligned to globalised cities and their modernity. DP, a health visitor, stated: 'I've been over [to local school] myself sometimes for meetings and there's a whole array of different coloured children from different nationalities and I think it is great, multiculturalism.' So, for these people, Dover, although connected to France, had previously been excluded from wider trends of diversity and cosmopolitanism.

In addition to the newly emerging connections to Europe through migration, the Tunnel has also produced a marked shift in more localised spatial relations, which further disconnected the border from the town. MJ described the breakdown of this relationship.

> So more and more people are crossing from France in vehicles than were in the past. So they are not walking from the port up the high street, buying whatever they want from Marks and Sparks and then going home. They are coming across in a car, so they are much more able to move around east Kent and further afield. So it isn't about Dover–Calais anymore.

As high-speed rail links have disconnected Dover from the border, local spatial imaginaries or the ordering/othering (van Houtum and van Naerssen, 2002) in which the border was centrally placed have also been disrupted. Other local imaginaries emerged, which situated Dover in opposition to nearby towns, with their growing reputation as up-and-coming commuter areas, and which discursively produced it as the 'other'. Other local towns were often regarded as more desirable places – so construed by a cross-section of the community, including by SN, the Nepali wife of a soldier in a Gurkha regiment whom we introduced in chapter 3:

Now we stay in Dover, but in June we are going to Canterbury as we have already bought a house for us. ... Because it is city centre, there is lots of scope and opportunity for job as well, part-time or full-time, and there are lots of schools around Canterbury centre.

A sixteen-year-old boy from Folkestone referred to his home town as 'not as bad as Dover'. PS, originally from Scotland, spoke of his reluctance to move from London to Dover to work in a local NGO.

My first impressions were ... the economy was a lot worse here, was worse than I had anticipated and what I had experienced in most other places [...] I certainly was surprised at the place that the economy was too bad for charity shops. That was my first experience of seeing the town. ... it was a different country than I had realised.

His reference to 'a different country' – different from the cities he had previously lived in – captures the 'left behind' and the 'stuckness' themes that seemed to characterise Dover in local imaginaries. This grey zone was not solely related to economic decline but also to the multilayered (re)borderings that had begun to shape life in the town since the 1990s.

Conclusion

In this chapter we have explored in detail some of the grey zones that have emerged in Britain (and beyond, in the case of Calais) as a result of a wide range of multiscalar contemporary de- and rebordering processes. Our bordering scapes highlight that 'limbo' or 'stuckness' are both socially and geographically variable. We explored these variations in three different sites: Calais, London, and Dover. We argued that these grey zones appear in the increasing gulf between international frameworks designed to protect vulnerable and displaced people and nation-states' internal and external bordering legislations, as well as resulting from the uneven incorporation of different locations into national and global economies.

In our seventh bordering scape, focused on Calais, we described the contesting political agendas that brought about the cyclical policies of concentrating the migrants in a camp and then dispersing them. We examined the complex routine as well as precarity that constitute life in the camp and how even within the camp, certain groups are more 'stuck' and vulnerable than others, and how crossing the border

158

has become both part of and the impossible goal of everyday life in the camp.

In our eighth bordering scape, we showed how, even after succeeding in crossing the border and arriving in the United Kingdom, many migrants find themselves embedded in the grey zones of life in the United Kingdom without settled immigration status for years. We show how precarity is reaching into every area of life, affecting migrants' mental, emotional, and physical well-being. While their rights may not be protected by the state, many other areas are managed and controlled by the authorities or their representatives, including private companies that administer asylum accommodation, for example. We showed how no-choice accommodation and lack of access to the labour market engender dependency, which is often used in public discourse to highlight the 'cost' of asylum seekers to the state. Yet their 'stuckness' is enforced by the nation-state, has an ideological basis, and is at odds with the philosophy (if not the actual legality) of international agreements. What we also showed, however, is that the experiences of the grey zones are also shaping migrants' situated gazes and revising their perspectives on the past, the present, and the future.

Our final bordering scape analysed a different type of grey zone: the post-borderland borderscape of Dover. Here stuckness is linked to debordering processes that moved the border away from the town and caused higher than average levels of unemployment, an increasing immobility, a growing sense of disconnection and resentment towards the evolving diversity of the population. The stuckness we found in Dover is a form of left-behindness and marginalisation in the state policy agenda. This kind of stuckness and its contestation were undoubtedly among the reasons why the town became a target for the UK Independence Party (UKIP), which initiated the Brexit campaign.

6

Conclusion
Understanding Bordering

In the previous five chapters we presented specific theoretical, methodological, historical, and empirical contexts, which we then put to use for the benefit of understanding bordering processes. Taken together, the analyses in this book can be summed up into four major complementary arguments.

First, rather than operating on the margins of state and society, contemporary borderings, working as they do in the context of neoliberal globalisation, itself in (multiple) crisis, are central to and constitutive of multiscalar political, economic and social processes.

Secondly, within their local, regional, and global context, the constructions, reproductions, and transformations of bordering processes are shaped by, and in turn shape, different shifting and contesting political projects of governance and belonging.

Thirdly, both locally and globally, contemporary multiscalar bordering processes have been a major axis in the development of intersectional social, economic, and political inequalities.

Fourthly, in order to understand contemporary borderings fully as social, political, and economic phenomena, we need to encompass, in a dialogical and epistemological manner, the gazes of differentially situated social agents.

In our concluding chapter we go over these arguments, which cut across the ways the bordering scapes discussed in this book have been experienced by the people we interviewed and observed in our research. At the end we ponder over the old Marxist dictum that one needs to change the world, not just to understand it, and we share a few thoughts on our understanding of bordering and possible ways of working towards positive social and political change.

Bordering as central to and constitutive of social processes

Throughout the book we have argued that, to understand contemporary borderings, we need to change our views of borders and borderings from seeing them as operating on the margins of state and society to considering them major constitutive features of contemporary social, economic, and political dynamics. The analytical marginalisation of borders and bordering has been partly due to methodological nationalism (Beck, 2007; Buscher and Urry, 2009). In a Westphalian construction of the world, states are regarded as containers of society (Taylor, 1994) and the role of borders and bordering is to outline, delineate, separate, and link mostly autonomous societies.

This view was never entirely true, and in chapter 2 we discussed how the construction of state borders as enclosures has been a particular historical outcome of the rise of the nation-states as well as a product of colonial–imperial practices. However, we also argued that, with the rise of contemporary neoliberal globalisation and its crises and with the global compression of time–space brought about by technological innovations, crossing borders and other forms of border work have come to occupy major parts of people's everyday lives. This has been caused by several practices, all very different.

One major change has been in people's lifestyle – primarily but not exclusively in the Global North. Tourism, crossing international borders during holidays, and taking shopping trips abroad have come to be routine activities in the lives of larger and larger sections of the population and even major components of a person's leisure time and lifestyle (McCabe, 2002; Edensor, 2007).

Another big change has been the shift in national and global employment patterns. More and more people have to cross borders for work, education, and training purposes. While migration has been a constant human activity throughout history, never before was there such a widespread dependence of national economies on an international and (probably even more importantly for our discussion here) transnational body of workers – from company executives to professionals to temporary unskilled workers. Individuals and their families incorporate border crossing into their daily lives as frequent flyers, as seasonal workers, or as migrants and refugees in search of permanent settlement, after crossing the border in 'regular' or 'irregular' ways.

The consequent dispersion of families and communities in different diasporas, as well as in the homelands, gives bordering a central role in the formation of subjectivities, even if the microchip revolution in communication and transportation enables people to transcend physical borders by creating a virtual domain of identity and belonging (Papacharissi, 2010). For people with transnational families and communities, how easily they are able to cross borders – if at all – affects both their subjectivities and their everyday practices in major ways.

Crossing borders, however, is only one way in which bordering has come to play a major part in people's everyday lives. Given the enormous political economy that has developed in what we described as 'intelligent firewalls' in the regulation of bordering (these are explored in chapter 3), there is a very large number of people whose livelihoods depend on regulating and controlling the borders, surveilling border crossers, and working in servicing facilities around border-crossing points – on ferries and trains as well as in shopping areas constructed especially to serve border crossers.

Yet, as described in chapter 5, a growing number of people all over the globe have their daily lives centred on bordering not through employment or leisure time, but because they are stuck on the border. They may be trying to cross it in legal or illegal ways, spending their lives in grey zones and limbospaces of informal squats, detention centres, or worse. As Schatzki (2001) has put it, they have come to embody the borders.

One cannot understand the full, constitutive, and central role of contemporary bordering, however, by compartmentalising this phenomenon in the ways we have done till now. As described in chapter 4, everyday bordering has become a major governance technology, controlling diversity and constructing hierarchies of exclusion and exploitation as well as managing discourses on diversity in the population. As such, it affects not only migrants and racialised minorities; and it affects other people not only when they actually cross a border or are in employment in a border zone. Bordering has become a new citizenship duty and a major influence on social and communal solidarities. This is just one outcome of what Sassen (2006: 403) has described as an unsettling rearticulation of territory, authority, and rights in the global neoliberal (dis)order, social and political.

This central facet of everyday bordering is directly linked to our second argument – that the constructions, reproductions, and transformations of bordering processes are shaped by different political projects of governance and belonging, all of a contesting nature and all constantly changing.

Bordering as political discourse and practice of governance and belonging

Bordering is embedded in every construction of political communities, although, as we have seen in chapter 2, continuous territorial borders have been a product of very specific historical circumstances, which sometimes had very little, if at all, to do with the people living in these territories, and especially in the borderlands. Delineating any territorial boundaries for any political project of governance, whether a nation-state, an empire, or even a municipality, requires both borders and boundaries of governance. At the same time it relies, at least in part, explicitly or implicitly, on political projects of belonging that furnish criteria as to who can belong and who cannot.

Nevertheless, one of the things we have found in our study of contemporary bordering is that there is often an inherent tension between political projects of governance and political projects of belonging. This is because often the particularity of political projects of belonging tends to undermine the supposedly universal constructions of governance in parliamentary democracies, even within the boundaries of the state.

Such tensions can be found even in the law itself. The bordering scapes experienced for example by Nepali and European Roma minorities in Britain, described in chapter 3, illustrate how racialised origins affect citizenship rights and duties – including the actual right to live permanently in a country. Interestingly, in this example, the tension between the egalitarian rule of law and the citizenship rights of particular racialised groups is affecting two contesting political projects of belonging that have shaped the British political community: that of the British Empire and that of the European Union. Differential applications of the law on whether children of irregular migrants in the United States are entitled to state education reflect a similar tension.

Often, however, even if the universality of law is formally maintained, its everyday applications contest it. Such applications can vary from a formal policy of profiling border crossers, which results in the concentration of surveillance and interrogation on individuals who do not seem to belong (Romero, 2008; Nagra and

163

Maurutto, 2016), to a situation where such discrimination is not part of any formal policy but can be observed statistically. An example of the latter is the proportion of immigration officers' raids on businesses owned by members of ethnic minorities, migrants or not (Bowling and Phillips, 2003; Muller, 2016).

Of course, such a tension exists not only in the relationships between state officials and members of the public. Part of the development of everyday bordering into a governance technology – a technology of controlling diversity and discourses on diversity in society – consists of transforming citizens into unpaid and untrained border guards. As described in chapter 4, this development of a 'hostile environment', supposedly targeted at 'illegal workers', in reality heightens racism and intolerance to migrants in general, and also to anyone who might look or sound as if they 'do not belong', as did the victims of the Windrush scandal. Moreover, the hostile environment has also affected social solidarity and cohesion in society overall, driving wedges of suspicion and fear not only between families and communities, but also within them. This is one of the main causes of the major impact that everyday bordering has on local and global social inequalities.

Throughout the book we have seen the differential effects of the double crisis of governability and governmentality brought about by neoliberal globalisation. In relation to issues of bordering, we have also witnessed the continuing contestations of political projects of governance and belonging that promote universal human rights and citizenship rights and of projects that consider autochthonic belonging to be the precondition for any sense of entitlement.

As we discussed, following Arendt (1943) and Agamben (1998), refugees, and more generally all those with 'irregular' citizenship status, disturb the easy conflation of territory, state, and people (Yuval-Davis, 1997, 2011). One of the main results of this contestation is the growth, throughout the Global South and metropolitan North, of 'grey zones' in which life is hard, stuck, and precarious. Another is the fact that this precariousness, at least in part, is caused by shifting power relations between those who seek to protect the rights and aid the lives of those in these zones and those who dehumanise them or reduce them to the 'bare lives' Agamben talks about.

As we were finishing writing this book, Donald Trump announced the virtually immediate cessation of US funds for the United Nations Relief and Works Agency for Palestine Refugees in the Near East (UNWRA), which supports about 5 million Palestinian refugees and their descendants, settled in permanently temporary camps since the 1948 and then the 1967 wars. In principle, there is a strong argument that the status of refugee should not be a permanent one. Being a refugee should rather be a temporary protection, until people can go back and live in their countries of origin, once the political situation changes for the better or – more often – as a transitional step towards settling down in their new countries of residence and obtaining permanent residency and then citizenship.

As we've discussed earlier, in recent decades the status of refugee has tended to become more and more precarious, being accorded for fixed periods of time, usually five or ten years. However, more often than not, the temporariness of the refugee status has resulted not in safe (re)settlement, but in pushing people back into the grey zones.

Trump's argument that the refugee status should not pass from one generation to another would have been valid if, concurrently with the radical cut of the funds for UNRWA, he had pressurised Israel into allowing the beneficiaries of these funds to return to their places of origin and reclaim full citizenship and ownership of their houses and lands, and if he had asked the Arab states to naturalise the refugees and to give them full citizenship in the states in which they reside. Instead, this cutting of funds is just one extreme step towards pushing millions of people into bare lives spent in the grey zones. This is the ultimate step (short of systematic genocide) of contemporary bordering.

Bordering as an outcome and a cause of social inequalities

As discussed throughout the book, the experience of bordering varies hugely among those who have economic and political capital and those who do not. At the same time, differential access to border crossing exacerbates and further widens preexisting social, political, and economic inequalities.

Neoliberal economies rely upon the free mobility of corporate managers and professionals (e.g. Harvey, 2007a; Mezzadra and Neilson, 2012). At the same time, multinational corporations' investment in particular sites depends on the desirability of these sites in regional and global contexts. Such desirability depends in part on the existing infrastructure, on access to potential consumers, and on local expertise. Other potential attractions are directly linked to social inequalities. A few examples would be relatively low wage rates for the local workers; for businesses and high earners, instead, convenient tax ratings, which sharpen local inequalities; and relaxed health and safety regulations, which afford lower levels of protection for workers.

However, bordering policies themselves have an important influence on the working of the neoliberal economy. Filtering – the modus operandi of bordering discussed in chapter 3 – regulates the flows of both regular and irregular workers, affecting the conditions and remunerations of different jobs. These flows create niches of 'grey' or 'black' economy in which formal regulations related to working conditions, such as minimum wage and length of working shifts, are not adhered to. Some branches of the neoliberal economy, for instance catering or the building industry, often come to rely upon practices that are a direct result of the bordering regulations.

All this relates to more general trends of the global migration flows and of the filtering regulations related to bordering. The differential regimes of passport and visa control have created a loose, self-reproducing global stratification system in which the carriers of particular passports (mostly from the North) have relatively easy access to cross-border locations, while others (mostly from the South) can hardly ever gain such access, unless they have relatively large political and especially economic resources at their disposal.

The impact that these differentiations in access to border crossing has on social inequalities does not end once the borders have been crossed. From an international perspective, those who manage to cross the border successfully and obtain better employment and higher payment often send remittances back to their families. These affect social inequalities within their countries of origin as well as the overall economic situation of recipient countries with a high rate of remittances (Taylor and Wyatt, 1996; Yang, 2008).

Locally, however, in the countries of immigration, the social, cultural, economic, and civic status of workers affects and exacerbates local inequalities, influencing people's differential access to various public as well as private resources. As described in chapters 4 and 5, even when irregular migrants have formal rights to request emergency health services or to report criminal assault to the police, the fear that their details might be sent to the immigration services would prevent them from using such rights even when their lives are threatened. Since they cannot rent property legally, people without documentation are compelled to live in unsafe, overcrowded accommodation, from which unregulated landlords profit. In the case of the Windrush scandal, landlords, employers, and welfare administrators, in their bordering roles, denied the rights of black Britons who previously did not need documentary proof of citizenship.

Given that the 'common pot' of resources in the privatised and reconfigured welfare state is shrinking under neoliberal governance and that the growing surveillance of public services is part and parcel of the 'hostile environment' of everyday bordering, this matter of differential access drastically affects many migrants' chances of obtaining good housing, healthcare, and general improvements to their precarious everyday lives; and this is especially true of migrants with irregular legal status. It is for this reason that we need to explore and understand the effects of bordering from the differentially situated gazes of the migrants and of the locals who are affected by them.

Bordering as a situated endeavour

Throughout the book we have demonstrated the ways in which people who are differentially positioned experience borders and bordering in different ways. This is important not only for understanding why bordering and inequalities are intimately connected but also because, as the various empirical bordering scapes in the book have illustrated, without encompassing these multifarious experiences in a dialogical and epistemological manner we cannot fully understand what bordering is. The dichotomous notion of legality that we found in the border officers we interviewed, for example, is as relevant to an understanding of bordering as the much more comprehensive and nuanced idea of legality expressed by the restaurant owner whose business suffers as a result of peak time raids and of his incapacity to hire a chef for his specialist cuisine. Similarly, the Home Office's determination to do away with 'sham marriages' and thus to oblige marriage registrars to report on all cases of marriage with a non-EEA national is as important as the unease of the priest who feels that his pastoral role is being disrupted or undermined by his border-guarding role. Moreover, bordering cannot be understood without encompassing the effect of racialisation on landlords, who are afraid of criminal responsibility and thus choose not to let their flats to anyone without an EEA passport – or, as in some of the Windrush cases, to anyone whom they suspect of not having UK citizenship. Nor can bordering be understood without incorporating into our analysis the situated gazes of the racialised migrants themselves. The implication of viewing bordering just from perspectives of hegemonic political projects of governance, of belonging, or indeed of what benefits neoliberal economy is that social scientists add to the exclusionary project of everyday bordering. On the other hand, viewing bordering just from the situated gazes of precarious border crossers prevents us from understanding the different political, economic, and social interests that construct, reproduce, and control the complex technologies of contemporary local, regional, and global bordering. Any attempt to challenge and change these borderings in a more inclusive direction, in accordance with human rights and social justice principles, would have to be based on an all-encompassing understanding.

Bordering and transversal political epistemology

As explained in our introduction, the epistemology of situated intersectionality is not relativist, validating each situated knowledge on its own terms. Rather it is dialogical, encompassing and respecting all situated gazes as means of approaching the truth (Collins, 1990).

However, this does not mean that, as social scientists researching the phenomena of bordering, we are neutral. Situated intersectionality is an epistemological alternative to the positivist one and we take on board Haraway's (1991) famous affirmation that 'there is no view from nowhere'. Hence we agree with her and with many other feminist and antiracist social scientists that research is, in itself, a social, and very often also a political relationship, which needs to be acknowledged and reflected upon. As researchers we, like any other people, have each our own social positionings, identities, and emotional attachments, as well as our own imaginaries and normative value systems. It is for this reason that, by engaging in our study of bordering, we have also engaged in what some of us call transversal politics.

Transversal politics (e.g. Cockburn and Hunter, 1999; Yuval-Davis, 1997, 2006) is a politics of solidarity across state borders and social boundaries. Unlike in identity politics, the participants in this dialogue are not seen as 'representatives' of their collectivities but rather as advocates, and there is recognition of the fact that people who share similar socioeconomic positionings and membership of particular collectivities can still differ widely in their identifications, in their social attachments, and in their normative value systems.

Transversal dialogues are supported by processes of rooting and shifting. 'Rooting' means that each participant in the dialogue is reflectively aware of his or her own positionings, including those that express relative power vis-à-vis the other participants in the dialogue, and of his or her own emotional attachments, identifications, and normative value systems. 'Shifting' means that each participant in the dialogue respects the others as being of equal value while they have different positionings. It also implies that everyone is listening, empathising, and trying to imagine the situation as experienced from the others' different standpoints.

Transversal dialogical epistemology, unlike the intersectional one, in which the more differentially the gazes are situated the better, is limited by normative values shared among the participants in dialogue across borders and boundaries. This is intended to develop a common understanding of what social and political change would be necessary to promote the normative and political goals of all the participants. Therefore transversal political dialogue benefits from being informed by situated intersectional dialogue but differs from it in its purpose. It is also important to emphasise that transversal dialogical understanding is a necessary but not a sufficient condition for political action. People and groupings that are differentially situated might have different priorities, given their particular social and political contexts. Transversal dialogical understanding guarantees solidarity, but not necessarily common action.

During our research on bordering we have worked transversally with many individuals and organisations with whom we share the same human rights and social justice approach to the question of bordering. The clearest example, however, of our transversal political work during our bordering research is the film we produced while working on it. It was made in collaboration with three different activist organisations that are working on different aspects of bordering issues in London: Southall Black Sisters (SBS), Migrants' Rights Network (MRN), and Refugee and Migrant Forum of Essex and London (RAMFEL). This collaboration was based on many years of close political cooperation during which we have developed a transversal understanding based on mutual trust and respect. One of the important common grounds we have developed while working with these and other similar organisations (such as the Runnymede Trust or Hackney Migrants Centre) is expressed very aptly by de Noronha (2016): 'we have to examine the relationship between race, class and immigration status ... we cannot understand racism in Britain without factoring in immigration control, nor understand immigration control without attending to issues of racism'.

Our close political solidarity and cooperation does not necessarily mean, of course, that all our 'transversal allies' would necessarily agree with our conclusion below. Nevertheless, we trust that they will understand why we reached it and will respect it.

Resisting everyday bordering

As 'public social scientists' (e.g. Burawoy, 2005; Clawson, 2007), we cannot end this book on bordering without addressing explicitly the most obvious question: If we are so critical of the ways everyday borderings are taking place now, what do we suggest as an alternative, and how should we go about getting there? As Stephen Castles (2004) suggests, migration policies fail because they often are poorly conceived, narrow, and contradictory, frequently accompanied by unintended consequences. However, similar pitfalls would also confront any of us in opposing them or calling for alternative approaches. As Saskia Sassen (2006) has pointed out, we are dealing here with foundational changes in complex systems, and such changes are always only partly legible. Hence interpretation becomes critical in the account of that change.

Given our analytical and situated intersectional approach, we would not be satisfied with any single interpretative account. Our methodological perspective demands a combined inter- and intra-categorical, situated, multiscalar, multilocal, and multitemporal intersectional study, which any single study can only aspire to but cannot achieve. Therefore we are not going to reduce our suggestions on the topic of bordering to simplistic, 'universal' solutions, nor are we going to treat bordering as one single issue. Different local, regional, global, and historical contexts might favour some political responses more than others, and the political priorities of some situated people and groups with whom we share transversal political alliances might differ.

It is for this reason that shared political values are necessary but not sufficient guides for coordinated political action. All we can do here is point to some of the normative signposts that we believe should direct various political activisms aimed at resisting the destructive effects of contemporary bordering, and emphasise that these signposts emanate from our overall arguments in this book. And, as Rita Chadha from RAMFEL has warned us in our film *Everyday Borders*, we should avoid working in 'silos' – tackling issues separately, in an uncon-nected and decontextualised way.

First, we do not believe that one can just do away with the consti-tutive role of bordering in local and global social, economic, and political structures and processes. We do not believe that a world *sans frontières* (as it appears in the visions of many organisations that oppose contemporary bordering regimes and technologies) would necessarily be a more just world. While we have shown in this book the many ways in which contemporary borderings reflect and magnify local and global inequalities and injustices, much of the intensification of these inequalities and injustices has been linked to deregulations of borders, especially in the Global South and especially around goods and services – but also in relation to displacing and moving large numbers of people locally, in the 'near abroad', and globally. Indeed, Bridget Anderson (2017) points out that 'migration' has come to signify 'problematic mobility', intensifying at a time of global impoverishment and lack of security.

We need to remember that human mobility concerns not only individual freedoms, but is closely related to political projects of governance and belonging as well as to the operation of neoliberal capitalism. Nett points out that the removal of borders might result in 'raw Darwinism' (Nett, 1971: 226; see also Salazar's contribution in Abrams et al., 2017). Moreover, if we include in our situated intersectional understanding the impact of bordering on the majority of 'stayers' rather than on the 'movers', the real – and the imagined – sense of safety that borderings provide cannot be dismissed out of hand, given the importance of this question in contemporary, especially autochthonic, political projects of belonging.

Moreover, when discussing individuals' right of free movement as an ethical political value, one cannot disconnect this right from other civil, political, and especially social rights. Only a minimalist liberal perspective that does not see governance institutions – local, national, or global – as responsible for the basic material needs of the people under their authority would consider free human mobility to be just about freedom of movement and not related to other citizenship rights. Such a perspective is not concerned with how and to what extent people can satisfy basic needs such as for food and shelter; it believes instead in the ultimate power of market forces of supply and demand to minimise extreme human suffering at the cost of unregu-lated human mobility – a perspective we definitely do not share.

It is for this reason that Shahram Khosravi, in a debate on this question that took place in the congress of the International

Anthropological Association (Abrams et al., 2017: 150), claims that the way to ensure free human mobility is not 'open borders' but 'no borders', the corollary of which is 'no homelands'. Only political projects of governance and belonging that ensure the provision of resources and rights to people all over the globe, rather than a Westphalian social order in which states act as mutually exclusive 'containers' of such resources and rights, can start to address this issue. Significantly, as some of the active participants in this debate have pointed out, the UN Human Declaration of Human Rights endorses the right of free movement within, but not between, sovereign nation-states, something that needs to be urgently addressed if we are to be able to tackle the extreme injustices linked with contemporary borderings in which the right of free movement is virtually guaranteed to the relatively few rich northerners but is limited and effectively denied to most of the others.

It is therefore clear that the way to combat these extreme injustices caused by bordering regimes is to work towards such global political projects in opposition to rather than in collusion with neoliberal globalisation. As we have pointed out in this book, together with many other bordering scholars and activists (e.g. Pécoud and De Guchteneire, 2007; see also Papastergiadis, 2000), fighting the economic and political policies that perpetuate inequality is one of our highest priorities, because such policies are often more important than migration policies in shaping migration. Neoliberal globalisation is not about universal human mobility but rather about the differential filtering of border crossing – about making borders invisible to the 'high flyers' but creating bordering limbospaces for many others, using bordering as a mechanism of controlling labour markets – legal and illegal, local and global. This same political economy has created the context of shrinking public resources and of growing privatisation of states. Local, regional, and global social movements have developed to oppose social injustices that emanated from the hegemony of neoliberal globalisation – NGOs such as Global South against Borders, Medicins sans Frontières, Helsinki Citizens Assembly, Avaaz, and many more. However, the entanglement of private and public finances and structures renders the feasibility of short-term defeat of the neoliberal global capitalist system, even in crisis, highly improbable at the moment.

So, while the task to organise against neoliberalism locally and globally should have high political priority, it cannot replace the need for struggles against the specific effects of contemporary borderings everywhere, every day. Such struggles should focus on the impact of bordering both on individual people's lives (and deaths), and on collective social and political convivialities and solidarities. They should be directed against both political projects of governance and political projects of belonging that sustain them.

In terms of political projects of governance, this means finding ways to push back bordering from the centre to the margins. It means changing everyday bordering legislations that, while explicitly aimed at creating a 'hostile environment' for 'illegal migrants', in practice create a hostile environment for everyone, transforming the notion of citizenship. It means including the grey zones into a realm inhabited by people with full civil, political, social, cultural, and economic rights.

Pushing bordering back should be done not by marginalising or denying people's mobility rights, since border crossing has become a central and very desirable feature of contemporary life. Rather it should be done by negotiating and struggling for bottom-up, dialogical political projects of governance and belonging. Since, as Parmar (2018) argues, contemporary borderings mirror existing racial and economic hierarchies that govern transnational mobility and dictate who has the right to belong, we must expose and challenge the prevailing neoliberal order and hierarchies of belonging.

In these struggles, discrimination and exclusion on the basis of gender, race, religion, origin, class, stage in the life cycle, immigration status, and other major intersectional axes of social inequality would not determine the filtering firewall effects of bordering. We, the authors of this book, as migrants or as members of migrant families and communities, with transnational homes and belonging, have a special interest in seeing such political and social changes taking place.

When dealing with political projects of belonging, it is especially important to tackle the topic of growing autochthonic political movements – both politically and by sustaining alternative imaginaries of society and community. We should see permeable and shifting boundaries as opportunities for growth rather than as inherently dangerous and unsafe things. We should not regard belonging as categorically and irreversibly ascribed status but understand it as a quality acquired via active participation. These are all ambitious aims, which can be achieved only by chipping away at the three fronts of neoliberalism, everyday bordering, and autochthonic politics. However, because in the concrete reality of our contemporary world all three are entangled and shaping each other, success in one area would make success in the other two just a little bit easier. The only way to keep fighting for social justice without getting burned out, even at dark times, to paraphrase Gramsci, is by keeping the pessimism of the intellect and the optimism of the will.

References

Abbott, D. 2016. 'Need to distract everyone from the NHS funding crisis? Blame foreigners'. *New Statesman*, 5 October 2016. https://www.newstatesman.com/politics/staggers/2016/10/need-distract-everyone-nhs-funding-crisis-blame-foreigners.

Abrams, S. B., Bianco, F., Khosravi, S., Salazar, N., and de Genova, N. 2017. 'The free movement of people around the world would be Utopian: IUAES World Congress 2013'. *Identities*, 24(2): 123–55.

Adesina, Z. and Brennan, C. 2017. 'Forged IDs: Landlord laws "fuelling black market"'. *BBC Inside Out*, 16 October 2017. http://www.bbc.co.uk/news/uk-england-london-41593684.

Afouxenidis, A., Petrou, M., Kandylis, G., Tramountanis, A., and Giannagi, D. 2017. 'Dealing with a humanitarian crisis: Refugees on the eastern EU border on the island of Lesvos'. *Journal of Applied Security Research*, 12(1): 7–39.

Agamben, G. 1995. 'We Refugees'. *Symposium*, 49(2): 114–19.

Agamben, G. 1998. *Homo sacer: Sovereign power and bare life*. Stanford, CA: Stanford University Press.

Against Borders for Children, 2016. 'We won! DfE are ending the nationality school census!' 10 April 2018. https://www.schoolsabc.net/2018/04/we-won.

Agier, M. 2011. *Managing the undesirables: Refugee camps and humanitarian government*. Cambridge: Polity.

Ahmed, S. 2014. *Cultural politics of emotion*. Edinburgh: Edinburgh University Press.

Akbari, S. C. 2009. *Idols in the East: European representations of Islam and the Orient, 1100–1450*. Ithaca, NY: Cornell University Press.

Akbari, S. C., Herzog, T., Jütte, D., Nightingale, C., Rankin, W., and Weitzberg, K. 2017. 'AHR conversation: Walls, borders, and boundaries in world history'. *American Historical Review*, 122(5.1): 1501–53.

Albert, M. 1998. 'On boundaries, territory and postmodernity: An international relations perspective'. *Geopolitics*, 3(1): 53–68.

Albert, M., Jacobson, D., and Lapid, Y. 2001. *Identities, borders, orders: Rethinking international relations theory*. Minneapolis: University of Minnesota Press.

Aldama, A. J., Sandoval, C., and García, P. J., eds. 2012. *Performing the US Latina and Latino borderlands*. Bloomington: Indiana University Press.

Aliverti, A. 2014. 'Enlisting the public in the policing of immigration'. *British Journal of Criminology*, 55(2): 215–30.

Al-Jazeera, 2011. 'Plea for "massive aid" for Africa refugees'. News Africa, 10 July. https://www.aljazeera.com/news/africa/2011/07/2011710112312872979.html.

Amilhat-Szary, A. L. and Giraut, F., eds. 2015. *Borderities and the politics of contemporary mobile borders*. London: Palgrave Macmillan.

Amoore, L. 2006. 'Biometric borders: Governing mobilities in the war on terror'. *Political Geography*, 25(3): 336–51.

Andreas, P. 2003. 'Redrawing the line: Borders and security in the twenty-first century'. *International Security*, 28(2): 78–111.

Anderson, Ben. 2016. 'Neoliberal affects'. *Progress in Human Geography*, 40(6): 734–53.

Anderson, Benedict. 1991 [1983]. *Imagined communities: Reflections on the origins and spread of nationalism*. London: Verso.

Anderson, Benedict. 1998. *The spectre of comparisons: Nationalism, Southeast Asia, and the world*. London: Verso.

Anderson, Bridget. 2013. *Us and them: The dangerous politics of immigration*. Oxford: Oxford University Press.

Anderson, Bridget. 2017. 'Toward a new politics of migration?'. *Ethnic and Racial Studies*, 40(9): 171–84.

Anderson, David. 2016. *The terrorism acts in 2015: Report of the independent reviewer on the operation of the Terrorism Act 2000 and Part 1 of the Terrorism Act 2006*. Richmond: HMSO.

Anderson, J., O'dowd, L., and Wilson, T. M. 2002. 'Introduction: Why study borders now?'. *Regional & Federal Studies*, 12(4): 1–12.

Anderson, M. and Bort, E. 2001. 'Theory'. In M. Anderson and E. Bort, *The Frontiers of the European Union* (pp. 13–44). Basingstoke: Palgrave Macmillan.

Andersson, R. 2014. 'Time and the migrant other: European border controls and the temporal economics of illegality'. *American Anthropologist*, 116(4): 795–809.

Andreas, P. 2003. 'Redrawing the line: Borders and security in the twenty-first century'. *International Security*, 28(2): 78–111.

Angeli, D., Dimitriadi, A., and Triandafyllidou, A. 2014. 'Assessing the cost-effectiveness of irregular migration control policies in Greece'. Midas Report, October, Open Society Foundation.

Anthias, F. 2012. 'Transnational mobilities, migration research and intersectionality'. *Nordic Journal of Migration Research*, 2(2): 102–10.

Anthias, F. and Yuval-Davis, N. 1983. 'Contextualizing feminism: Gender, ethnic and class divisions'. *Feminist Review*, 15: 62–75.

Antonsich, M. 2010. 'Searching for belonging: An analytical framework'. *Geography Compass*, 4(6): 644–59.

Anzaldúa, G. 1987. *Borderlands: La frontera*, vol. 3. San Francisco, CA: Aunt Lute.

Arendt, H. 1943. 'We refugees'. *Menorah Journal*, 31(1): 69–77.

Arendt, H. 1973. *The origins of totalitarianism*. Orlando: Houghton Mifflin Harcourt.

176

Arton Capital. 2017. https://www.artoncapital.com/investors/?gclid=EAIaIQob
ChMIuqmOxvGU3wIVAyUrCh3mdwFwEAAYASAAEgL1D_D_BwE.

Aslund, A. 1992. *Post-communist economic revolutions: How big a bang?*
Washington, DC: Center for Strategic and International Studies.

Atkinson, R., Burrows, R., Glucksberg, L., Ho, H. K., Knowles, C., and Rhodes,
D. 2017. 'Minimum city? The deeper impacts of the "super-rich" on urban
life'. In R. Forrest, S. Koh, and B. Wissink, eds, *Cities and the super-rich* (pp.
253–71). New York: Palgrave Macmillan.

Aure, M. 2011. 'Borders of understanding: Re-making frontiers in the Russian–
Norwegian contact zone'. *Ethnopolitics*, 10(2): 171–86.

Avni, N., and Yiftachel, O. 2013. 'The new divided city? Planning and 'gray
space' between global north-west and south-east'. In S. Parnell and S. Oldfield,
eds, *The Routledge Handbook on Cities of the Global South* (pp. 487–505).
London: Routledge.

van Baar, H. 2017. 'Contained mobility and the racialization of poverty in
Europe: The Roma at the development–security nexus'. *Social Identities*,
24(4): 442–58.

Back, L. 2015. 'Why everyday life matters: Class, community and making life
livable'. *Sociology*, 49(5): 820–36.

Back, L. and Sinha, S. 2018. *Migrant city*. London: Routledge.

Bakewell, O. 2008. 'Research beyond the categories: The importance of policy
irrelevant research into forced migration'. *Journal of Refugee Studies*, 21(4):
432–53.

Balachandran, G. 2012. *Globalizing labour? Indian seafarers and world shipping,
c. 1870–1945*. New Delhi: Oxford University Press.

Baldwin, M. P. 2001. 'Subject to empire: Married women and the British
Nationality and Status of Aliens Act'. *Journal of British Studies*, 40(4): 522–56.

Balibar, É. 1991. '*Es gibt keinen Staat in Europa*: Racism and politics in Europe
today'. *New Left Review*, 186: 5–19.

Balibar, É. 2004. *We, the people of Europe? Reflections on transnational
citizenship*. Princeton, NJ: Princeton University Press.

Barfield, T. L. 2001. 'The shadow empires: Imperial state formation along the
Chinese–Nomad frontier'. In S. E. Alcock, T. N. D. Altroy, K. D. Morrison,
and C. M. Sinopoli, eds, *Empires: Perspectives from archaeology and history*
(pp. 10–41). Cambridge: Cambridge University Press.

Barkin, J. S. and Cronin, B. 1994. 'The state and the nation: Changing norms
and rules of sovereignty in international relations'. *International Organization*,
48(1): 107–30.

Barth, F. 1998. *Ethnic groups and boundaries: The social organization of culture
difference*. Long Grove, IL: Waveland Press.

Batchelor, C. A. 1998. 'Statelessness and the problem of resolving nationality
status'. *International Journal of Refugee Law*, 10(1–2): 156–72.

Bauböck, R. 2006. *Migration and citizenship: Legal status, rights and political
participation*. Amsterdam: Amsterdam University Press.

Baud, M. and van Schendel, W. 1997. 'Toward a comparative history of borderlands'. *Journal of World History*, 8(2): 211–42.

Bauman, Z. 2000. 'Time and space reunited'. *Time & Society*, 9(2–3): 171–85.

Bauman, Z. 2004. *Wasted lives: Modernity and its outcasts*. Cambridge: Polity.

BBC News. 2017. 'Volunteers could guard some UK borders, Home Office says'.
31 October. http://www.bbc.co.uk/news/uk-42527750.

BBC One. 2014. 'The one show'. 24 November. https://www.bbc.co.uk/programmes/b04ptzvb.

Beck, U. 2007. 'The cosmopolitan condition: Why methodological nationalism fails'. *Theory, Culture & Society*, 24(7–8): 286–90.

Beck, U. and Sznaider, N. 2010. 'Unpacking cosmopolitanism for the social sciences: A research agenda'. *British Journal of Sociology*, 61: 381–403.

Belger, T. 2017. 'Newlyweds heartbroken after US wife denied visa by "cruel" loophole'. *Liverpool Echo*, 5 August. http://www.liverpoolecho.co.uk/news/liverpool-news/newlyweds-heartbroken-after-wife-denied-13436705#ICID=sharebar_twitter.

Bell, B. and Machin, S. 2013. 'Immigrant enclaves and crime'. *Journal of Regional Science*, 53: 118–41.

Bello, W. F., Cunningham, S., and Rau, B. 1994. *Dark victory: The United States, structural adjustment, and global poverty*. London: Pluto.

Beyer, P. 1994. *Religion and globalization*. London: SAGE.

Bhabha, H. 2015 [1994]. *Debating cultural hybridity: Multicultural identities and the politics of anti-racism*. London: Zed Books.

Bhambra, G. 2016. 'Brexit, the Commonwealth, and exclusionary citizenship'. Open Democracy, 8 December. https://www.opendemocracy.net/gurminder-k-bhambra/brexit-commonwealth-and-exclusionary-citizenship.

Bhatt, C. 2007. 'Frontlines and interstices in the global war on terror'. *Development and change*, 38(6): 1073–93.

Bichler, S. and Nitzan, J. 2017. 'Oil and blood in the Orient'. Research note. https://www.econstor.eu/bitstream/10419/172198/1/20171200_bn_blood_and_oil_in_the_orient_redux.pdf.

Bickell, B. 2016. 'Government must encourage Chinese tourists to put UK on their itinerary'. *The Telegraph*, 3 September. http://www.telegraph.co.uk/business/2016/09/03/government-must-encourage-chinese-tourists-to-put-uk-on-their-it.

Bigo, D. 2001. 'The Möbius ribbon of internal and external security (ies)'. *Identities, borders, orders: Rethinking international relations theory*, 18: 91–116.

Billig, M. 1995. *Banal nationalism*. London: SAGE.

Blakkisrud, H. and Kolstø, P. 2011. 'From secessionist conflict towards functioning state: Processes of state- and nation-building in Transnistria'. *Post-Soviet Affairs*, 27(2): 178–210.

Blinder, 2017. 'Migration to the UK: Asylum'. The Migration Observatory, 26 October. http://www.migrationobservatory.ox.ac.uk/resources/briefings/migration-to-the-uk-asylum.

Bloch, A., Kumarappan, L., and McKay, S. 2015. 'Employer sanctions: The impact of workplace raids and fines on undocumented migrants and ethnic enclave employers'. *Critical Social Policy*, 35(1): 132–51.

Bloch, A. and McKay, S. 2015. 'Employment, social networks and undocumented migrants: The employer perspective'. *Sociology*, 49(1): 38–55.

Bloch, A. and McKay, S. 2016. *Living on the margins: Undocumented migrants in a global city*. Bristol: Policy Press.

Bloch, A. and Schister, L. 2005. 'At the extremes of exclusion: Deportation, detention and dispersal'. *Ethnic and Racial Studies*, 28(3): 491–512.

Block, D. 2004. Globalization, transnational communication and the Internet. *International Journal on Multicultural Societies*, 6(1): 13–28.

Blunt, A. 2005. 'Cultural geography: Cultural geographies of home'. *Progress in Human Geography*, 29(4): 505–15.

Bolt, D. 2016. 'Inspection report on Border Force operations at east coast seaports. July to November 2016: Presented to Parliament pursuant to Section 50 (2) of the UK Borders Act 2007'. OGL. https://www.gov.uk/government/uploads/system/uploads/attachment_data/file/631668/An-inspection-of-Border-Force-operations-at-east-coast-seaports.pdf

Border Force. 2013. 'Children travelling to the UK'. Information leaflet, July 2013. https://www.gov.uk/government/publications/children-travelling-to-the-uk.

Border security: Canada front line, series 1–3. 2012–14. Vancouver: Force Four Entertainment. TV show. http://www.imdb.com/title/tt2518480.

Bousfield, D. 2005. 'The logic of sovereignty and the agency of the refugee: Recovering the political from "Bare Life"'. YCISS Working Paper No. 36. Toronto: York University.

Bowen, J. T. 2008. 'Moving places: The geography of warehousing in the US'. *Journal of Transport Geography*, 16: 379–87.

Bowen, J. T. 2012. 'A spatial analysis of FedEx and UPS: Hubs, spokes, and network structure'. *Journal of Transport Geography*, 24: 419–31.

Bowling, B. and Phillips, C. 2003. 'Policing ethnic minority communities'. LSE. http://eprints.lse.ac.uk/9576.

Bradshaw M. and Stenning, A. C. 2004. 'Introduction'. In M. Bradshaw and A. Stenning, eds, *East Central Europe and the former Soviet Union: The post-socialist states* (pp. 1–32). Harlow: Pearson Education.

Brah, A. and Phoenix, A. 2004. 'Ain't I a woman? Revisiting intersectionality'. *Journal of International Women's Studies*, 5(3): 75–86.

Brambilla, C. 2010. 'Borders still exist! What are borders?' In B. Riccio and C. Brahmbilla, eds, *Transnational migration, cosmopolitanism and dis-loated borders* (pp. 73–86). Rimini: Guaraldi.

Brambilla, C. 2014. 'Shifting Italy/Libya borderscapes at the interface of EU/Africa borderland: A "genealogical" outlook from the colonial era to post-colonial scenarios'. *ACME: An International Journal for Critical Geographies*, 13(2): 220–45.

Brambilla, C. 2015. 'Exploring the critical potential of the borderscapes concept'. *Geopolitics*, 20(1): 14–34.

Brambilla, C., Laine, J., Scott. J. W., and Bocchi, G., eds. 2015. *Borderscaping: Imaginations and practices of border making*. Aldershot: Ashgate.

Braun, G. 1996. 'Les Traductions françaises des traités de Westphalie de 1648 à la fin de l'Ancien Régime'. *XVIIe Siècle*, 190: 131–55.

Brenner, N. 1998. 'Global cities, glocal states: Global city formation and state territorial restructuring in contemporary Europe'. *Review of International Political Economy*, 5(1): 1–37.

Brenner, N. 1999. 'Globalisation as reterritorialisation: The re-scaling of urban governance in the European Union'. *Urban Studies*, 36(3): 431–51.

Brenner, N. and Theodore, N. 2002. 'Cities and the geographies of "actually existing neoliberalism"'. *Antipode*, 34(3): 349–79.

Broeders, D. 2007. 'The new digital borders of Europe: EU databases and the surveillance of irregular migrants'. *International sociology*, 22(1): 71–92.

Brooks, R. and Waters, J. 2011. *Student mobilities: Migration and the internationalization of higher education*. Basingstoke: Palgrave.

Brooks, R. and Waters, J. 2015. 'The hidden internationalism of elite English schools'. *Sociology*, 49(2): 212–28.

Brown, W. 2009. *Regulating aversion: Tolerance in the age of identity and empire*. Princeton, NJ: Princeton University Press.

Brown, W. 2015. *Undoing the demos: Neoliberalism's stealth revolution*. Brooklyn, NY: Zone Books.

Brunet-Jailly, E. 2012. 'Securing borders in Europe and North America', in T. M. Wilson and H. Donnan, eds, *Companion to Border Studies* (pp. 100–18). Oxford: Wiley Blackwell.

Bryan, B., Dadzie, S., and Scafe, S. 1985. *The heart of the race: Black women's lives in Britain*. London: Virago.

Bürkner. H. J. 2018. 'Imaginaries ready for use: Framings of the bordered intersectionalised everyday provided by the EU's sectoral policies', *Political Geography*, 66: 189–98.

Büscher, M. and Urry, J. 2009. 'Mobile methods and the empirical'. *European Journal of Social Theory*, 12(1): 99–116.

Bullough, O. 2018. 'The real Goldfinger: The London banker who broke the world'. *Guardian*, 7 September. https://www.theguardian.com/news/2018/sep/07/the-real-goldfinger-the-london-banker-who-broke-the-world.

Bulmer, S. 2014. 'Germany and the Eurozone crisis: Between hegemony and domestic politics'. *West European Politics*, 37(6): 1244–63.

Bunyan, T. 1991. 'Towards an authoritarian European state'. *Race and Class*, 32(3): 19–30.

Burawoy, M. 2005. 'For public sociology'. *American Sociological Review*, 70(1): 4–28.

Burikova, Z. and Miller, D. 2010. *Au pair*. Cambridge: Polity.

Burns, R. I. 1995. 'The *guidaticum* safe-conduct in medieval Arago-Catalonia: A mini-institution for Muslims, Christians and Jews'. *Medieval Encounters*, 1(1): 51–113.

Burrows, Roger, 2013. 'The new gilded ghettos: The geodemographics of the super-rich'. Discover Society. http://discoversociety.org/2013/12/03/the-new-gilded-ghettos-the-geodemographics-of-the-super-rich.

Bush, George W. 2002. State of the Union Address. https://georgewbush-white-house.archives.gov/news/releases/2002/01/20020129-11.html.

Calhoun, C. 2003a. 'Belonging' in the cosmopolitan imaginary. *Ethnicities*, 3(4): 531–53.

Calhoun, C. 2003b. 'The elusive cosmopolitan ideal'. *Berkeley Journal of Sociology*, 47: 3–26.

Capps, R., Marc, R. Rosenblum, C. R., and Chishti, M. A. 2011. *Delegation and divergence: A study of 287(G) state and local immigration enforcement*. Washington, DC: Migration Policy Institute.

Carruthers, S. L. 2005. 'Between camps: Eastern bloc "escapees" and Cold War borderlands'. *American Quarterly*, 57(3): 911–42.

Carter, B. and Fenton, S. 2010. 'Not thinking ethnicity: A critique of the ethnicity paradigm in an over-ethnicised sociology'. *Journal for the Theory of Social Behaviour*, 40(1): 1–18.

Casas-Cortes, C., Cobarrubias, S., and Pickles, J. 2013. 'Re-bordering the neighbourhood: Europe's emerging geographies of non-accession integration'. *European Urban and Regional Studies*, 20(1): 37–58.

Cassidy, K. L. 2013. 'Gender relations and cross-border small trading in the

Ukrainian–Romanian borderlands'. *European Urban and Regional Studies*, 20(1): 91–108.

Cassidy, K. 2017. 'Border crossings, shame and (re)narrating the past in the Ukrainian-Romanian Borderlands'. In H. Donnan, M. Hurd, and C. Leutloff-Grandits, eds, *Migrating borders and moving times: Temporality and the crossing of borders in Europe* (pp. 58–79). Manchester: Manchester University Press.

Cassidy, K., Yuval-Davis, N., and Wemyss, G. 2018a. 'Debordering and everyday (re) bordering in and of Dover: Post-borderland borderscapes'. *Political Geography*, 66: 171–9.

Cassidy, K., Yuval-Davis, N., and Wemyss, G. 2018b. 'Intersectional Border(ing)s'. *Political Geography*, 66: 139–41.

Castells, M. 2000. Materials for an exploratory theory of the network society1. *British Journal of Sociology*, 51(1): 5–24.

Castles, S. 2004. 'Why migration policies fail'. *Ethnic and Racial Studies*, 27(2): 205–27.

Castles, S., De Haas, H., and Miller, M. J. 2014. *The age of migration: International population movements in the modern world*. Basingstoke: Palgrave Macmillan.

Certeau, M. de. 1984 [1980]. *The practice of everyday life*. Berkeley: University of California Press.

Ceuppens, B. and Geschiere, P. 2005. 'Autochthony: Local or global? New modes in the struggle over citizenship and belonging in Africa and Europe'. *Annual Review of Anthropology*, 34: 385–407.

Chakrabarty, D. 2000. 'Witness to suffering: Domestic cruelty and the birth of the modern subject in Bengal'. In T. Mitchell, ed., *Questions of modernity* (pp. 49–86). Minneapolis: University of Minnesota Press.

Channel 5. 2014. 'The sham wedding crashers'. Episode 4 of *Black market Britain undercover sting*. 30 October 2014.

Charsley, K. 2012. 'Transnational marriage'. In K. Charsley, ed., *Transnational marriage: New perspectives from Europe and beyond* (pp. 3–22). London: Routledge.

Charsley, K. and Benson, M. C. 2012. 'Marriages of convenience or inconvenient marriages: Regulating spousal migration to Britain'. *Journal of Immigration, Asylum and Nationality Law*, 26(1): 10–26.

Chatterjee, P. 1993. *The nation and its fragments: Colonial and postcolonial histories*. Princeton, NJ: Princeton University Press.

Chauvin, P., Simonnot, N., Douay, C., and Vanbiervliet, F. 2015. 'Access to healthcare for the most vulnerable in a Europe in social crisis'. Doctors of the World/Médecins du Monde International Network Position Paper. https://www.hal.inserm.fr/inserm-00992172/document.

Chrisafis, A. 2011. 'Marine Le Pen emerges from father's shadow'. *Guardian*, 22 March. https://www.theguardian.com/world/2011/mar/21/marine-lepen-defends-republic.

Claessens, S. and Kodres, L. 2014. 'The regulatory responses to the global financial crisis: Some uncomfortable questions'. IMF Working Paper 14/46. Washington, DC: International Monetary Fund.

Clarke, M. 2016. *Planes, passports and porkie pies, slice one: Stirring tales of UK border control (but not as shown on TV)*. Kibworth Beauchamp, UK: Matador.

181

Clawson, D., ed. 2007. *Public sociology: Fifteen eminent sociologists debate politics and the profession in the twenty-first century*. Berkeley: University of California Press.

Clayton, G. 2010. 'The UK and extraterritorial control: Entry clearance and juxtaposed controls'. In B. Ryan and V. Mitsilegas, *Extraterritorial control: Legal challenges* (pp. 397–430). Leiden: Martinus Nijhoff.

Cockburn, C. and Hunter, L. 1999. 'Transversal politics and translating practices', *Soundings* (Special issue: *Transversal Politics*), *12*: 89–93.

Cohen, R. 1991. 'Citizens, denizens and helots: The politics of international migration flows in the post-war world'. In R. Cohen, ed., *Contested domains: Debates in international labour studies* (pp. 151–80). London: Zed Books.

Coleman, M. 2012. 'From border policing to internal controls in the United States'. In H. Donnan and T. Wilson, eds, *The companion to border studies* (pp. 419–37). Oxford: Wiley Blackwell.

Collett, E. 2016. 'The paradox of the EU–Turkey refugee deal'. Migration Policy Institute, March. https://www.migrationpolicy.org/news/paradox-eu-turkey-refugee-deal.

Collins, P. H. 1990. *Black feminist thought, consciousness and the politics of empowerment*. London: Harper Collins.

Collins, P. H. and Bilge, S. 2016. *Intersectionality*. Cambridge: Polity.

Collinson, P. 2017. 'Half of landlords in one London borough fail to declare rental income'. *Guardian*, 13 August. https://www.theguardian.com/business/2017/aug/13/half-of-landlords-in-one-london-borough-fail-to-declare-rental-income.

Comaroff, J. and Comaroff, J. L. eds. 2001. *Millennial capitalism and the culture of neoliberalism*. Durham, NC: Duke University Press.

Conlon, D. 2011. 'Waiting: Feminist perspectives on the spacings/timings of migrant (im)mobility'. *Gender, Place and Culture*, *18*(3): 353–60.

Cons, J. 2016. *Sensitive space: Fragmented territory at the India–Bangladesh border*. Seattle: University of Washington Press.

Cooper, A., Perkins, C., and Rumford, C. 2014. 'The vernacularization of borders'. In R. Jones and C. Johnson, eds, *Placing the border in everyday life* (pp. 15–32). Farnham, UK: Ashgate.

Cooper, A. and Rumford, C. 2011. *Cosmopolitan borders: Bordering as connectivity*. Farnham: Ashgate.

Cooper, F. and Stoler, A. L., eds. 1997. *Tensions of empire: Colonial cultures in a bourgeois world*. Berkeley: University of California Press.

Corporate Watch. 2016. 'Byron Burgers sending millions to owners offshore while workers are deported'. https://corporatewatch.org/byron-burgers-sending-millions-to-owners-offshore-while-workers-are-deported.

Corporate Watch. 2017. 'The round-up: Rough sleeper immigration raids and charity collaboration'. https://corporatewatch.org/the-round-up-rough-sleeper-immigration-raids-and-charity-collaboration-2.

Cowden, S. and Sahgal, G. 2017. 'Why fundamentalism'. *Feminist Dissent*, *2*: 7–38.

Craig, G. 2010. *Child slavery now: A contemporary reader*. Policy Press: Portland.

Crenshaw, K. 1989. 'Demarginalizing the intersection of race and sex: A black feminist critique of antidiscrimination doctrine, feminist theory and antiracist politics'. University of Chicago Legal Forum. https://chicagounbound.uchicago.edu/uclf/vol1989/iss1/8.

182

Crotty, J. 2009. 'Structural causes of the global financial crisis: A critical assessment of the "new financial architecture"'. *Cambridge Journal of Economics*, *33*: 563–80.

Croxton, D. 1999. 'The Peace of Westphalia of 1648 and the origins of sovereignty'. *International History Review*, *21*(3): 569–91.

Czaika, M. and Neumayer, E. 2017. 'Visa restriction and economic globalisation'. *Applied Geography*, *84*: 75–82.

D'Aoust, A. M. 2013. 'In the name of love: Marriage migration, governmentality, and technologies of love'. *International Political Sociology*, *7*(3): 258–74.

D'Aoust, A. M. 2017. 'A moral economy of suspicion: Love and marriage migration management practices in the United Kingdom'. *Environment and Planning D: Society and Space*, *36*(1): 40–59. doi: 10.1177/0263775817716674.

Darling, J. 2011. 'Domopolitics, governmentality and the regulation of asylum accommodation'. *Political Geography*, *30*(5): 263–71.

Darling, J, 2016a. 'Asylum in austere times: Instability, privatization and experimentation within the UK asylum dispersal system'. *Journal of Refugee Studies*, *29*(4): 483–505.

Darling, J. 2016b. 'Privatising asylum: Neoliberalisation, depoliticisation and the governance of forced migration'. *Transactions of the Institute of British Geographers*, *41*(3): 230–43.

Datta, S. 2017. 'The end of privacy: Aadhaar is being converted into the world's biggest surveillance engine'. Scroll.in, 24 March. https://scroll.in/article/832592/the-end-of-privacy-aadhaar-is-being-converted-into-the-worlds-biggest-surveillance-engine.

Datta-Ray, S. K. 2016. 'Far too many others: Brexit has led to a baleful focus on non-EU immigrants'. *Telegraph India*, 13 August. https://www.telegraphindia.com/opinion/far-too-many-others/cid/1452120.

Davis, G. and Guma, G. 1992. *Passport to freedom: A guide to world citizenship*. Washington, DC: Seven Locks Press.

DCLG = Department for Communities and Local Government. 2016. *English Housing Survey Private Rented Sector Report, 2014–15*. https://www.gov.uk/government/uploads/system/uploads/attachment_data/file/570848/Private_Rented_Sector_Full_Report.pdf.

Deardon, L. 2017. 'Bangladesh is now the single biggest country of origin for refugees on boats as new route to Europe'. *Independent*, 5 May. https://www.independent.co.uk/news/world/europe/refugee-crisis-migrants-bangladesh-libya-italy-numbers-smuggling-dhaka-dubai-turkey-detained-a7713911.html.

Delanty, G. 2006. 'Borders in a changing Europe: Dynamics of openness and closure'. *Comparative European Politics*, *4*(2–3): 183–202.

Deloitte. 2013. *Tourism, jobs and growth: The economic contribution of the tourist economy in the UK*. Oxford Economics. https://www.visitbritain.org/sites/default/files/vb-corporate/Documents-Library/documents/Tourism_Jobs_and_Growth_2013.pdf.

Department for Transport. 2013. 'Transport Statistics Great Britain: 2013'. 12 December. https://assets.publishing.service.gov.uk/government/uploads/system/uploads/attachment_data/file/264679/tsgb-2013.pdf.

Department for Transport. 2017. 'Transport Statistics Great Britain: 2017'. 23 November. https://assets.publishing.service.gov.uk/government/uploads/system/uploads/attachment_data/file/664323/tsgb-2017-print-ready-version.pdf.

Derrida, J. 1997. *Deconstruction in a nutshell: A conversation with Jacques Derrida*. New York: Fordham University Press.

DeVerteuil, G., May, J., and von Mahs, J. 2009. 'Complexity not collapse: Recasting the geographies of homelessness in a "punitive" age'. *Progress in Human Geography*, 33(5): 646–66.

DfE = Department for Education. 2017. *School census, 2016 to 2017: Guide, version 1.6*. April 2017. https://www.gov.uk/government/uploads/system/uploads/attachment_data/file/609375/School_census_2016_to_2017_guide_v1_6.pdf.

Dicken, P. 1992. 'International production in a volatile regulatory environment: The influence of national regulatory policies on the spatial strategies of transnational corporations'. *Geoforum*, 23(3): 303–16.

Dicken, P. 2003. *Global shift: Reshaping the global economic map in the 21st century*. London: SAGE.

Dinan, D. 2004. *Europe recast: A history of European Union*. Basingstoke: Palgrave Macmillan.

Doevenspeck, M. 2011. 'Constructing the border from below: Narratives from the Congolese-Rwandan state boundary'. *Political Geography*, 30(3): 129–42.

Dona, G. 2015. 'Making homes in limbo: Embodied virtual "homes" in prolonged conditions of displacement'. *Refuge: Canada's Journal on Refugees*, 31(1): 67–73.

Donnan, H. and Wilson, T. M. 1999. *Borders: Frontiers of identity, nation and state*. Oxford: Berg.

Dover District Council. 2015. 'State of the district, 2015. Chapter F: Economy, business and employment'. https://www.dover.gov.uk/Corporate-Information/Facts-and-Figures/PDF/SOTD-Chapter-F-Economy-Business-and-Employment.pdf.

Dugan, E. 2017. 'This woman always thought she was British: Now, after 30 years, the Home Office says she's not'. Buzzfeed, 8 July. https://www.buzzfeed.com/emilydugan/this-woman-always-thought-she-was-british-now-after-30?utm_term=.qs3RY24GP#.aarkK4dqQ.

Dugard, J. 1980. 'South Africa's independent homelands: An exercise in denationalization'. *Denver Journal of International Law and Policy, 10*: 11–36.

Dummett, A. and Nicol, A. 1990. *Subjects, citizens, aliens and others: Nationality and immigration law*. London: Weidenfeld & Nicholson.

Dunaway, W. 1996. *The first American frontier: Transition to capitalism in southern Appalachia, 1700–1860*. Chapel Hill: University of North Carolina Press.

Dundon-Smith, D. M. and Gibb, R. A. 1994. 'The Channel Tunnel and regional economic development'. *Journal of Transport Geography*, 2(3): 178–89.

Dzenovska, D. 2017. '"We want to hear from you": Reporting as bordering in the political space of Europe'. In N. de Genova, ed., *The borders of "Europe": Autonomy of migration, tactics of bordering* (pp. 283–98). London: Duke University Press.

Eatwell, R. 2011. *Fascism: A history*. London: Pimlico.

Economist. 2009. 'Greed and fear'. *Economist*, 22 January. https://www.economist.com/special-report/2009/01/22/greed-and-fear

Edenborg, E. 2016. 'Nothing more to see: Contestations of belonging and visibility in Russian media'. PhD thesis, Lund University and Malmo University.

Edensor, T. 2007. 'Mundane mobilities, performances and spaces of tourism'. *Social & Cultural Geography*, 8(2): 199–215.

Edkins, J. 2000. 'Sovereign power, zones of indistinction, and the camp'. *Alternatives*, 25(1): 3–25.

Eilenberg, Michael 2012. *At the edges of the state: Dynamics of state formation in the Indonesian borderlands*. Leiden: KITLV Press.

Elden, S. 2009. *Terror and territory: The spatial extent of sovereignty*. Minneapolis: University of Minnesota Press.

Elgot, J. 2017. 'MP stopped at border over daughter's name urges passport reform'. *Guardian*, 6 September. https://www.theguardian.com/uk-news/2017/sep/06/mp-stopped-at-border-over-daughters-name-urges-passports-reform.

Elias, N. and Scotson, J. L. 1965. *The established and the outsider: A sociological enquiry into community problems*. London: Cass.

Engbersen, G. 2012. 'Migration transitions in an era of liquid migration'. In M. Okolski, ed., *European Immigrations: Trends, Structures and Policy Implications* (pp. 91–105). Amsterdam: Amsterdam University Press.

Esping-Andersen, G. 1990. *The three worlds of welfare capitalism*. Princeton, NJ: Princeton University Press.

European Commission. 2017. 'Managing the refugee crisis: The facility for refugees in Turkey'. https://ec.europa.eu/home-affairs/sites/homeaffairs/files/what-we-do/policies/european-agenda-migration/background-information/docs/20160713/factsheet_managing_the_refugee_crisis_the_facility_for_refugees_in_turkey_en.pdf

Fassin, D. 2005. 'Compassion and repression: The moral economy of immigration policies in France'. *Cultural Anthropology*, 20(3): 362–87.

Fassin, D. 2009. 'Les Économies morales revisitées'. *Annales: Histoire, Sciences Sociales*, 6: 1237–66.

Fassin, D. 2013. *Enforcing order: An ethnography of urban policing*. Cambridge: Polity.

Fassin, D., ed. 2015. *At the heart of the state: The moral world of institutions*. London: Pluto.

Fayman, S., Metge, P., Spiekermann, K., Wegener, M., Flowerdew, T., and Williams, I. 1995. 'The regional impact of the Channel Tunnel: Qualitative and quantitative analysis'. *European Planning Studies*, 3(3): 333–56.

Featherstone, M. 1992. 'The heroic life and everyday life'. *Theory, Culture & Society*, 9(1): 159–82.

Fekete, L. 2009. *A suitable enemy: Racism, migration and Islamophobia in Europe*. London: Pluto.

Feldman, R. 2018. *What price safe motherhood? Charging for NHS maternity care in England and its impact on migrant women*. Maternity Action. https://www.maternityaction.org.uk/wp-content/uploads/WhatPriceSafeMotherhoodFINAL.pdf.

Fenster, T. 2004. 'Belonging, memory and the politics of planning in Israel'. *Social & Cultural Geography*, 5(3): 403–17.

Fisher, M. 2004. *Counterflows to colonialism: Indian travellers and settlers in Britain, 1600–1857*. Delhi: Permanent Black.

Fitzi, G., Mackert, J., and Turner, B. 2018. *Populism and the crisis of democracy*. London: Routledge.

Flores, E. 2017. 'Walls of separation: An analysis of three "successful" border walls'. *Harvard International Review*, 27 July. http://hir.harvard.edu/article/?a=14542.

Foucault, M. 2007. *Security, territory, population: Lectures at the College de France, 1977–1978*, trans. Graham Burchell. Basingstoke: Palgrave Macmillan.

Foucher, M. 1998. 'The geopolitics of European frontiers'. In M. Anderson and E. Bort, eds, *The Frontiers of Europe* (pp. 235–50). London: Pinter.

Fraser, N. 2017. 'The end of progressive neoliberalism'. *Dissent*, 2. https://www.dissentmagazine.org/online_articles/progressive-neoliberalism-reactionary-populism-nancy-fraser.

Frederiksen, M. D. and Knudsen, I. H. 2015. 'Introduction: What is a grey zone and why is Eastern Europe one?' In I. H. Knudsen and M. D. Frederiksen, eds, *Ethnographies of grey zones in Eastern Europe* (pp. 1–22). London: Anthem Press.

Friedman, J. 1995. 'Global system, globalisation and the parameters of modernity'. In M. Featherstone, S. Lash, and R. Robertson, eds, *Global modernities* (pp. 69–90). London: SAGE.

Fryer, P. 1984. *Staying power: The history of black people in Britain*. Chicago, IL: University of Alberta.

Fukuyama, F. 1992. *The end of history and the last man*. New York: Macmillan.

Furlong, R. 2008. 'EU migrants relocating to the UK'. BBC online, 26 March. http://news.bbc.co.uk/1/hi/uk/7312814.stm.

Gammeltoft-Hansen, T. 2011. *Access to asylum: International refugee law and the globalization of migration control*. Cambridge: Cambridge University Press.

Garcelon, M. 2001. 'Colonizing the subject: The genealogy and legacy of the Soviet internal passport'. In J. Caplan and J. Torpey, eds, *Documenting Individual Identity* (pp. 83–100). Princeton, NJ: Princeton University Press.

García, M. C. 2006. *Seeking refuge: Central American migration to Mexico, the United States, and Canada*. Berkeley: University of California Press.

Gayle, D. 2016. 'Pupil data shared with Home Office to "create hostile environment" for illegal migrants'. *Guardian*, 15 December. https://www.theguardian.com/uk-news/2016/dec/15/pupil-data-shared-with-home-office-to-identify-illegal-migrants.

Gayle, D. 2017. 'Ex-NHS chief backs doctors' warning over ID checks on patients'. *Guardian* online. https://amp.theguardian.com/society/2017/oct/11/ex-nhs-chief-backs-doctors-warning-id-checks-patients.

Geddes, A. and Scholten, P. 2016. *The politics of migration and immigration in Europe*. London: SAGE.

Genova, N. de. 2012. 'Border, scene and obscene'. In T. M. Wilson and H. Donnan, eds, *A Companion to Border Studies* (pp. 492–504). Oxford: Wiley Blackwell.

Genova, N. de. 2013. 'Spectacles of migrant "illegality": The scene of exclusion, the obscene of inclusion'. *Ethnic and Racial Studies*, 36(7): 1180–98.

Genova, N. de, ed. 2017. *The borders of 'Europe': Autonomy of migration, tactics of bordering*. Durham, NC: Duke University Press.

Gentleman, A. 2018. 'Trafficked, beaten, enslaved: The life of a Vietnamese cannabis farmer'. *Guardian*, 31 January 2018. https://www.theguardian.com/world/2018/jan/31/trafficked-beaten-ensaved-life-of-cannabis-farmer-vietnam.

Geschiere, P. 2009. *The perils of belonging: Autochthony, citizenship, and exclusion in Africa and Europe*. Chicago, IL: University of Chicago Press.

Giddens, A. 1985. *The nation-state and violence: Volume two of A contemporary critique of historical materialism*. Berkeley: University of California Press.

Giddens, A. 1998. *The third way*. Cambridge: Polity.

Gill, N. 2009. 'Presentational state power: Temporal and spatial influences over asylum sector decision makers'. *Transactions of the Institute of British Geographers*, 34(2): 215–33.

Gill, P. 2017. *Democracy, law and security: Internal security services in contemporary Europe*. London: Routledge.

Gilroy, P. 2004. *After empire: Multiculture or postcolonial melancholia*. Abingdon: Routledge.

Godin, M., Moller Hamsen, K., Lounasmaa, A., Squire, C., and Zaman, T., eds. 2017. *Voices from the 'Jungle': Stories from the Calais refugee camp*. London: Pluto.

Gonzales, R. G. and Sigona, N. 2017. 'Mapping the soft borders of citizenship'. In R. G. Gonzales and N. Sigona, eds, *Within and beyond citizenship: Borders, membership and belonging* (pp. 1–16). Abingdon: Routledge.

Goodley, S. 2013. 'Kazakh oligarch accuses president of kidnapping wife and daughter'. *Guardian*, 2 June. https://www.theguardian.com/world/2013/jun/02/kazakh-oligarch-accuses-president-kidnapping.

Gough, J. 2002. Neoliberalism and socialisation in the contemporary city: Opposites, complements and instabilities. *Antipode*, 34(3): 405–26.

Government of Canada. 2017. 'Notice: Government of Canada eliminates conditional permanent residence'. Ottawa, 28 April. https://www.canada.ca/en/immigration-refugees-citizenship/news/notices/elminating-conditional-pr.html.

Gov.UK. 2015. 'PM announces significant changes to visitor visas for Chinese tourists for the benefit of the British economy'. Press release, 25 October. https://www.gov.uk/government/news/pm-announces-significant-changes-to-visitor-visas-for-chinese-tourists-for-the-benefit-of-the-british-economy.

Gov.UK. 2018. Immigration rules, Appendix K: Shortage occupation list, 25 February 2016, updated 12 January 2018. https://www.gov.uk/guidance/immigration-rules/immigration-rules-appendix-k-shortage-occupation-list.

Gowan, P. 1995. 'Neo-liberal theory and practice for Eastern Europe', *New Left Review*, 213: 3–60.

Gower, M. and McGuiness, T. 2017. 'The financial (minimum income) requirement for partner visas'. House of Commons Library Briefing Paper No. 06724, 22 February.

Graham, H. 2017. 'Private firms banned from forcing asylum seekers to share bedrooms in Newcastle'. *Chronicle*, 21 March. https://www.chroniclelive.co.uk/news/north-east-news/private-firms-banned-forcing-asylum-12771797.

Gramsci, A. 1971. *Selections from the prison notebooks of Antonio Gramsci*, ed. and trans. Q. Hoare and G. Nowell. London: Lawrence & Wishart.

Grant, S. and Peel, C. 2015. '"No passport equals no home": An independent evaluation of the "Right to Rent" scheme'. Joint Council for the Welfare of Immigrants. https://www.jcwi.org.uk/sites/default/files/documets/No%20Passport%20Equals%20No%20Home%20Right%20to%20Rent%20Independent%20Evaluation_0.pdf.

Grayson, J. 2016. 'Solidarity activism, campaigning and knowledge production: Challenging Refugee Inc.: The case of G4S and corporate asylum markets'. *Concept: The Journal of Contemporary Community Education Practice Theory*, 7(2): 1–10.

Grayson, J. 2017. 'Daisy and the £4 billion asylum housing contracts'. Institute of Race Relations, 30 November. http://www.irr.org.uk/news/daisy-and-the-4-billion-asylum-housing-contracts.

Green, S. 2009. 'Lines, traces and tidemarks: Reflections on forms of borderliness'. *EastBordNet Working Papers*, 1(1): 1–19. doi: 10.7765/9781526125910.00012.

Green, S. 2015. 'Making grey zones at the European peripheries'. In I. H. Knudsen and M. D. Frederiksen, eds, *Ethnographies of Grey Zones in Eastern Europe: Relations, Borders and Invisibilities* (pp. 173–86). London: Anthem Press.

Grewcock, M. 2014. 'Australian border policing: Regional "solutions" and neocolonialism'. *Race and Class*, 55(3): 71–8.

Griffiths, M. B. E. 2017. 'Seeking Asylum and the politics of family'. *Families, Relationships and Societies*, 6(1): 153–6.

Grosz, E. A. 1999. *Becomings: Explorations in Time, Memory, and Futures*. Cornell, NY: Cornell University Press.

Grove, J. 2012. 'Home Office to strip London Met of highly trusted status'. *Times Higher Education*, 26 August. https://www.timeshighereducation.com/news/home-office-to-strip-london-met-of-highly-trusted-status/420965.article.

Grove-White, R. 2014. 'Immigration Act 2014: What next for migrants' access to NHS care?' Social Healthcare Association, 28 May. https://www.sochealth.co.uk/2014/05/28/immigration-act-2014-next-migrants-access-nhs-care.

Guardian Staff and Agencies. 1999. 'UK News: Furious Al-Fayed denied British citizenship again'. *Guardian*, 6 May. https://www.theguardian.com/uk/1999/may/06/3.

Guild, E. 2009. *Security and migration in the 21st century*. Cambridge: Polity.

Häkli, J. 2015. 'The border in the pocket: The passport as a boundary object'. In A.-L. Amilhat-Szary and F. Giraut, eds, *Borderities and the politics of contemporary mobile borders* (pp. 85–99). London: Palgrave Macmillan.

Hall, A. and Mendel, J. 2012. 'Threatprints, threads and triggers: Imaginaries of risk in the "war on terror"'. *Journal of Cultural Economy*, 5(1): 9–27.

Hall, S. 1988. *The hard road to renewal: Thatcherism and the crisis of the left*. London: Verso.

Hall, S. and Held, D. 1989. 'Citizens and citizenship'. In S. Hall and M. Jacques, eds, *New times: The changing face of politics in the 1990s* (pp. 173–88). London: Verso.

Hall, S., and Massey, D. 2010. 'Interpreting the Crisis'. *Soundings*, 44: 57–71.

Hall, S. M. 2015. 'Migrant urbanisms: Ordinary cities and everyday resistance'. *Sociology*, 49(5): 853–69.

Halpern, J. 2015. *War against the people*. London: Pluto.

Hancock, A. M. 2016. *Intersectionality: An intellectual history*. New York: Oxford University Press.

Haraway, D. 1991. *Simians, cyborgs and women: The reinvention of women*. London: Free Association Press.

Harney, A. 2017. 'Behind Kushner Companies, a Chinese agency skirts visa-for-investment rules'. Reuters, 12 May. http://uk.reuters.com/article/us-china-kushner-qiaowai-insight-idUKKBN1882EI.

Harvey, D. 1989. *The conditions of postmodernity: An enquiry into the origins of cultural change*. Oxford: Blackwell.

Harvey, D. 1999. 'Time–space compression and the postmodern condition'. *Modernity: Critical Concepts*, 4: 98–118.

Harvey, D. 2007a. *A brief history of neoliberalism*. New York: Oxford University Press.

Harvey, D. 2007b. 'Neoliberalism as creative destruction'. *The Annals of the American Academy of Political and Social Science*, 610(1): 21–44.

Havlíček, T., Jeřábek, M., and Dokoupil, J., eds. 2018. *Borders in Central Europe after the Schengen Agreement*. Cham, Switzerland: Springer International.

Hawkins, O. 2018. 'Asylum statistics'. Briefing Paper, House of Commons Library, 23 January. SN01403.pdf.

Hawley, E. W. 2015. *The New Deal and the problem of monopoly*. Princeton, NJ: Princeton University Press.

Held, D. and Mcgrew, A. 2005. 'The great globalization debate: An introduction'. In D. Held and A. Mcgrew, eds, *The global transformations reader: An introduction to the globalization debate* (pp. 1–50). Malden, MA: Polity.

Heller, A. 1984. *Everyday life*. London: Routledge & Kegan Paul.

Heller, C. and Pezzani, L. 2017. 'Liquid traces: Investigating the deaths of migrants at the EU's maritime frontier'. In N. De Genova, ed., *The borders of "Europe": Autonomy of migration, tactics of bordering* (pp. 95–119). Durham, NC: Duke University Press.

Highmore, B., ed. 2012. *Everyday life: Critical concepts in media and cultural studies*, vols 1–4. London: Routledge.

Hindu. 2017. 'Illegal Bangladeshi immigrants held with Aadhaar cards'. *Hindu*, 18 January. http://www.thehindu.com/news/cities/bangalore/illegal-bangladeshi-immigrants-held-with-aadhaar-cards/article21859950.ece.

Hjelmgaard, K. 2018. 'From 7 to 77: There's been an explosion in building border walls since World War II'. *USA Today*, 24 May. https://eu.usatoday.com/story/news/world/2018/05/24/border-walls-berlin-wall-donald-trump-wall/553250002.

HMSO. 2014. Chapter 22, *Immigration Act 2014*. London: TSO.

Hobolt, S. B. 2016. 'The Brexit vote: A divided nation, a divided continent'. *Journal of European Public Policy*, 23(9): 1259–77.

Hobsbawm, E. 1987. *The age of empire*. London: Weidenfeld & Nicolson.

Holmes, C. 1991. *A tolerant country: Immigrants, refugees and minorities in Britain*. London: Faber & Faber.

Holmes, C. 2015. *A tolerant country? Immigrants, refugees and minorities, vol. 1*. London: Routledge.

Holmes, C. 2018. 'Central American migrant caravan begins crossing US border: 5 essential reads'. The Conversation, 1 May. https://theconversation.com/central-american-migrant-caravan-begins-crossing-us-border-5-essential-reads-95824.

Holmes, S. A. 1988. 'Immigration fueling cities' strong growth'. *New York Times*, 1 January, pp. A1–A13.

Home Affairs Committee Report. 2010. 'Counter-terrorism measures in British airports'. http://www.publications.parliament.uk/pa/cm200910/cmselect/cmhaff/311/31102.htm.

Home Office. 2013a. 'Impact assessment: Tackling illegal immigration in privately rented accommodation'. https://assets.publishing.service.gov.uk/government/uploads/system/uploads/attachment_data/file/226713/consultation.pdf.

Home Office. 2013b. 'Sham marriages and civil partnerships: Background information and proposed referral and investigation scheme'. November 2013.

Home Office. 2018. 'Asylum support'. Gov.UK. https://www.gov.uk/asylum-support/what-youll-get.

Houtum, H. van. 2010. 'Human blacklisting: The global apartheid of the EU's external border regime'. *Environment and Planning D: Society and Space*, 28(6): 957–76.

Houtum, H. van, Kramsch, O. T., and Zierhofer, W. eds. 2005. *B/ordering space*. Aldershot: Ashgate.

Houtum, H. van and van Naerssen, T. 2002. 'Bordering, ordering and othering'. *Tijdschrift voor economische en sociale geografie*, 93(2): 125–36.

Howard, P. N., Duffy, A., Freelon, D., Hussain, M. M., Mari, W., and Maziad, M. 2011. 'Opening closed regimes: What was the role of social media during the Arab Spring?' https://ssrn.com/abstract=2595096. doi: 10.2139/ssrn.2595096.

Howard, P. N. and Hussain, M. M. 2013. *Democracy's fourth wave? Digital media and the Arab Spring*. New York: Oxford University Press.

Hozić, A., and True, J. 2017. 'Brexit as a scandal: Gender and global trumpism'. *Review of International Political Economy*, 24(2): 270–87.

Hudson, A. 1998. 'Beyond the borders: Globalisation, sovereignty and extra-territoriality'. *Geopolitics*, 3(1): 89–105.

Hutton, A. 2013. 'Sham marriage police storm real wedding'. *Camden New Journal*, 7 November. http://archive.camdennewjournal.com/news/2013/nov/exclusive-sham-marriage-police-storm-real-wedding.

Huysmans, J. 2000. 'The European Union and the securitization of migration'. *Journal of Common Market Studies*, 38(5): 751–77.

Hyndman, J. and Giles, W. 2011. 'Waiting for what? The feminization of asylum in protracted situations'. *Gender, Place & Culture*, 18(3): 361–79.

Hyndman, J. and Giles, W. 2016. *Refugees in extended exile: Living on the edge*. London: Taylor & Francis.

Hyndman, J. and Mountz, A. 2008. 'Another brick in the wall? Neo-refoulement and the extemalization of asylum by Australia and Europe'. *Government and Opposition*, 43(2): 259–69.

Hynes, P. and Sales, R. 2010. 'New communities: Asylum seekers and dispersal'. In A. Bloch and J. Solomos, eds, *Race and ethnicity in the 21st century* (pp. 39–61). Palgrave Macmillan: Basingstoke.

Ibrahim, A. 2016. *The Rohingyas: Inside Myanmar's Hidden Genocide*. Oxford: Oxford University Press.

ICIBI = Independent Chief Inspector of Borders. 2016. 'An inspection of the "hostile environment" measures relating to driving licences and bank accounts: January to July 2016'. https://assets.publishing.service.gov.uk/government/uploads/system/uploads/attachment_data/file/567652/ICIBI-hostile-environment-driving-licences-and-bank-accounts-January-to-July-2016.pdf.

Ignatieff, M. 2001. *Human rights as politics and idolatry*. Princeton, NJ: Princeton University Press.

IIFJIG = International Initiative for Justice in Gujarat Team. 2003. *Threatened existence: A feminist analysis of the genocide in Gujarat*. https://www.onlinevolunteers.org/gujarat/reports/iijg/2003/annexures.pdf.

Inda, J. X. and Rosaldo, R. 2008. 'Tracking global flows'. In J. X. Inda and R. Rosaldo, eds, *The anthropology of globalization: A reader* (pp. 3–46). Oxford: Wiley Blackwell.

International Labour Organisation and Walk Free Foundation. 2017. *Global estimates of modern slavery: Forced labour and forced marriage*. Geneva: ILO,

WFF and IOM. https://www.ilo.org/wcmsp5/groups/public/---dgreports/---dcomm/documents/publication/wcms_575479.pdf.

IOM = International Organization for Migration. 2018a. 'Missing migrants project: Tracking deaths along migratory routes'. http://missingmigrants.iom.int/region/mediterranean.

IOM = International Organization for Migration. 2018b. *World migration, 2008: Managing labour mobility in the evolving global economy.* World Migration Report Series. Geneva: IOM. https://publications.iom.int/system/files/pdf/wmr_1.pdf.

Irish Examiner. 2018. Border counties at risk of economic decline despite broader economic growth, report shows. 25 July. https://www.irishexaminer.com/breakingnews/business/border-counties-at-risk-of-economic-decline-despite-broader-economic-growth-report-shows-857657.html.

Janiewski, D. 1995. 'Gendering, racializing and classifying: Settler colonization in the United States, 1590–1990'. In D. Stasiulis and N. Yuval-Davis, eds, *Unsettling settler societies: Articulations of gender, race, ethnicity and class* (pp. 132–60). London: SAGE.

Jaspers, S. and Buchanan-Smith, M. 2018. *Darfuri migration from Sudan to Europe: From displacement to despair.* London: Research and Evidence Facility (REF) Consortium. https://www.odi.org/sites/odi.org.uk/files/resource-documents/12385.pdf.

Jessop, B. 2013a. 'Putting neoliberalism in its time and place: A response to the debate'. *Social Anthropology*, 21(1): 65–74.

Jessop, B. 2013b. 'Recovered imaginaries, imagined recoveries: A cultural political economy of crisis construals and crisis management in the North Atlantic financial crisis'. In M. Benner, ed., *Before and beyond the global economic crisis: Economics, politics and settlement* (pp. 234–54). Cheltenham: Edward Elgar.

Jessop, R. D. 2002. *The future of the capitalist state.* Cambridge: Polity.

Jones, D. S. 2014. *Masters of the universe: Hayek, Friedman, and the birth of neoliberal politics.* Princeton, NJ: Princeton University Press.

Jones, H. 2014. 'Operation Centurion: The communication of fear and resistance. Mapping Immigration Controversy', posted on 26 June. https://mappingimmigrationcontroversy.com/2014/06/26/operation-centurion-the-communication-of-fear-and-resistance.

Jones, H., Gunaratnam, Y., Bhattacharyya, G., Davies, W., Dhaliwal, S., Forkert, K., Jackson, E., and Saltus, R. 2017. *Go home? The politics of immigration ccontroversies.* Manchester: Manchester University Press.

Jones, R. 2009. 'Geopolitical boundary narratives, the global war on terror and border fencing in India'. *Transactions of the Institute of British Geographers*, 34(3): 290–304.

Jones, R. 2011. 'Border security, 9/11 and the enclosure of civilisation'. *Geographical Journal*, 177(3): 213–17.

Jones, R. 2012. *Border walls: Security and the war on terror in the United States, India, and Israel.* Zed Books: London.

Jones, R. 2014. 'Border wars: Narratives and images of the US–Mexico border on TV'. In R. Jones and C. Johnson, eds, *Placing the border in everyday life* (pp. 185–204). Abingdon: Ashgate.

Jones, R. 2016. *Violent borders: Refugees and the right to move.* New York: Verso.

Jones, R. and Johnson, C., eds. 2014. *Placing the border in everyday life.* Abingdon: Ashgate.

Jørgensen, M. B. 2012. 'Danish regulation on marriage migration: Policy understandings of transnational marriages'. In K. Charsley, ed., *Transnational marriage: New perspectives from Europe and beyond* (pp. 60–78). London: Routledge.

Jouet, M. 2016. 'Why evangelicals like Trump: Fundamentalist approaches to evangelicalism have long fostered anti-intellectual and authoritarian mindsets.' *New Nation*, 13 May. https://newrepublic.com/article/133488/evangelicals-like-trump.

Juss, S. S. 1993. *Immigration, nationality and citizenship.* Mansell: London.

Juss, S. S. 1997. *Discretion and deviation in the administration of immigration control.* Sweet & Maxwell: London.

Kaldor, M. 2013. *New and old wars: Organised violence in a global era.* Hoboken, NJ: John Wiley & Sons, Inc.

Kamalizad, A. 2017. 'Meet the border angels, the group trying to save migrants' lives'. *Mother Jones*, 20 October. http://www.motherjones.com/politics/2017/10/meet-the-border-angels-the-group-trying-to-save-migrants-lives.

Kamayani. 2017. 'Jharkhand: Another woman dies of hunger after Aadhaar disrupts delivery of ration and pension #KillerAadhaar'. Kractivist, posted 2 January. http://www.kractivist.org/jharkhand-another-woman-dies-of-hunger-after-aadhaar-disrupts-delivery-of-ration-and-pension-killeraadhaar.

Kaufman, E. 2017. 'Why the fear of islamization is driving populist right support and what to do about it'. LSE Blog. http://blogs.lse.ac.uk/europpblog/2017/03/18/why-the-fear-of-islamization-is-driving-populist-right-support-and-what-to-do-about-it.

Kaur, A. 2018. 'Trumpism, Immigration and Globalisation'. *RSIS Commentary*, 18. https://www.rsis.edu.sg/wp-content/uploads/2018/02/CO18018.pdf.

Keith, L. and Van Ginneken, E. 2015. 'Restricting access to the NHS for undocumented migrants is bad policy at high cost'. *BMJ*, 350. doi: 10.1136/bmj.h3056.

KentOnline. 2014. 'KCC leader Paul Carter set for thousands of migrants from Bulgaria and Romania as working restrictions lifted'. KentOnline, 1 January. http://www.kentonline.co.uk/deal/news/county-set-for-influx-of-10736.

Khaira, R. 2017. 'Rs 500, 10 minutes, and you have access to billion Aadhaar details'. *Tribune*, 3 January. https://www.tribuneindia.com/news/nation/rs-500-10-minutes-and-you-have-access-to-billion-aadhaar-details/523361.html.

Khajuria, R. K. 2017. '"Invisible" laser walls to bolster security along border with Pakistan in J-K. *Hindustan Times*, 13 May. https://www.hindustantimes.com/india-news/with-invisible-laser-walls-india-bolsters-security-along-border-with-pakistan/story-dBHI8AgYqFJAlhVxxQXYZO.html.

Kimmerling, B. and Migdal, J. S. 1993. *Palestinians: The making of a people.* New York: Free Press.

Kingfisher, C. and Maskovsky, J. 2008. 'Introduction: The limits of neoliberalism', *Critique of Anthropology, 28*(2): 115–26.

Kirk, D. and Huyck, E. 1954. 'Overseas migration from Europe since World War II'. *American Sociological Review, 19*(4): 447–56.

Kirkup, J. and R. Winnett, 2012. 'Theresa May interview: "We're going to give illegal migrants a really hostile reception"'. *Telegraph*, 25 May. https://www.telegraph.co.uk/news/uknews/immigration/9291483/Theresa-May-interview-Were-going-to-give-illegal-migrants-a-really-hostile-reception.html.

Knudsen, I. H. and Frederiksen, M. D., eds. 2015. *Ethnographies of grey zones in Eastern Europe: Relations, borders and invisibilities*. London: Anthem Press.

Kofman, E. and Meetoo, V. 2008. 'Family migration'. In *World Migration Report 2008: Managing Labour Mobility in the Evolving Labour Economy* (pp. 151–72). Geneva: International Organization for Migration.

Kofman, E. and Sales R. 1992. 'Towards fortress Europe?' *Women's Studies International Forum*, 15(1): 29–39.

Koopman, S. 2011. 'Alter-geopolitics: Other securities are happening'. *Geoforum*, 42(3): 274–84.

Kornai, J. 1994. 'Transformational recession: The main causes'. *Journal of Comparative Economics* 19(3): 39–63.

Kristof, L. K. D. 1959. 'The nature of frontiers and boundaries'. *Annals of the Association of American Geographers*, 49: 269–82.

Kron, S. 2011. 'The border as method: Towards an analysis of political subjectivities in transmigrant spaces'. In D. Wastl-Walter, ed., *The Ashgate Research Companion to Border Studies* (pp. 103–20). Aldershot: Ashgate.

Kushner, T. 2012. *The battle of Britishness: Migrant journeys, 1685 to the present*. Manchester: Manchester University Press.

Lahav, G. and Guiraudon, V. 2000. 'Comparative perspectives on border control: Away from the border and outside the state'. In P. Andreas and T. Snider, eds, *The wall around the West: State borders and immigration controls in North America and Europe* (pp. 55–77). Lanham, MD: Rowman & Littlefield.

Lal, S. and Wilson, A. 1986. But my cows aren't going to England: A study in how families are divided. Manchester: Manchester Law Centre.

Lammy, D. 2018. 'Don't let Rudd's departure distract from a toxic policy that needs to die'. *Guardian*, 30 April. https://www.theguardian.com/commentisfree/2018/apr/30/amber-rudd-departure-toxic-policy-windrush-generation-home-secretary-david-lammy.

Lash, S. and Urry, J. 1994. *Economy of signs and space*. London: SAGE.

Lather, P. 1997. *Getting smart*. London: Routledge.

Latour, B. 2000. 'When things strike back: A possible contribution of science studies to social studies'. *British Journal of Sociology*, 51(1): 107–24.

Lattimore, O. 1937. 'Origins of the Great Wall of China: A frontier concept in theory and practice'. *Geographical Review*, 27(4): 529–49.

Lavie, S. and Swedenburg, T. 1996. 'Between and among the boundaries of culture: Bridging text and lived experience in the third timespace'. *Cultural Studies*, 10(1): 154–79.

Lefebvre, H. 1987. *Everyday* life (Yale French Studies 73). New Haven, CT: Yale University Press.

Lefebvre, H. 1991. *The production of space*. Oxford: Blackwell.

Legg, S. 2017. 'Decolonialism'. *Transactions of the Institute of British Geographers*, 42(3): 345–8.

Leinbach, T. R. and Bowen, J. T. 2004. 'Airspaces: Air transport, technology, and society'. In D. B. Brunn, S. L. Cutter, and J. W. Harrington, eds, *Geography and technology* (pp. 285–314). Dordrecht: Kluwer.

Leun, J. van der 2006. 'Excluding illegal migrants in the Netherlands: Between national policies and local implementation'. *West European Politics*, 29(2): 310–26.

Levy, C. 2010. 'Refugees, Europe, camps/states of exception: "Into the zone", the European Union and extraterritorial processing of migrants, refugees and asylum-seekers (theories and practice)'. *Refugee Survey Quarterly*, 29(1): 92–119.

Lewis, H., Dwyer, P., Hodkinson, S., and Waite, H. 2015. 'Hyper-precarious lives: Migrants, work and forced labour in the Global North'. *Progress in Human Geography*, 39(5): 580–600.

Liberty, ed. 2018. *A guide to the hostile environment*. April. https://www.liberty humanrights.org.uk/sites/default/files/HE%20web.pdf

Lindner, P. 2007. 'Localising privatisation, disconnecting locales: Mechanisms of disintegration in post-socialist rural Russia'. *Geoforum*, 38(30): 494–504.

Lipsky, M. 1980. *Street-level bureaucracy: Dilemmas of the individual in public services* New York: Russell Sage Foundation.

Loomba, A. 1998. *Colonialism/Postcolonialism*. New York: Routledge.

Loomba, A. 2004 [1998]. 'Situating colonial and postcolonial studies'. In J. Rivkin and M. Ryan, eds, *Literary theory: An anthology* (pp. 1100–11). Oxford: Wiley Blackwell.

Loyd, J. 2014. *Health rights are civil rights: Peace and justice activism in Los Angeles, 1963–1978*. Minneapolis: University of Minnesota Press.

Lutz, H., Herrera Viva, M. T., and Spuil, L. eds. 2011. *Framing intersectionality: Debates on a multi-faceted concept in gender studies*. Burlington, VT: Ashgate.

Maguire, M., Frois, C., and Zurawski, N., eds. 2014. *Anthropology of security: Perspectives from the frontline of policing, counter-terrorism and border control*. London: Pluto.

Maher, S. 2016. *Salafi-Jihadism: The history of an idea*. New York: Oxford University Press.

Maidment, J. 2017. 'Theresa May commits Tories to cutting net migration to the UK to the tens of thousands'. *Telegraph*, 20 April. http://www.telegraph.co.uk/news/2017/04/20/theresa-may-commits-tories-cutting-net-migration-uk-tens-thousands.

Manhotra, D. 2016. 'State takes steps to prevent illegal immigrants from getting Aadhaar'. *Tribune*, 17 March. http://www.tribuneindia.com/news/jammu-kashmir/community/state-takes-steps-to-prevent-illegal-immigrants-from-getting-aadhaar/209709.html.

Manjikian, L. 2010. 'Refugee "in-betweenness": A proactive existence'. *Refuge*, 27(1): 50–59.

Mann, M. 2004. *Fascists*. Cambridge: Cambridge University Press.

Manson, S. M. 2001. 'Simplifying complexity: A review of complexity theory'. *Geoforum*, 32(3): 405–14.

Marshall, T. H. 1950. *Citizenship and social class*. Cambridge: Cambridge University Press.

Martinez, O. J. 1994. 'The dynamics of border interaction'. *Global boundaries, World boundaries*, 1: 1–15.

Massey, D. 1983. 'Power-geometry and a progressive sense of place'. In J. Bird, B. Curtis, T. Putnam, and L. Tickner, eds, *Mapping the futures: Local cultures, global change* (pp. 59–69). London: Routledge.

Massey, D. 1994. *Place, space and gender*. Minneapolis: University of Minnesota Press.

Massey, D. 1995. *Spatial divisions of labor: Social structures and the geography of production*. London: Psychology Press.

Massey, D. 2005. *For space*. London: SAGE.

Mathisen, R. W. 2006. 'Peregrini, barbari, and cives romani: Concepts of citizenship and the legal identity of barbarians in the later Roman Empire'. *American Historical Review*, 111(4): 1011–40.

Mayblin, L. 2014. 'Asylum, welfare and work: Reflections on research in asylum and refugee studies'. *International Journal of Sociology and Social Policy*, 34(5–6): 375–91. doi: 10.1108/IJSSP-11–2013–0113.

McBride, S. 2005. *Paradigm shift: Globalization and the Canadian state*. Halifax, NS: Fernwood.

McCabe, S. 2002. 'The tourist experience and everyday life'. In G. M. S. Dann, ed., *The tourist as a metaphor of the social world* (pp. 61–75). Wallingford: CABI Publishing.

McCall, C. 2018. 'Brexit, bordering and people on the island of Ireland'. *Ethnopolitics* 17(3): 292–305.

McCall, L. 2005. 'The complexity of intersectionality'. *Signs: Journal of Women in Culture and Society*, 30(3): 1771–800.

McDermott, K. and Agnew, J. 1996. *The Comintern: A history of international communism, from Lenin to Stalin*. London: Macmillan.

McGuinness, T. and Gower, M. 2017. *The Common Travel Area and the special status of Irish nationals in UK law*. Briefing Paper 7661, House of Commons Library. CBP-7661.pdf.

McLean, I. 2003. 'Two analytical narratives about the history of the EU'. *European Union Politics*, 4(4): 499–506.

Medecins sans Frontières. 2016. 'Update on Calais 'Jungle' refugee camp'. MSF, 27 May. http://www.msf.org/en/article/france-update-calais-jungle-refugee-camp.

Megoran, N. 2012. 'Rethinking the study of international boundaries: A biography of the Kyrgyzstan–Uzbekistan boundary'. *Annals of the Association of American Geographers*, 102(2): 464–81.

Melin, R. 2016. '"Debordering" and "rebordering": Discriminatory and racial discourses of borders under globalisation'. *International Journal of Migration and Border Studies*, 2(1): 59–76.

Metykova, M. 2010. 'Only a mouse click away from home: Transnational practices of Eastern European migrants in the United Kingdom'. *Social Identities*, 16(3): 325–38.

Meyer, J. W. 2007. 'Globalization: Theory and trends'. *International Journal of Comparative Sociology*, 48(4): 261–73.

Mezzadra, S. and Neilson, B. 2012. 'Between inclusion and exclusion: On the topology of global space and borders'. *Theory, Culture & Society*, 29(4–5): 58–75.

Mezzadra, S. and Neilson, B. 2013. *Border as method, or the multiplication of labour*. Durham, NC: Duke University Press.

Mitropoulos, A. 2017. 'Bordering colonial uncertainty'. *PoLAR: Political and Legal Anthropology Review*. https://polarjournal.org/bordering-colonial-uncertainty.

Moravcsik, A. and Vachudova, M. A. 2003. 'National interests, state power, and EU enlargement'. *East European Politics and Societies*, 17(1): 42–57.

Morris, H. 2017. 'EU escalates "visa war" with US with Americans set to lose visa-free travel to Europe'. *Telegraph*, 2 March. http://www.telegraph.co.uk/travel/news/us-nationals-to-be-forced-to-apply-to-visas-eu-reciprocity.

Moss, T., Pettersson, G., and van de Walle, N. 2006. 'A review essay on aid dependency and state building in sub-Saharan Africa: An aid-institutions paradox'. Working Paper 74, Center for Global Development. https://www.cgdev.org/sites/default/files/5646_file_WP_74.pdf.

Mould, O. 2017. 'The Calais Jungle: A slum of London's making'. *City*, *21*(3–4): 388–404.

Mountz, A. 2011. 'Islands as enforcement archipelago: Haunting, sovereignty, and asylum on islands'. *Political Geography*, *30*: 118–28.

Muller, A. 2016. 'Workplace immigration checks and raids: What needs to be done'. Migrant Tales, 13 September. http://www.migranttales.net/migrants-rights-network-workplace-immigration-checks-and-raids-what-needs-to-be-done.

Mustasaari, S. 2016. 'Best interests of the child in family reunification: A citizenship test disguised'. In A. Griffiths, S. Mustasaari, and A. Mäki-Petäjä-Leinonen, eds, *Subjectivity, citizenship and belonging: Identities and intersections* (pp. 123–45). Abingdon: Routledge.

Nagar, R., Lawson, V., McDowell, L., and Hanson, S. 2002. 'Locating globalization: Feminist (re) readings of the subjects and spaces of globalization'. *Economic Geography*, *78*: 257–84.

Nagra, B. and Maurutto, P. 2016. 'Crossing borders and managing racialized identities: Experiences of security and surveillance among young Canadian Muslims'. *Canadian Journal of Sociology*, *41*(2), 165–93.

Nash, C. and Reid, B. 2010, 'Border crossings: New approaches to the Irish border'. *Irish Studies Review*, *18*(3): 265–84.

Nash, K. 2009. 'Between citizenship and human rights'. *Sociology*, *43*(6): 1067–83.

Nayak, A. 2011. 'Geography, race and emotions: Social and cultural intersections'. *Social & Cultural Geography*, *12*(6): 548–62.

Neal, A. W. 2009. 'Securitization and risk at the EU border: The origins of FRONTEX'. *JCMS: Journal of Common Market Studies*, *47*(2): 333–56.

Neal, S. and Murji, K. 2015. 'Sociologies of everyday life: Editors' introduction to the special issue'. *Sociology*, *49*(5): 811–19.

Neate, R. 2014. 'Kazakh billionaire to be extradited over alleged £3bn fraud, French court rules'. *Guardian*, 9 January. https://www.theguardian.com/business/2014/jan/09/kazakh-extradited-fraud-mukhtar-ablyazov.

Nett, R. 1971. 'The civil right we are not ready for: The right of free movement of people on the face of the earth'. *Ethics*, *81*(3): 212–27.

Newman, D. 2006. 'Borders and bordering: Towards an interdisciplinary dialogue'. *European Journal of Social Theory*, *9*(2): 171–86.

Newman, D. and Paasi, A. 1998. 'Fences and neighbours in the postmodern world: Boundary narratives in political geography'. *Progress in Human Geography*, *2*: 186–207.

Nickell, S. 2004. 'Poverty and worklessness in Britain'. *Economic Journal*, *114*(494): C1–C25.

Nicol, A. 1993 'Nationality and immigration'. In R. Blackburn, ed., *Rights of citizenship* (pp. 254–70). London: in Mansell.

Nightingale, C. H. 2012. *Segregation: A global history of divided cities*. Chicago, IL: University of Chicago Press.

Nightingale, C. H. 2017. 'AHR conversation: Walls, borders, and boundaries in world history'. *American Historical Review*, *122*(5.1): 1501–53.

Nixon, R. and Qiu, L. 2018. 'Trump's evolving words on the wall'. *New York*

Times, 18 January. https://www.nytimes.com/2018/01/18/us/politics/trump-border-wall-immigration.html.

Noiriel, G. 1991. *La Tyrannie du national: Le droit d'asile en Europe, 1793–1993*. Calmann-Lévy: Paris.

Noronha, L. de. 2016. 'Deportations and multi-status Britain', *Discover Society*, 4 October. https://discoversociety.org/2016/10/04/deportation-and-multi-status-britain.

Northedge, F. S. 1986. *The League of Nations: Its life and times, 1920–1946*. Leicester: Leicester University Press.

Norton, P. 2016. 'How could Brexit impact independent schools?'. *Telegraph*, 28 June. http://www.telegraph.co.uk/education/2016/06/28/how-could-brexit-impact-independent-schools.

O'Byrne, D. J. 2001. 'On passports and border controls'. *Annals of Tourism Research*, 28(2): 399–416.

O'Carroll, L. 2016. 'Immigration raid on Byron Hamburgers rounds up 35 workers'. *Guardian*, 27 July. https://www.theguardian.com/uk-news/2016/jul/27/immigration-raid-on-byron-hamburgers-rounds-up-30-workers.

O'Carroll, L. 2018. 'Brexit and the Irish border question explained'. *Guardian*, 19 September. https://www.theguardian.com/uk-news/2018/sep/19/brexit-and-the-irish-border-question-explained.

Ohmae, K. 1990. 'Managing in a global environment: An excerpt from *The Borderless World*'. *McKinsey Quarterly*, 3: 3–19.

Ong, A. 2003. *Buddha in hiding: Refugees, citizenship, and the New America*. Berkeley: University of California Press.

Ong, A. 2006. *Neoliberalism as exception: Mutations in citizenship and sovereignty*. Durham, NC: Duke University Press.

ONS = Office of National Statistics. 2013. *Detailed country of birth and nationality analysis from the 2011 Census of England and Wales*. http://webarchive.nationalarchives.gov.uk/20160107124139/http://www.ons.gov.uk/ons/dcp171776_310441.pdf.

Osborne, H. 2016. 'Landlords "don't understand right to rent immigration checks"'. *Guardian*, 1 February. https://www.theguardian.com/money/2016/feb/01/landlords-do-not-understand-rules-immigration-checks-association.

Ostry, J. D., Loungani, P., and Furceri, D. 2016. 'Neoliberalism: Oversold?'. *Finance & Development*, 53(2). http://www.imf.org/external/pubs/ft/fandd/2016/06/ostry.htm.

Overbeek, H. W. ed. 2002. *Restructuring hegemony in the global political economy: The rise of transnational neo-liberalism in the 1980s*. Abingdon: Routledge.

Oxfam. 2016. 'Tax battles: The dangerous global race to the bottom on corporate tax'. Oxfam Policy Paper, 12 December. https://www.oxfam.org/sites/www.oxfam.org/files/bp-race-to-bottom-corporate-tax-121216-en.pdf.

Ozolins, U. 2003. 'The impact of european accession upon language policy in the Baltic States'. *Language Policy*, 2: 217–38.

Paasi, A. 1998. 'Boundaries as social processes: Territoriality in the world of flows'. *Geopolitics*, 3(1): 69–88.

Paasi, A. 2005. 'The changing discourses on political boundaries: Mapping the backgrounds, contexts and contents'. In H. van Houtum, O. T. Kramsch, and W. Zierhofer, eds, *B/ordering Space* (pp. 17–31). Adershot: Ashgate.

Paasi, A. 2009. 'Bounded spaces in a "borderless world": Border studies, power and the anatomy of territory'. *Journal of Power*, 2(2): 213–34.

Paasi, A. 2012. 'Border studies reanimated: Going beyond the territorial/ relational divide'. *Environment and Planning A*, 44(10): 2303–9.

Paasi, A. and Prokkola, E.-K. 2008. 'Territorial dynamics, cross border work and everyday life in the Finnish–Swedish border area'. *Space and Polity*, 12(1): 13–29.

Pain, R. and Staeheli, L. 2014. 'Introduction: Intimacy-geopolitics and violence'. *Area*, 46(4): 344–60.

Painter, J. 2006. 'Prosaic geographies of stateness'. *Political Geography*, 25(7): 752–74.

Panitch, L. 1994. 'Globalisation and the state'. *Socialist Register*, 30(30): 60–93.

Panitch, L. 1996. 'Rethinking the role of the state'. *Globalization: Critical Reflections*, 83: 96–7.

Panitch, L. and Gindin, S. 2012. *The making of global capitalism*. New York: Verso.

Papacharissi, Z., ed. 2010. *A networked self: Identity, community, and culture on social network sites*. New York: Routledge.

Papastergiadis, N. 2000. *The turbulence of migration: Globalization, deterritorialization, and hybridity*. Cambridge: Polity.

Pappe, I. 2007. *The ethnic cleansing of Palestine*. Oxford: Oneworld Publications.

Park, H. 2015. 'Which states make life easier or harder for illegal immigrants'. *New York Times*, 29 March. https://www.nytimes.com/interactive/2015/03/30/us/laws-affecting-unauthorized-immigrants.html.

Parker, N. et al. 2009. 'Lines in the sand? Towards an agenda for critical border studies'. *Geopolitics*, 14(3): 582–7.

Parmar, A. 2018, 'Borders as mirrors: Racial hierarchies and the politics of migration'. Paper presented at the conference 'Borders, Racisms and Harms', University of London, 2 May.

Patel, C. and Peel, C. 2017. *Passport please: The impact of the right to rent checks on migrants and ethnic minorities in England*. London: Joint Council for the Welfare of Immigrants.

Peck, J. and Tickell, A. 2002. 'Neoliberalizing space'. *Antipode*, 34(3): 380–404.

Pécoud, A. and Guchteneire, P. de, eds. 2007. *Migration without borders: Essays on the free movement of people*. Paris: UNESCO.

Pegg, D. 2017. 'The "golden visa" deal: "We have in effect been selling off British citizenship to the rich"'. *Guardian*, 4 July. https://www.theguardian.com/uk-news/2017/jul/04/golden-visa-immigration-deal-british-citizenship-home-office.

Pellander, S. 2014. '"An acceptable marriage": Marriage migration and moral gatekeeping in Finland'. *Journal of Family Issues*, 8(3): 159–66. doi: 10.2478/njmr-2018-0021.

Perdue, P. 1998. 'Boundaries, maps, and movement: Chinese, Russian, and Mongolian empires in early modern central Eurasia'. *International History Review*, 20(2): 263–86.

Perera, S. 2007. 'A Pacific zone? (In)security, sovereignty, and stories of the Pacific borderscape'. In P. K. Rajaram and C. Grundy-Warr, eds, *Borderscapes: Hidden geographies and politics and territory's edge* (pp. 201–27). Minneapolis, MN: University of Minnesota Press.

Perkmann, M. and Sum, N. L. 2002. 'Globalization, regionalization, and cross-border regions: Scales, discourses and governance'. In M. Perkmann and N. L. Sum, eds, *Globalization, regionalization, and cross-border regions* (pp. 3–21). Basingstoke: Palgrave Macmillan.

Petras, J. F. and Veltmeyer, H. 2001. *Globalization unmasked: Imperialism in the 21st century*. London: Zed Books.

Philo, G., Briant, E., and Donald, P. 2013. *Bad news for refugees*. London: Pluto.

Piasecki, K. 2014. 'The birth of new ethnoses? Examples from Northern Europe'. *Our Europe*, 3: 7–20.

Picciotto, S. 1991. 'The internationalisation of the state'. *Capital & Class*, 15(1): 43–63.

Pickering, S. 2006. 'Border narratives'. In S. Pickering and L. Weber, eds, *Borders, mobility and technologies of control* (pp. 45–62). Dordrecht: Springer.

Pickles, J. and Smith, A., eds. 1998: *Theorizing transition: The political economy of post-communist transformation*. London: Routledge.

Pine, F. 2015. 'Living in the grey zones: When ambiguity and uncertainty are the ordinary'. In I. H. Knudsen and M. D. Frederiksen, eds, *Ethnographies of grey zones in Eastern Europe: Relations, borders and invisibilities* (pp. 25–40). London: Anthem Press.

Pink, S. 2012. *Situating everyday life: Practices and places*. London: SAGE.

Pisano, J. 2009. 'From iron curtain to golden one: Remaking identity in the European Union borderlands'. *East European Politics and Societies*, 23(2): 266–90.

Plaut, M. 2006. 'Ethiopia's Oromo Liberation Front'. *Review of African Political Economy*, 33(109): 587–93.

Pötzsch, H. 2015. 'The emergence of iBorder: Bordering bodies, networks and machines'. *Environment and Planning D: Space and Society*, 33: 101–18.

Poole, L. and Adamson, K. 2008. *Report on the situation of the Roma community in Govanhill, Glasgow*. Glasgow: Oxfam.

Pooley, C. G. and Whyte, I. D. 1991. *Migrants emigrants and immigrants: A social history of migration*. London: Routledge.

Poon, T. S. C. 1996. 'Dependent development: The subcontracting networks in the tiger economies'. *Human Resource Management Journal*, 6(4): 38–49.

Popescu, G. 2012. *Bordering and ordering the twenty-first century: Understanding borders*. Lanham, MD: Rowman & Littlefield.

Potter, J., in collaboration with Docs Not Cops. 2018. 'Patients not passports: No borders in the NHS!'. *Justice, Power and Resistance*, 2(2): 417–29.

Potter, J. and Milner, A. 2018. 'Tuberculosis: Looking beyond "migrant" as a category to understand experience'. Race Equality Foundation Briefing Paper: A Better Health Briefing 44. https://www.researchgate.net/profile/Jessica_Potter/publication/326155664_Tuberculosis_looking_beyond_%27migrant%27_as_a_category_to_understand_experience/links/5b3b70a2aca2720785062bac/Tuberculosis-looking-beyond-migrant-as-a-category-to-understand-experience.pdf.

Press Association. 2016. 'Postcode lottery' revealed in NHS care'. *Guardian*, 8 September. https://www.theguardian.com/society/2016/sep/08/postcode-lottery-revealed-in-nhs-care.

Pries, L. 2001. 'The approach of transnational social spaces: Responding to new configurations of the social and the spatial'. In L. Pries, ed., *New transnational social spaces: International migration and transnational companies in the early twenty-first century* (pp. 3–36). London: Routledge.

Radstone, S. 2007. *The sexual politics of time: Confession, nostalgia, memory.* Abingdon: Routledge.

Rai, S. M. 2015. 'Political performance: A framework for analysing democratic politics'. *Political Studies, 63*(5): 1179–97.

Ramadan, A. 2013. 'Spatialising the refugee camp'. *Transactions of the Institute of British Geographers, 38*(1): 65–77.

Rand, G. and Wagner, K. A. 2012. 'Recruiting the "martial races": Identities and military service in colonial India'. *Patterns of Prejudice, 46*(3–4): 232–54.

Refugee Council. 2017. 'The facts about asylum'. Refugee Council. https://www.refugeecouncil.org.uk/policy_research/the_truth_about_asylum/facts_about_asylum_-_page_5.

Reichmuth, J. and Berster, P. 2018. 'Past and future developments of the global air traffic'. In M. Kaltschmitt and U. Neuling, eds, *Biokerosene* (pp. 13–31). Berlin: Springer.

Rex, J. 1995. 'Multiculturalism in Europe and America'. *Nations and Nationalism, 1*(2): 243–59.

Rex, J. 1996. *Ethnic minorities in the modern nation state: Working papers in the theory of multiculturalism and political integration.* London: Macmillan.

Rivzi, F. and Lingard, B. 2010. *Globalizing educational policy.* London: Routledge.

Robertson, R. 1992. *Globalization: Social theory and global culture.* London: SAGE.

Rodrigue, J. P. 2006. 'Transportation and the geographical and functional integration of global production networks'. *Growth and Change, 37*(4): 510–25.

Romero, L. G. 2016. 'How the US is outsourcing border enforcement to Mexico'. The Conversation, 29 November. https://theconversation.com/how-the-us-is-outsourcing-border-enforcement-to-mexico-69272.

Romero, M. 2008. 'Crossing the immigration and race border: A critical race theory approach to immigration studies'. *Contemporary Justice Review, 11*(1): 23–37.

Rosaldo, R. 1997. 'Cultural citizenship, inequality, and multiculturalism'. In V. F. Flores and R. Benmayor, eds, *Latino cultural citizenship: Claiming identity, space, and rights* (pp. 27–38). Boston, MA: Beacon.

Ross, T. 2015. 'Nicky Morgan orders immigration review to examine "education tourism"'. *Telegraph*, 16 August. http://www.telegraph.co.uk/news/uknews/immigration/11805477/Nicky-Morgan-orders-immigration-review-to-examine-education-tourism.html.

Ross, T. 2016. 'Migration pressure on schools revealed'. *Telegraph*, 7 May. http://www.telegraph.co.uk/news/2016/05/07/migration-pressure-on-schools-revealed.

Rothschild, J. 2017. *East Central Europe between the two world wars.* Seattle: University of Washington Press.

Royal Airport Concierge. 2017. 'About us'. http://www.royalairportconcierge.com/biography.

Rumford, C. 2006. 'Theorizing borders'. *European Journal of Social Theory, 9*(2): 155–69.

Rumford, C. 2008. 'Introduction: Citizens and borderwork in Europe'. *Space and Polity, 12*(1): 1–12.

Rumford, C. 2009. 'Introduction: Citizens and borderwork in Europe'. In

C. Rumford, ed., *Citizens and borderwork in contemporary Europe* (pp. 1–12). London: Routledge.

Rumford, C. 2013. *Citizens and borderwork in contemporary Europe*. London: Routledge.

Rygiel, K., Baban, F., and Ilcan, S. 2016. 'The Syrian refugee crisis: The EU–Turkey "deal" and temporary protection'. *Global Social Policy*, 16(3): 315–20.

Ryymin, T. and Ludvigsen, K. 2013. 'From equality to equivalence? Norwegian health policies towards immigrants and the Sámi, 1970–2009'. *Nordic Journal of Migration Research*, 3(1): 10–18.

Saad-Filho, A. and Johnston, D. 2005. *Neoliberalism: A critical reader*. Chicago, IL: University of Chicago Press.

Sachs, J. 1990. 'What is to be done?' *Economist* (London), 13 January, pp. 19–24.

Sack, R. D. 1986. *Human territoriality: Its theory and history*. Cambridge: Cambridge University Press.

Sahgal, G. and Yuval-Davis, N. eds. 1992. *Refusing holy orders: Women and fundamentalism in Britain*. London: Virago.

Sahlins, P. 1989. *Boundaries: The making of France and Spain in the Pyrenees*. Berkeley & Los Angeles, CA: University of California Press.

Said, E. 1978. *Orientalism*. New York: Pantheon.

Saint, T. 2003. *Refusal Shoes*. London: Serpent's Tail.

Sassen, S. 1995. 'On concentration and centrality in the global city'. In P. L. Knox and P. J. Taylor, eds. *World cities in a world system* (pp. 63–78). New York: Cambridge University Press.

Sassen, S. 2006. *Territory, authority, rights: From medieval to global assemblages*. Princeton, NJ: Princeton University Press.

Sassen, S. 2014. *Expulsions: Brutality and complexity in the global economy*. Cambridge, MA: Harvard University Press.

Sassen, S. 2015a. 'Bordering capabilities versus borders: Implications for national border'. In A.-L. Amilhat-Szary and F. Giraut, eds, *Borderities and the politics of contemporary mobile borders* (pp. 23–52). London: Palgrave Macmillan.

Sassen, S. 2015b. *Losing control? Sovereignty in the age of globalization*. New York: Columbia University Press.

Sassen, S. 2016. 'At the systemic edge: Expulsions'. *European Review*, 24(1): 89–104.

Schatzki, T. R. 2001. 'Practice-minded orders'. In T. R. Schatzki, K. K. Cetina, and E. Von Savigny, eds, *The practice turn in contemporary theory* (pp. 42–55). Abingdon: Routledge.

Schierup, C. U., Hansen, P., and Castles, S. 2006. *Migration, citizenship, and the European welfare state: A European dilemma*. London: Oxford University Press.

Scholte, J. A. 2005. *Globalization: A critical introduction*. Basingstoke: Palgrave Macmillan.

Scholten, S. 2015. *The privatisation of immigration control through carrier sanctions: The role of private transport companies in Dutch and British immigration control*. Leiden: Brill Nijhoff.

Scott, J. C. 1987. *Weapons of the weak: Everyday forms of peasant resistance*. New Haven, CT: Yale University Press.

Shelter, 2016. *Research report: Survey of private landlords*. Shelter England, 18

February. https://england.shelter.org.uk/__data/assets/pdf_file/0004/1236820/
Landlord_survey_18_Feb_publish.pdf.

Shepherd, J. 2012. 'Stranded: The students and staff hit by the crackdown on "bogus" colleges'. *Guardian*, 14 May. https://www.theguardian.com/education/2012/may/14/students-private-colleges-closures-immigration.

Sheppard, E. 2002. 'The spaces and times of globalization: Place, scale, networks, and positionality'. *Economic Geography*, 78(3): 307–30.

Shirer, W. L. 1991. *The rise and fall of the Third Reich: A history of Nazi Germany*. New York: Random House.

Sigona, N. 2015. 'Campzenship: Reimagining the camp as a social and political space'. *Citizenship Sudies*, 19(10): 1–15.

Simmons, R., Thomson, R., and Russell, L. 2014. *Education, work and social change: Young people and marginalisation in post-industrial Britain*. London: Palgrave Macmillan.

Simons, R. A., Wu, J., Xu, J., and Fei, Y. 2015. 'Chinese investment in US real estate markets using the EB-5 Program'. *Economic Development Quarterly*, 30(1): 75–87.

Smith, A. 1986. *The ethnic origins of nations*. Oxford: Blackwell.

Smith, E. and Marmo, M. 2014. *Race, gender and the body in British immigration control: Subject to examination*. London: Palgrave Macmillan.

Sohn, C. 2014. 'The border as a resource in the global urban space: A contribution to the cross-border metropolis hypothesis'. *International Journal for Urban and Regional Research*, 38(5): 1697–711.

Sokol, M. 2001. 'Central and Eastern Europe a decade after the fall of statesocialism: Regional dimensions of transition processes'. *Regional Studies*, 35(7): 645–55.

Steden, R. van and Sarre, R. 2007. 'The growth of private security: Trends in the European Union'. *Security journal*, 20(4): 222–35.

Stenning, A. 2005. 'Re-placing work: Economic transformations and the shape of a community in post-socialist Poland'. *Work, Employment & Society*, 19(2), 235–59.

Stenning, A. and Hörschelmann, K. 2008. 'History, geography and difference in the post-socialist world: Or, do we still need post-socialism?' *Antipode*, 40(2): 312–35.

Stephen, M. D. 2014. 'Rising powers, global capitalism and liberal global governance: A historical materialist account of the BRICs challenge'. *European Journal of International Relations*, 20(4): 912–28.

Stewart, J., Bendall, M. E., and Morgan, C. V. 2015. 'Jobs, flags, and laws: How interests, culture, and values explain recruitment into the Utah Minuteman Project'. *Sociological Perspectives*, 58(4): 627–48. doi: 10.1177/0731121414557700.

Stoetzler, M and Yuval-Davis, N. 2002. 'Standpoint theory, situated knowledge and the situated imagination'. *Feminist Theory*, 3(3): 315–34.

Stoller, P. 2009. *The power of the between: An anthropological odyssey*. Chicago, IL: University of Chicago Press.

Strauss M. J. 2015. 'Nations outside their borders: How extraterritorial concessions reinforce sovereignty'. In A.-L. Amilhat-Szary and F. Giraut, eds, *Borderities and the politics of contemporary mobile borders* (pp. 53–67). London: Palgrave Macmillan.

Szary, A.-L. and Giraut, F. 2015. 'Borderities: The politics of contemporary mobile borders'. In A.-L. Szary and F. Giraut, eds, *Borderities and the politics of contemporary mobile borders* (pp. 1–19). London: Palgrave Macmillan.

Taylor, A. J. P. 1966. *From Sarajevo to Potsdam*. New York: Harcourt, Brace and World.

Taylor, C. 2004. *Modern social imaginaries*. Durham, NC: Duke University Press.

Taylor, J. E. and Wyatt, T. J. 1996. 'The shadow value of migrant remittances, income and inequality in a household-farm economy'. *The Journal of Development Studies*, 32(6): 899–912.

Taylor, P. J. 1994. 'The state as container: Territoriality in the modern world-system'. *Progress in Human Geography*, 18(2): 151–62.

Tazzioli, M. 2017. 'Calais after the jungle: Migrant dispersal and the expulsion of humanitarianism'. Open Democracy, 20 July. https://www.opendemocracy.net/beyondslavery/martina-tazzioli/calais-after-jungle-migrant-dispersal-and-expulsion-of-humanitarianis.

Tervonen, M. and Enache, A. 2017. 'Coping with everyday bordering: Roma migrants and gatekeepers in Helsinki'. *Ethnic and Racial Studies*, 40(7): 1114–31.

Tett, G. 2009. 'Lost through destructive creation'. *Financial Times*, 10 March.

Thandi, S. S. 2007. 'Migrating to the "mother country", 1947–1980'. In M. H. Fisher, S. Lahiri, and S. S. Thandi, *A South-Asian history of Britain: Four centuries of peoples from the Indian sub-continent* (pp. 159–82). Oxford: Greenwood World Publishing.

Tilly, C. 1992. *Coercion, capital, and European states, ad 990–1990*. Oxford: Blackwell.

Toje, H. 2006. 'Cossack identity in the new Russia: Kuban Cossack revival and local politics', *Europe-Asia Studies* 58(7): 1057–77.

Torpey, J. 1997. 'Revolutions and freedom of movement: An analysis of passport controls in the French, Russian, and Chinese Revolutions'. *Theory and Society*, 26: 837–68.

Torpey, J. 2000. *The invention of the passport: Surveillance, citizenship and the state*. Cambridge: Cambridge University Press.

Townsend, M. 2018a. 'Border treaty blamed for Calais migrant surge that has led to violence'. *Guardian*, 3 February. https://www.theguardian.com/world/2018/feb/03/border-treaty-migrant-surge-calais-violence.

Townsend, M. 2018b. 'Police face first "super-complaint" over immigration referrals' *Guardian*, 15 December. https://www.theguardian.com/uk-news/2018/dec/15/police-face-immigration-data-sharing-super-complaint.

Travis, A. and Gayle, D. 2016 'Individual children's details passed to Home Office for immigration purposes'. *Guardian*, 8 February. https://www.theguardian.com/uk-news/2016/oct/12/individual-childrens-details-passed-to-home-office-for-immigration-purposes.

Travis, A. and Taylor, D. 2017. 'PM accused of closing door on child refugees as "Dubs" scheme ends'. *Guardian*, 8 February. https://www.theguardian.com/world/2017/feb/08/dubs-scheme-lone-child-refugees-uk-closed-down.

Triandafyllidou, A., ed. 2016. *Irregular migration in Europe: Myths and realities*. London: Routledge.

Triandafyllidou, A. and Maroukis, T. 2012. *Migrant smuggling: Irregular migration from Asia and Africa to Europe*. London: Palgrave.

Trump, D. 2016. 'President-Elect Donald Trump victory rally in Orlando, Florida'. December 16. C-Span. https://www.c-span.org/video/?420255-1/president-elect-donald-trump-holds-rally-orlando-florida.

Trump, D. 2018. 'State of the Union Address, January 30, 2018'. https://www.whitehouse.gov/briefings-statements/president-donald-j-trumps-state-union-address.

Tsing, A. 2000: 'Inside the economy of appearances'. *Public Culture, 12*: 115–44.

Turner, F. J. 1996. 'The significance of the frontier in American history' [1893]. In F. J. Turner, *The frontier in American history* (pp. 1–38). New York: Dover Publications.

UKCISA. 2017. '97% go home when visas expire'. UK Council for International Student Affairs, 25 August. https://www.ukcisa.org.uk/studentnews/1002/Major-announcements-on-international-students-97-go-home-when-visas-expire (accessed October 2017; no longer on the site).

UKVI = UK Visas and Immigration. 2015a. 'List of "bogus colleges" closed'. Home Office, 31 August. Document released under the Freedom of Information Act. Reference: 36608. https://www.whatdotheyknow.com/request/list_of_bogus_colleges_closed.

UKVI = UK Visas and Immigration. 2015b. 'Tier 4 sponsors whose status appeared as revoked from 2010 to 2014'. https://www.gov.uk/government/publications/tier-4-sponsors-whose-status-appeared-as-revoked-from-2010-to-2014.

UKVI = UK Visas and Immigration. 2018a. 'Tier 1 (Investor) of the Points Based system: Policy'. https://www.gov.uk/government/uploads/system/uploads/attachment_data/file/672532/T1__I__Guidance_01_2018_final_PDF.pdf.

UKVI = UK Visas and Immigration. 2018b. 'Tier 2 of the points based system: Policy'. https://www.gov.uk/government/uploads/system/uploads/attachment_data/file/673762/Tier_2_Policy_Guidance_01_2018__2_.pdf.

UNHCR. 2011. *UNHCR statistical database online*. Geneva: United Nations High Commissioner for Refugees.

UNHCR. 2016a. 'Mediterranean death toll soars, 2016 is deadliest year yet'. United Nations High Commission for Refugees, 25 October. http://www.unhcr.org/afr/news/latest/2016/10/580f3e684/mediterranean-death-toll-soars-2016-deadliest-year.html.

UNHCR. 2016b. *Mixed movements in South-East Asia, 2016*. UNHCR Regional Office for South-East Asia. https://unhcr.atavist.com/mm2016.

UNHCR 2016c 'Global forced displacement hits record high'. United Nations High Commission for Refugees. 30 June. https://www.unhcr.org/hk/en/3078-global-forced-displacement-hits-record-high.html.

UNHCR. 2017. *UNHCR statistical database online*. Geneva: United Nations High Commissioner for Refugees.

UNWTO. 2016. *UNWTO Annual report 2016*. World Tourism Organization. Madrid. http://cf.cdn.unwto.org/sites/all/files/pdf/annual_report_2016_web_0.pdf.

Urry, J. 1990. *The tourist gaze: Leisure and travel in contemporary societies*. London: SAGE.

Urry, J. 2005. 'The complexity turn'. *Theory, Culture & Society*, 22(5): 1–14.

Urry, J. 2007. *Mobilities*. Cambridge: Polity.

Urry, J. 2014. *Offshoring*. Cambridge: Polity

Valdez, I. M., Coleman, I., and Akbar, A. 2017. 'Missing in action: Practice, paralegality, and the nature of immigration enforcement'. *Citizenship Studies*, 21: 5, 547–69.

Vallet, E. 2016. *Borders, fences and walls: State of insecurity?* London: Routledge.

Vaughan-Williams, N. 2008. 'Borderwork beyond inside/outside? Frontex, the citizen-detective and the war on terror'. *Space and Polity*, 12(1): 63–79.

Vaughan-Williams, N. 2011. 'Off-shore biopolitical border security: The EU's global response to migration, piracy and "risky" subjects'. In L. Bialasiewicz, ed., *Europe in the world: EU geopolitics and the making of European space* (pp. 185–200). Farnham: Ashgate.

Vaz, K. 2014. 'Evidence to the Home Affairs Select Committee: The work of the Immigration Directorates (Q4 2013)'. Parliament TV, 24 June 2014.

Vine, J. 2014a. 'Evidence to the Home Affairs Select Committee: The work of the Immigration Directorates (Q4 2013)'. Parliament TV, 24 June 2014.

Vine, J. 2014b. 'The rights of European citizens and their spouses to come to the UK: Inspecting the application process and tackling the abuse'. Policy paper, 19 June 2014. https://www.gov.uk/government/publications/the-rights-of-european-citizens-and-their-spouses-to-come-to-the-uk-inspecting-the-application-process-and-the-tackling-of-abuse.

Visram, R. 2002. *Asians in Britain: 400 years of history*. London: Pluto.

Vollmer, B., Güntner, S., Lukes, S., and J. Wilding, 2016. 'Bordering practices in the UK welfare system'. *Critical Social Policy*. doi: 10.1177/0261018315622609.

Walby, S. 2003. 'The myth of the nation-state: Theorizing society and polities in a global era', *Sociology*, 37(1): 531–48.

Walby, S. 2007. 'Complexity theory, systems theory, and multiple intersecting social inequalities'. *Philosophy of the Social Sciences*, 37(4): 449–70.

Walby, S. 2009. *Globalization and inequalities: Complexity and contested modernities*. London: SAGE.

Walters, W. 2006. 'Rethinking borders beyond the state'. *Comparative European Politics*, 4(2–3): 141–59.

Wallerstein, I. 1974. *The modern world-system: Capitalist agriculture and the origins of the European world-economy in the sixteenth centenary*. Berkeley: University of California Press.

Ward, K. and England, K. 2007. 'Introduction: Reading neoliberalization'. In K. Ward and K. England, eds, *Neoliberalization: States, networks, peoples* (pp. 1–22). Oxford: Blackwell.

Ware, V. 2012. *Military migrants: Fighting for YOUR country*. Basingstoke: Palgrave Macmillan.

Webber, F. 2012. Borderline justice: The fight for refugee and migrant rights. London: Pluto.

Weizman, E. 2012. *Hollow land: Israel's architecture of occupation*. New York: Verso Books.

Wellink, A. H. E. M. 2009. 'The future of supervision'. Speech delivered at a FSI High Level Seminar, Cape Town, South Africa, 29 January. https://www.dnb.nl/en/news/news-and-archive/speeches-2009/dnb212415.jsp.

Wemyss, G. 2006. 'The power to tolerate: Contests over Britishness and belonging in east London'. *Patterns of Prejudice*, 40(3): 215–36.

Wemyss, G. 2009. *The invisible empire: White discourse, tolerance and belonging*. London: Ashgate.

Wemyss, G. 2015a. 'Everyday bordering and raids every day: The invisible empire and metropolitan borderscapes'. In C. Brambilla, J. Laine, J. W. Scott, and G. Bocchi, eds, *Borderscaping: Imaginations and Practices of Border Making* (pp. 187–98). Farnham: Ashgate.

Wemyss, G. 2015b. 'The new Immigration Bill and the criminalization of work and everyday bordering'. Glasgow Refugee and Migration Network, 16 June. https://gramnet.wordpress.com/2015/06/16/the-new-immigration-bill-the-criminalization-of-work-and-everyday-bordering.

Wemyss, G., 2018. 'Compliant environment': Turning ordinary people into border guards should concern everyone in the UK'. The Conversation, 20 November. https://theconversation.com/compliant-environment-turning-ordinary-people-into-border-guards-should-concern-everyone-in-the-uk-107066.

Wemyss, G., Cassidy, K., and Yuval-Davis, N. 2017. 'Welcome to Britain in 2017, where everybody is expected to be a border guard'. The Conversation, 7 April. https://theconversation.com/welcome-to-britain-where-everybody-is-expected-to-be-a-border-guard-75148.

Wemyss, G. and Cassidy, K. 2017. '"People think that Romanians and Roma are the same": Everyday bordering and the lifting of transitional controls'. *Ethnic and Racial Studies*, 40(7): 1132–50.

Wemyss, G., Yuval-Davis, N., and Cassidy, K. 2018. '"Beauty and the beast": Everyday bordering and sham marriage discourse'. *Political Geography*, 66: 171–9.

White, M. and Harding, L. 2001. 'Passport row lands Mandelson in trouble'. *Guardian*, 24 January. https://www.theguardian.com/uk/2001/jan/24/labour.mandelson.

Whittaker, C. R. 1994. *Frontier of the Roman Empire: A social and economic study*. London: Johns Hopkins University Press.

Widdecombe, A. 2014. *Strictly Ann: The autobiography*. London: Weidenfold & Nicolson.

Wilding, J. 2017. 'Revealed: Legal advice for asylum seekers disappearing due to legal aid cuts. The Conversation, 15 November. https://theconversation.com/revealed-legal-advice-for-asylum-seekers-disappearing-due-to-legal-aid-cuts-86897.

Williams, R. 1977. *Marxism and literature*. Oxford: Oxford University Press.

Williams, L. 2012. 'Transnational marriage migration and marriage migration: An overview'. In K. Charsley, ed., *Transnational marriage: New perspectives from Europe and beyond* (pp. 23–37). London: Routledge.

Willsher, K. 2018. 'May and Macron to sign new Calais border treaty'. *Guardian*, 17 January 2018. https://www.theguardian.com/world/2018/jan/17/may-and-macron-to-sign-new-calais-border-treaty.

Wilson, A. R. 2013. *Situating intersectionality: Politics, policy, and power*. New York: Palgrave Macmillan.

Wimmer, A. 1997. 'Who owns the state? Understanding ethnic conflict in post-colonial societies'. *Nations and nationalism*, 3(4): 631–66.

Wolf, E. 1982. *Europe and the people without history*. Berkeley: University of California Press.

Wonders, N. A. 2006. 'Global flows, semi-permeable borders and new channels of inequality'. In S. Pickering and L. Weber, eds, *Borders, mobility and technologies of control* (pp. 63–86). Dordrecht: Springer.

Woods, M. 2007. 'Engaging the global countryside: Globalization, hybridity and the reconstitution of rural place'. *Progress in Human Geography, 31*(4): 485–507.

Wray, H. 2011. 'An ideal husband? Marriages of convenience, moral gatekeeping and immigration to the UK'. In E. Guild and P. Minderhoud, eds, *The first decade of EU migration and asylum law* (pp. 351–74). Leiden: Martinus Nijhoff.

Wray, H. 2012. 'Any time, any place, anywhere: Entry clearance, marriage migration and the border'. In K. Charsley, ed., *Transnational marriage: New perspectives from Europe and beyond.* (pp. 41–59). London: Routledge.

Wray, H. 2015. 'The "pure" relationship, sham marriages and immigration control'. In J. Miles, R. Probert, and P. Mody, eds, *Marriage rites and rights* (pp. 141–65). Oxford: Hart.

Wray, H. 2016. *Regulating Marriage migration into the UK: A stranger in the home.* London: Routledge.

Wright, M. 2010. 'Gender and geography II'. *Progress in Human Geography, 33*: 379–86.

Yang, D. 2008. 'International migration, remittances and household investment: Evidence from Philippine migrants' exchange rate shocks'. *Economic Journal, 118*(528): 591–630.

Yassin-Kassab, R. and Al-Shami, L. 2018. *Burning country: Syrians in revolution and war.* London: Pluto.

Yeo, C. 2017. 'Another massive increase in immigration and nationality application fees for 2017–18'. Free Movement. https://www.freemovement.org.uk/increase-immigration-nationality-application-fees-2018-19.

Yeung, H. 1998. 'Capital, state and space: Contesting the borderless world'. *Transactions of the Institute of British Geographers, 23*: 291–309.

Yiftachel, O. 2009. 'Theoretical notes on "gray cities": The coming of urban apartheid?'. *Planning Theory, 8*(1): 88–100.

Yiftachel, O. 2011. 'Critical theory and gray space'. In N. Brenner, P. Marcuse, and M. Mayer, eds, *Cities for people, not profit: Critical urban theory and the right to the city* (150–70). New York: Routledge.

Yiftachel, O. 2016. 'The Aleph–Jerusalem as critical learning'. *City, 20*(3), 483–94.

Yildiz, C. and De Genova, N. 2017. 'Un/Free mobility: Roma migrants in the European Union'. *Social Identities, 24*(4): 425–41.

Young, C. and Brown, W. H. 1995. 'The African colonial state in comparative perspective'. *History: Reviews of New Books, 24*(1): 39–40.

Yuval-Davis, N. 1997. *Gender and nation.* London: SAGE.

Yuval-Davis, N. 2006. 'Intersectionality and feminist politics'. *European Journal of Women's Studies, 13*(3): 193–209.

Yuval-Davis, N. 2007. 'Human/Women's rights and feminist transversal politics'. In M. Marx Ferree and A. M. Tripp, eds, *Transnational feminisms: Women's global activism and human rights* (pp. 275–95). New York: New York University Press.

Yuval-Davis, N. 2011. *The politics of belonging: Intersectional contestations.* London: SAGE.

Yuval-Davis, N. 2012. 'The double crisis of governability and governmentality'. *Soundings, 52*: 88–99.

Yuval-Davis, N. 2013. 'A situated intersectional everyday approach to the study of bordering'. Euborderscapes, Working Paper no. 2. http://www.euborderscapes. eu/fileadmin/user_upload/Working_Papers/EUBORDERSCAPES_Working_ Paper_2_Yuval-Davis.pdf.

Yuval-Davis, N. 2015a. 'Situated intersectionality and social inequality'. *Raisons politiques*, 2: 91–100.

Yuval-Davis, N. 2015b. 'Want to know how to kill a multicultural society? Turn its ordinary citizens into borderguards'. *Independent*, 15 December. https://www. independent.co.uk/voices/want-to-know-how-to-kill-a-multicultural-society- turn-its-ordinary-citizens-into-border-guards-a6774151.html.

Yuval-Davis, N. 2016. 'Those who belong and those who don't: Physical and mental borders in Europe'. *Green European Journal*. https://www. greeneuropeanjournal.eu/those-who-belong-and-those-who-dont-physical- and-mental-borders-in-europe.

Yuval-Davis, N. and Kaptani, E. 2009. 'Identity, performance and social action: Participatory theatre among refugees'. In M. Wetherell, ed., *Identity and Social Action* (pp. 56–74). London: Palgrave.

Yuval-Davis, N. and Stoetzler, M. 2002. 'Imagined boundaries and borders: A gendered gaze'. *European Journal of Women's Studies*, 9(3): 329–44.

Yuval-Davis, N. and Vieten, U. 2018. 'Citizenship, entitlement and autoch- thonic political projects of belonging in the age of Brexit'. In S. G. Ellis, ed., *Enfranchising Ireland? Identity, citizenship and state* (pp. 107–24). Dublin: The Royal Irish Academy.

Yuval-Davis, N. Varjú, V., Tervonen, M., Hakim, J., and Fathi, M. 2017. 'Press discourses on Roma in the UK, Finland and Hungary'. *Ethnic and Racial Studies*, 40(7): 1151–69.

Yuval-Davis, N., Wemyss, G., and Cassidy, K. 2016. 'Changing the racialized "common sense" of everyday bordering'. Open Democracy UK, February. https://www.opendemocracy.net/uk/nira-yuval-davis-georgie-wemyss- kathryn-cassidy/changing-racialized-common-sense-of-everyday-bord.

Yuval-Davis, N., Wemyss, G., and Cassidy, K. 2017. 'Introduction to the special issue: Racialized bordering discourses on European Roma'. *Ethnic and Racial Studies*, 40(7): 1–11.

Yuval-Davis, N. Wemyss, G., and Cassidy, K. 2018. 'Everyday bordering, belonging and the re-orientation of British immigration legislation'. *Sociology*, 52(2): 228–44.

Zamindar, V. F. Y. 2007. *The long partition and the making of modern South Asia: Refugees, boundaries, histories*. New York: Columbia University Press.

Zembylas, M. 2010. 'Agamben's theory of biopower and immigrants/refugees/ asylum seekers: Discourses of citizenship and the implications for curriculum theorizing'. *Journal of Curriculum Theorizing*, 6(2): 31–45.

Index

209